ISBN 978-1-331-55718-0
PIBN 10205549

1 MONTH OF
FREE
READING

at
www.ForgottenBooks.com

By purchasing this book you are eligible for one month membership to ForgottenBooks.com, giving you unlimited access to our entire collection of over 700,000 titles via our web site and mobile apps.

To claim your free month visit:

www.forgottenbooks.com/free205549

Similar Books Are Available from
www.forgottenbooks.com

PHILIP MELANCHTHON

CHAPTER I

BIRTH AND EARLY YEARS

Bretten—Claus Schwartzerd—His Sons—Philip Schwartzerd Born—
His Brother and Sisters—His First School—John Unger—Death
of Philip's Father and Grandfather—Reuchlin—Pforzheim—
Studies Greek—Name Changed.

NEAR Carlsruhe, the capital of Baden, in the
beautiful valley of the Kraichgau, is the little
city of Bretten, with five thousand inhabitants.
Four hundred years ago it belonged to the Palatinate, and numbered three hundred families as the
sum total of its population.   For a town so small it
enjoyed much intercourse with the outside world,
since through its principal street passed a large part
of the merchandise carried from Italy to the lower
Rhine.   But the inhabitants of the town lived
mostly from the produce of their fertile fields.   They
were simple in their manners, upright in their lives,
and warmly attached to the Church.   Their relig-

ious faith was sincere; but it was coloured by the superstitions of the times, since in that little Palatine city so late as 1504, five persons were convicted of witchcraft and burned to death. However, the fame of Bretten does not rest on the beauty of its situation, nor on the probity of its inhabitants, nor on the number of witches it burned four hundred years ago; for as much could be said of many another town in the Palatinate. Its fame rests on the fact that on Thursday, the sixteenth of February, 1497, at just six minutes past seven o'clock in the evening, it gave birth to Philip Melanchthon, the *Preceptor of Germany*. An authentic old account runs thus:

" In the days of Count Palatine Philip, Elector on the Rhine, there lived in Heidelberg, at the foot of the mountain, an upright, pious man named Claus Schwartzerd, who, by his wife Elizabeth, had two sons, John and George, who from their youth up were carefully trained in the fear of God and in the practice of every virtue. John learned the trade of a locksmith; but George, who did everything which was bidden him with the utmost alacrity, and was a very active boy, so won the favour of the Elector, that his Electoral Grace took him to Court, and had him shown all kinds of handiwork, that he might learn what he most delighted in, and what could be made of him. Now, when the boy took delight in armour, and associated most with armourers, the Elector placed him under a master at Amberg to learn the trade. He learned so rapidly as to astonish everyone; and his companions grew so jealous of him that one day one of them burned him so dangerously with hot lead that his life was despaired of. It was only by divine grace and special care that he was saved.

"When the Elector learned what had happened he took him away, and sent him to Nuremberg to a master skilled in all kinds of armour, even to its most obscure parts. When the master showed special interest in the boy, the latter gave all the more heed and soon comprehended whatever was shown him, for he had so much skill that he could imitate with his hands whatever his eyes saw. He could forge his work as smooth as though it had been filed. He pursued his trade for several years, and was at length able to make everything pertaining to armour in the very best style. The Elector now called him back to Court and made him his armourer, or armour-bearer." [1]

The old account goes on to say that George Schwartzerd became so celebrated for his skill in the manufacture of armour, that such foreign potentates as the King of Poland, the Duke of Würtemberg, the Elector of Saxony, the Margrave of Baden, importuned the Elector Philip for his services.

"But the Elector, in order that he might attach George, who was now thirty years old, the more surely to his own country, began to look out for an honourable marriage for him, and to that end he negotiated with Hans Reuter, a distinguished citizen of Bretten, for his

---

[1] Short Report . . . written by the Professors of the University of Wittenberg, *Corpus Reformatorum*, 10 : 255. The *Corpus Reformatorum*, hereafter referred to as *C. R.*, contains in twenty-eight volumes, edited by Bretschneider and Bindseil, the works of Melanchthon, and many other valuable documents of the Reformation era.

daughter Barbara, a virtuous, well-bred maiden, who, by
the providence of the Almighty God, and the negotiations of the Elector, was promised to him in marriage.
They were married at Spires in the presence of many
knights who assembled to do them honour.

" The two loved each other dearly ; for George
Schwartzerd was an upright, pious, God-fearing man,
who served God earnestly, prayed devoutly, and observed the hours of prayer as diligently as a minister.
Often would he rise at midnight,.fall upon his knees, and
offer devout prayer.   No oath ever escaped his lips, and
no one ever saw or heard of his being drunk.   He lived
in wedlock four years without children; but after the
close of the fourth year, which was 1497, on Thursday
after *Invocavit*, his first son, Philip, our dear master and
teacher, was born in Bretten, in the house of the father-
in-law and grandfather, Hans Reuter.   Thus God blessed
this pious and God-fearing man with the gift of a son,
whom not one land, but many, yea, all Christendom, has
enjoyed and without doubt will enjoy to the end of the
world." [1]

Other children were born to George and Barbara
Schwartzerd, as, in 1499, a daughter named Anna,
who was married to Chilian Grumbach, and died in
Heilbronn ; George, about four years younger than
Philip, who became mayor of Bretten and wrote
several histories; Margaretha, born in 1506, married
first to Andrew Stichs, and, after his death, to the
electoral secretary, Hawerer, died in 1540; Barbara,
born in 1508 and married to Peter Kecheln.   The
grandchildren were many, and all shared that divine

---

[1] *C. R.*, 10 : 256.

HOUSE IN BRETTEN IN WHICH MELANCHTHON WAS BORN.

blessing promised to them that love God and keep
His commandments.

The fame of "the Heidelberg armourer," as
George Schwartzerd was called, still grew, and
foreign princes still sought to profit by his skill.
When the Emperor Maximilian, "the last knight,"
was holding a diet at Worms, he was challenged to
single combat by a bold young Italian hero named
Fandius Mandari. After he had assured himself of
the rank and valour of his challenger, Maximilian
ordered a suit of armour from George Schwartzerd,
entered the lists, and gained an easy victory. As a
consequence he was so much delighted with the
armour that he presented its maker with a coat of
arms, which represented a lion sitting on a shield
and helmet, holding tongs in the right fore-paw, and
a hammer in the left.

George Schwartzerd was retained in the service of
the Emperor Maximilian until the breaking out of
a war between Bavaria and the Palatinate, when
he took leave of his royal master, and returned to
the Elector Philip, who employed him in the secret
service against the enemy. Drinking water from a
poisoned well, he fell sick, and after lingering four
years, he died, at the age of forty-nine years, October
27, 1507.

This was a sad year for Barbara Schwartzerd and
her five little children. Only eleven days before the
death of her husband, her father had passed from
earth. Thus the boy Philip was bereft of his grandfather and of his father in his eleventh year. The
latter, three days before his death, called his children

to his bedside, and after bestowing his paternal blessing and commending them to the protection of their Heavenly Father, said: " I have seen many and great changes in the world, but greater ones are yet to follow, in which may God lead and guide you. Fear God, and do right."[1]

In order that Philip might not witness the death of his father, his mother sent him for a few days to Spires; but he never forgot the dying counsel of his father.

The education of his two boys was a matter that lay near the heart of George Schwartzerd. But being much from home he committed their intellectual and religious training to their grandfather, " a fine, intelligent man, who himself had studied," with the strict injunction that they should be kept at school and taught something useful. Accordingly Philip and his little brother George were sent to the town school, where they were well drilled in the rudiments of knowledge, and made rapid progress. But when the French plague broke out in the town, and the school-teacher was attacked by it, the grandfather took the boys out of school, and applied to his brother-in-law, the celebrated John Reuchlin (1455–1523), for a teacher who should instruct them at home. Reuchlin sent him John Unger of Pforzheim, who had acquired a good knowledge of the ancient languages. Unger was a conscientious, pious man, and a faithful teacher. He laboured earnestly to promote the moral and intellectual improvement of his pupils. He inculcated modesty, honesty, and the love of truth. His frequent com-

---

[1] C. R., 8 : 367.

mand was, " Be prudent and ready to yield." He drilled the boys thoroughly in grammar and syntax, using as a text-book the poems of the Italian Carmelite, Baptista of Mantua, since at that time very few of the Latin classics had been printed in Germany. Every mistake was corrected with the rod. Yet, notwithstanding the severity of his discipline, Unger enjoyed the confidence and affection of his pupils. In after years, when Philip had himself become the greatest linguist and the most illustrious scholar and teacher in Germany, he wrote thus of his own first preceptor in language ·

" I had a teacher who was an excellent linguist. He died two years ago.' He was an honest man. He taught the Gospel and suffered much for the Gospel's sake. He was pastor at Pforzheim. He drove me to the grammar, and required me to construct sentences. He made me give the rules of construction by means of twenty or thirty verses from the Mantuan. He would not allow me to pass over anything. Whenever I would make a mistake he plied the rod, and yet with the moderation that was proper. Thus he made me a linguist. He was a good man. He loved me as a son, and I him as a father. In a short time we shall meet, I hope, in eternal life. I loved him notwithstanding that he used such severity; though it was not severity, but parental correction which urged me to diligence. At evening I had to hunt the rules in order to recite. You see discipline was stricter then than now." [2]

The young Philip was a worthy pupil of so excel-

---

[1] Unger died at Pforzheim in 1553.
[2] *C. R.*, 25 : 448.

lent a teacher.   In disposition he was modest and amiable.   Though he would sometimes become irritated, he not unfrequently applied to himself the saying, " He cuts and stabs, and yet hurts nobody." In matters of intellect he had a quick perception, an acute penetration, a retentive memory, an ardent thirst for knowledge, and the ability to express his thoughts with accuracy and precision.   In school and out he was incessantly asking questions, and often would gather a few schoolfellows around him for the purpose of discussing what had been read and learned.   Philip was noted for proficiency in grammar; and when their grandfather observed the diligence of the boys, he bought them a *Missal*, that along with their other studies they might acquire a knowledge of the choral services of the Church. He also required them to take their place in the choir on all the Holy Days.

" At that time the great Bacchanti were roving through the country.   Whenever one came to Bretten the grandfather sent Philip to dispute with him.   It was seldom that anyone could withstand him.   This pleased the old man; and he took special delight in these contests.   The boy, too, became more confident, and grew in fondness for study.   The grandfather took care to buy books and other things, that the boy might not be impeded." [1]

And now that both the father and grandfather of Philip and George had departed this life, the education of the boys devolved upon their grandmother, Eliżabeth Reuter, the sister of Reuchlin, who was

[1] *C. R.*, 10 : 258.

then reckoned the best Greek and Hebrew scholar
in Germany. He had studied Greek at Paris, Or-
leans, and Poictiers, had taught at Basel and Tübingen, and had learned Hebrew in Rome. He was
Philip's granduncle, being the brother of his grandmother. Hence it was no small circumstance in the
boy's education when the grandmother determined
to remove with him to her native town of Pforzheim,
for here he would be sure to come more or less under
the influence of Reuchlin, who, though he resided
in Stuttgart as president of the Swabian Court of
the Confederates, frequently returned to his native
Pforzheim, in whose splendid Latin school he had
begun his education. The school at Pforzheim was
still one of the most celebrated in the Palatinate.
Its Rector was George Simler, a scholar of the celebrated Ludwig Dringenberg, and an alumnus of the
University of Cologne. Simler was an excellent
Latin scholar, and, besides, had a good knowledge of
Greek and Hebrew—a rare accomplishment at that
time. His assistant and co-labourer was John Hiltebrant, also a fine scholar, who during the vacation
lectured privately on the Greek language. It was
the custom to admit to the study of Greek only
the brightest and best pupils. Philip Schwartzerd
was soon selected as one of the favoured few. He
used his opportunity with so much diligence and
profit that in a short time he became tolerably pro-
ficient in Greek. Long years afterward he wrote:

" When a boy I heard two very learned men, George
Simler and Conrad Helvetius, alumni of the University

of Cologne; the one first explained to me the Latin and Greek poets, and introduced me to a purer philosophy, often referring during the lecture on Aristotle to the Greek. The other at Heidelberg first taught me the elements of astronomy."[1]

Simler also gave instruction in versification, and expounded the school-comedies of his friend Reuchlin, two of which he published at Pforzheim in 1508, with a commentary, and a dedication to their author. He and his assistant were exactly such teachers as are needed to prepare young men for the university. Under their efficient instruction Philip Schwartzerd surpassed all his schoolfellows, among whom were Simon Grynæus, the linguist and theologian of Basel, Berthold Haller, the Reformer of Bern, Francis Friedlieb of Ettlingen, who wrote a historico-geographical work on the German Empire, Nicholas Gerbel, and John Schwebel, natives of Pforzheim, the former afterward a jurist at Strassburg and the latter the Reformer of the territory of Zweibrücken. But the most important influence exerted on the mind of the future Preceptor of Germany at this time was the intimate relations with Reuchlin which he now enjoyed. He was brought in direct contact with this great Aristarchus of the literary world in the house of his grandmother. When Reuchlin saw that the twelve-year-old boy possessed such excellent talents, and showed such industry in study, he praised him, called him his son, placed his own red doctor's hat on his head, gave him a Greek

---

[1] *Declamatt.*, 135.

Grammar, and promised to send him a copy of his own Græco-Latin Lexicon, yet upon the condition that when he came again, Philip should present him with some Latin verses of his own composition.   In a short time Reuchlin returned to Pforzheim, where-upon Philip presented the verses and received the promised Lexicon, the first of its kind that had ap-peared in Germany.   As a further mark of his grati-tude, Philip, with some of his schoolfellows, studied one of Reuchlin's school-comedies, and while the author was at a banquet given by the monks of the place, he and his companions came and rendered the comedy so elegantly that all were pleased, espe-cially Reuchlin, who declared that so clever and learned a young man should no longer bear the homely name of Schwartzerd, meaning black earth, but shoud be called by its Greek equivalent, *Me-lanchthon*, the name by which he has since been known, and by which he shall henceforth be desig-nated in this book, though he himself after 1531, no doubt because of the easier pronunciation, wrote it *Melanthon*.[1]

---

[1] See *C. R.*, 1 : cxxxi.   *Melanchthon* is the spelling employed by Camerarius and by M.'s friends generally, though it does not appear that he himself was at any time pleased with it, since he rarely used it in early life, and throughout life signed the most of his letters simply Philippus, or *Φιλιππος*.

CHAPTER II

BECOMES A STUDENT AT HEIDELBERG

Universities — Heidelberg — Scholasticism — Melanchthon Matricu-
lates at Heidelberg—His Studies—His Companions—The New
Learning—Becomes Bachelor of Arts.

AT the beginning of the sixteenth century the
German universities were by no means what
they are now, the seats of the highest culture and
of the most advanced methods of instruction. In
the grade of their scholarship and in the character
of the work done by them, they were about equal
in the department of arts to the middle and upper
classes in the German gymnasia of the present time.
Boys then went to the university to learn what they
are now required to carry thither with them. All
the instruction was given in the Latin language;
but it was chiefly, if not exclusively, the corrupt
monks' Latin of the Middle Ages.

The Latin classics were but little read. Greek
and Hebrew were almost entirely ignored, and in
some places violently opposed. The philosophy
taught was that of Aristotle, exhibited for the most
part by means of defective and barbarous Latin

THE CASTLE AT HEIDELBERG.

translations; and theology had not yet been emancipated from the scholastic method.   The old contests between Realism and Nominalism were still raging, and when these contests could not be settled in the lecture-room, they were fought out by the students on the streets with their fists and canes.   Then little attention was given to composition and rhetoric. Logic was studied, not so much as an instrument for finding out truth, as for use in subtle and hairsplitting disputations.   The manners of the students were coarse, and their morals corrupt.   So much may be said of the universities in general.   Of Heidelberg in particular, though it was the oldest university in Germany west of Vienna and Prague, having been founded in 1386, it must be said that in learning and culture its relative rank was not high.   The Elector Philip, who had been quickened by the rising spirit of humanistic culture, had indeed sought to awaken a new intellectual life in his university.   His efforts in this direction had been nobly seconded by the Bishop of Worms, John von Dalberg; by John Wessel, a forerunner of Luther, who had sought to introduce a more liberal philosophy; by Rudolph Agricola, the dialectician; by Conrad Celtes, the poet; and especially by Jacob Wimpfeling, who sought to join humanistic learning to the scholastic theology.   John Reuchlin himself had for a time been a professor at Heidelberg, and his brother Dionysius had begun to introduce the study of Greek there.   But these friends and promoters of a broader and more liberal culture had been opposed and hindered in their work by the older professors,

and had made very little impression on the courses
of studies, or on the methods of teaching them.

Nevertheless, following the advice of Reuchlin
and Simler, Philip Melanchthon, now in his thirteenth year, turned his steps to the paternal city,
and on the fourteenth day of October, 1509, was
matriculated under the philosophical faculty in the
University of Heidelberg.[1]   He found a home with
Dr. Pallas Spangel, professor of theology, at whose
house he served wine to the Pomeranian guests on
the occasion of the marriage of Duke George of
Pomerania to the daughter of the Palatine Elector.[2]
The young and inexperienced student received assistance and encouragement from the learned doctor,
whom in after years he remembered with affection
as more favourable to the study of the liberal arts
than the rest of his colleagues who taught theology.[3]

Melanchthon's opinion of the studies and the
methods of study at Heidelberg is expressed in the
Preface to the Basel edition of his works, published
in 1541 :

" While yet a boy I was sent to the university, but the
young men were taught scarcely anything except *garrula
dialectice* and *particula physice*.   Inasmuch as I had
learned to write verse, with a kind of boyish avidity I
began to read the poets, and also history and the drama.
This habit gradually led me to the ancient classics.

---

[1] The record in the University Album is, " Philippus Schwartzerd
de Brethenn Spir. dyoc. xiiii. Octobris."   Bretten lay in the diocese
of Spires.   Hartfelder's *Philipp Melanchthon*, p. 12.

[2] *C. R.*, 11 : 1094.

[3] *Declamatt.*, ii., 204.

From these I acquired a vocabulary and style, but we boys had no instruction in composition We read everything without discrimination, but especially did we prefer modern works like those of Politian. My style took its complexion from these, and reproduced these harsher and less polished authors rather than the grace and beauty of the ancients." [1]

He tells us further that about this time he received as a present from Œcolampadius the three printed books of Rudolph Agricola's *Dialectics*, by the reading of which he was not only instructed, but also incited to examine and inquire more diligently into the order of the arguments in the orations of Cicero and Demosthenes. " In this way I was enabled to understand those orations better, to read them easier, and to comprehend their instruction."

It is evident from these reminiscences that Melanchthon pursued his studies largely by himself; and yet he acquired such a reputation for proficiency in Greek while at Heidelberg that when one day a professor proposed a question the solution of which required a knowledge of Greek, and cried out, " Where shall I find a Grecian ? " the students answered with one voice, " Melanchthon ! " " Melanchthon ! "

Yet Melanchthon did not occupy himself wholly with the ancient languages and with dialectics. He also studied philosophy, and when Conrad Helvetius came to Heidelberg and lectured on mathematics and astronomy, he found in Melanchthon one of his most appreciative hearers.

[1] *C. R.*, 4 : 715.

At this time, about the year 1510, he formed the acquaintance of Jacob Wimpfeling, who was at Heidelberg superintending the education of several young men from Strassburg.   Here Wimpfeling received intelligence of the death of Geiler von Kaisersberg.   Immediately he wrote a biographical sketch of the renowned Strassburg preacher, and to it added a number of elegies, including one from Melanchthon, whom he recommended to Count von Löwenstein as private tutor to his two sons.   It was in this same year that Wimpfeling published a book in defence of the scholastic theology against the satirical attack of Jacob Locker of Ingolstadt, and put into it a poem by Melanchthon, in which the young scholar calls upon the gods and heathen muses to yield to the true wisdom which alone can teach us who made the universe, and can show man how to lead a pious life.[1]

Melanchthon also at this time enjoyed the friendship of the poet Sorbil, of whom he said, nearly fifty years later, that no one in Germany had a better poetic vein.[2]

But the young Melanchthon was not an exclusive devotee of literature, philosophy, and science.   The deep religious sense of his innermost being, and the pious training of his childhood, found support and development in the sermons of Geiler, which had been commended to him by his uncle Reuchlin. In these sermons he came in contact with a devout and pious spirit which did not waste its energies in

---

[1] *C. R.*, 20 : 765.
[2] Schmidt's *Philipp Melanchthon*, p. 7

doubtful disputations, and in recounting old monks' fables, but rebuked sin and reasoned of righteousness and judgment to come in the homely and familiar language of every-day life. The impression made on the young student by the reading of these sermons was never effaced. In his Postils he refers to Geiler as saying that *Bischoff* (*bishop*), which according to German etymology means *bei den Schaffen* (*with the sheep*), according to its usage had come to mean *beiss das Schaff* [1] (*bite the sheep*).

This narrative of facts shows that Melanchthon, though but a boy in years, had taken rank among the learned, and that his associates were of that new generation which had risen to herald the coming of a brighter and better day for science and religion in Germany. Indeed he now stood on the dividing line between the Middle Ages and the modern era. But the day dawned so speedily, and the sun shot up toward the zenith so rapidly, that before Melanchthon had passed the meridian of his life, he had witnessed, and had acted a large part in effecting, one of the mightiest revolutions in culture, and one of the most beneficial reformations of religion, that the Christian world has ever known. The times were ready for the change, and the men were at hand to produce it. At the very time that Luther was expounding Aristotle in Wittenberg, and visiting Augustinian cloisters in Saxony, and climbing up Pilate's staircase at Rome, — at that very time, in the academic city by the Neckar, Philip Melanchthon, fourteen years his junior, was laying

---

[1] *C. R.*, 24 : 85.

that foundation in Latin, Greek, Logic, Rhetoric, Philosophy, Mathematics, and Astronomy, which qualified him to stand by the side of the solitary monk that shook the world. At this same time Melanchthon was forming friendships with young men, who, like himself, were destined to play an important part in the events of subsequent years, such as Peter Sturm, brother of Jacob Sturm, the celebrated statesman of Strassburg; Theobald Billican, Reformer of Nördlingen, then professor at Heidelberg and Marburg; and John Brentz, whose name will be forever associated with the renovation of Christianity in Würtemberg. Of Billican, Melanchthon wrote: " He was my schoolfellow, and in talents and eloquence he greatly surpassed me." Luther compared Brentz, in relation to himself, " to the still small voice following the whirlwind, earthquake, and fire." [1]

And now, after two years of study, the young Bretten matriculate, not yet fifteen years old, stood his examination under the rectorate of Dr. Leonhard Dietrich, and on the eleventh day of June, 1511, was made Bachelor of the Liberal Arts. Urged on by a noble thirst for knowledge, by a pardonable pride of his attainments, and by an ambition to become a teacher, he devoted himself with new zeal to the study of the scholastic philosophy, with the intention of taking the degree of Master of Arts. But at the end of a year his application was denied " on account of his youth and his boyish appearance." [2]

---

[1] Krauth's *Conservative Reformation*, p. 76, n.
[2] *C. R.*, 10 : 260.

CHAPTER III

STUDENT AND TEACHER AT TÜBINGEN

Melanchthon Leaves Heidelberg and Goes to Tübingen—Life and Studies at Tübingen—Melanchthon Becomes Master of Arts—Is Licensed to Teach—Lectures on the Classics—Becomes Proof-Reader, Editor, and Translator—Obscurantism—Melanchthon Attracts the Attention of Scholars.

PIQUED by the rejection of his application to become a candidate for the Master's degree, and thinking, doubtless, that there was not much more to be learned at Heidelberg, and believing that a change of climate might improve his health, Melanchthon resolved to emigrate to another university. Again following the advice of Reuchlin and Simler, he went to Tübingen, where he matriculated, September 17, 1512, John Schemer being Rector.

The University of Tübingen was founded in the year 1477 by Duke Eberhard the Bearded. It also was yet under the domination of the scholastic philosophy; but it had given a larger place than Heidelberg to humanistic culture. Here John Brassican, of Constance, taught Latin Grammar by a simple and practical method. Heinrich Bebel, in 1501 laureated by the Emperor Maximilian, lectured on poetry and eloquence.

Melanchthon heard these two with special delight, but he supplemented their deficiencies by reading Virgil and Cicero. He heard Francis Stadian on the philosophy of Aristotle, Simler on Jurisprudence and Logic, and Stöffler on Mathematics and Astronomy. He also heard lectures on Medicine, and read the words of Galen. Greek he pursued privately, assisted by Œcolampadius, who was fifteen years his senior. Hebrew he began at the suggestion of Reuchlin, who had written the first Hebrew Grammar that appeared in Germany. By the aid of this book Melanchthon pursued the study of Hebrew as far as was possible without further assistance. To this list of studies, already long, he joined that of Theology, which he always regarded as the crown of the sciences. Both Realism and Nominalism then had their representatives in the theological and in the philosophical faculty. At the close of the preceding century Gabriel Biel had taught Nominalism, and John Heynlin, Realism, both with renown.

The students lived in special quarters called *Bursen*, according as they belonged to the old school (Realism) or the new school (Nominalism). The symbol of the former was the eagle, that of the latter the peacock ; and many were the battles fought under the rival banners. Melanchthon read Occam assiduously, and became imbued with Nominalism. He also heard Jacob Lemp, " the old

JOHANNES COCHLÄUS.   EOBANUS HESSUS.

JOHANNES REUCHLINUS.

HANS SACHS.   CONRAD CELTES.

FROM ENGRAVING IN KREUSSLER'S "ANDENKEN IN MÜNZEN."

Doctor of Theology, who pictured transubstantiation on the blackboard."[1]   At the same time he deepened his spiritual life by reading Gerson, and found theological instruction in the writings of John Wessel, of whom he wrote in his Postils: " On many points of evangelical doctrine he taught exactly as we do, now that the Church is reformed, and that God has caused the glorious light of the Gospel to shine again in marvellous ways."[2]   He also kept up his intercourse with his learned uncle; often visiting him at Stuttgart, where he regaled himself in his uncle's library, or listened to his account of the persons and things he had seen in his wide intercourse with men.   And often did Reuchlin visit his nephew at Tübingen, living with him in his *Burse* and eating with him at the same table, " because he delighted in intercourse with young men."   Reuchlin gave Melanchthon a Latin Bible, which the latter carried with him whithersoever he went, " and read it carefully day and night."   Even during the church service, while the preacher was discoursing on the ethics of Aristotle, or relating monkish fables, he was reading in his Bible such explanations as no priest and no professor at Tübingen could give him.

Thus again it will be seen that Melanchthon's studies took a wide range.   He sought to know everything and to be a master in every science. Bretschneider sums up his student career at Tübingen as follows:

" He gave attention chiefly to Greek and Latin litera-

[1] *C. R.*, 4 : 718.
[2] *C. R.*, 24 : 309.

ture, to philosophy, history, eloquence, logic, mathematics, heard the theologians (particularly Lemp, who
taught the scholastic theology), the lecturers on law and
medicine, and read Galen so carefully that he could repeat most of his works from memory.'' [1]

His seventeenth birthday was now approaching,
and with it the fulfilment of the wish which had
been denied him at Heidelberg. On the twenty-
fifth day of January, 1514, as first among eleven
candidates, he received the degree of Master of the
Liberal Arts, and with it license as a *Privatdocent* to
lecture on the ancient classics to his own *Burse*, of
which he was regent. He began with Virgil and
Terence, to which Livy and Cicero were soon after
added. His didactic skill, his extraordinary thoroughness, his enthusiasm for classical literature,
awoke a new life in the university. Not content
with the discharge of his official duties, he gathered
round him a select circle of students for the cultivation of a purer Latinity, and for the study of the
Greek language.

He also became corrector to the printer, Thomas
Anshelm—a position which could be held then only
by a learned man. Here he had an opportunity to
employ his great learning in the interests of science.
He edited and almost completely re-wrote the
Chronicon, or *Universal History*, by John Naucler,
the Rector of the university, and made it one of the
most serviceable and widely read books of the age.
In March, 1516, he published, with Preface, a metri-

---

[1] *C. R.*, 1 : cxlvi.

cal arrangement of the Comedies of Terence, which had been hitherto published only as prose. In November of the same year he gave out a Preface to the *Dialogus Mythologicus* of Bartholomew of Cologne.

The next year, besides other literary labours, he translated a portion of Plutarch; and at the instance of Professor Stöffler he undertook the translation of Aratus, a part of which he put into Latin verse, and ceased only because he had resolved to undertake a greater work.

Stadian had been lecturing on Aristotle's *Analytica Posteriora*, which was then regarded as belonging to the Metaphysics. Melanchthon became convinced that this work belonged to Rhetoric, and succeeded in convincing his former professor of the correctness of his conclusions. Stadian then proposed that Melanchthon should prepare a new edition of Aristotle in the original, for the purpose of exhibiting, in his own true form, the great philosopher, "who, maimed, mutilated, and translated into barbarous Latin, had become more obscure than a sibylline oracle." [1]

Stadian, Reuchlin, Simler, Œcolampadius, and others, promised him assistance. But the work did not advance very far, as soon Melanchthon found his life-work in another field.

Meanwhile, and since 1509, Melanchthon had been a spectator, and more than a spectator, of one of the most shameful and bitter literary contests known to history. John Pfefferkorn, a converted Jew, and Jacob Hochstratten, a Dominican Inquisi-

[1] *C. R.*, 1 : 26, and 11 : 17.

tor, had insisted on the banishment of the Jews and the destruction of most of their writings.

The Emperor Maximilian, through the Elector of Mayence, required an opinion from Reuchlin. The great Hebraist defended the Hebrew literature against these self-appointed watchers on the walls of Zion. Pfefferkorn published Reuchlin's opinion with abusive comments, denounced him as a heretic, and had him brought to trial before the Bishop of Spires. The whole literary and theological world was now drawn into the contest. On the one side were the monks. On the other side were the brave and spirited champions of Humanism, such as Count Hermann of Neuenar, John Crotus, Peter Eberbach, Eoban Hess, Wilibald Pirkheimer, John Brassican, Richard Crotus, and the brave and brilliant Ulrich von Hutten. Reuchlin was acquitted by the court, but still the battle raged, until the valiant Francis von Sickingen forced the obscurant monks to pay the cost of prosecution, and to make the *amende honorable.*

What part Melanchthon took in this contest is not clear. He and his former teacher, John Hiltebrant, wrote Prefaces to *The Letters of Illustrious Men*, addressed to Reuchlin, and published by Anshelm in March, 1514, in order to show to the learned world the kind of man these Cologne obscurantists had attacked. Melanchthon praises the letters as models of epistolatory style, and adds that " Germany can behold nothing more glorious than the person of Reuchlin, whom the goddess of wisdom has adorned with the most splendid gifts."

As a counterpart to this book there soon appeared
Epistolæ Obscurorum Virorum (*The Letters of Obscure
Men*).   It is a book of satires, the most natural, the
most cruel, and hence the most effective ever written.   The very names of the writers, Hasenfusius,
Hasenmusius, Dollenkoppius, Lumplin, Schnar-
holtzius, Buntschuchmacherius, Eitelnarrabienus,
and the like, bespeak sarcasm and irony.   The book
was written in the barbarous monks' Latin of the
period, sometimes interlarded with German, as
follows :

> " Et ivi hinc ad Hagenau,
>   Da wurden mir die Augen blau,
>   Per te, Wolfgange Angst ;
>   Gott gib, dass du hangst,
>   Quia me cum baculo
>   Percusseras in oculo."

The satires mirror the ignorance, arrogance, immorality, and barbarity of the monks, their hate
of heretics and humanists, in a style which might
have tortured them to death had their ignorance
and stolidity not been so great that some of them
actually thought these letters had been composed
in their honour.   Hence they even assisted in their
circulation.

The question of the authorship of these letters
has not been settled.   They have been attributed
to Hutten, to Crotus Rubianus, and to other old
and young humanists.   One of the most amusing
and effective of the entire collection is entitled
*Carmen Rithmicale Magistri Philippi Schlauraff,
quod compilavit et comportavit, quando fuit Cursor*

in Theologia, et ambulavit per totam Alamaniam superiorem.[1]

Some have supposed that Melanchthon was the author of this piece, and under this supposition Bretschneider put it in the *Corpus Reformatorum*, though it is far more likely that it was written by Ulrich von Hutten. It represents a young Cologne Magister travelling over Germany in search of "poets," and everywhere treated with insults and blows. The prominence given to "Philip Melanchthon," in this poem shows that the young Tübingen Magister occupied a conspicuous place among the authors and humanists who were particularly hostile to the monkish pedantry of the day. A few extracts from this characteristic poem will interest the reader·

> "Tunc præterivi Studgardiam, quia habet ibi stanstiam
> *Reuchlin* ille hæreticus, qui fuit mihi suspectus.
> Tunc ad Tubingam abii, hic sedent multi socii,
> Qui novos libros faciunt et theologos vilipendunt:
> Quorum est vilissimus *Philippus Melanchthonius,*
> Sicut ego cognovi: et igitur Deo vovi,
> Si viderem illum mortuum, quod irem ad Sanctum Jacobum.
> Et *Paulus Vereander*, die schwuren alle mit einander,
> Quod vellent me percutere, si non vellem recedere.
> Sed quidam hic theologus cum nomine *Franciscus*
> Sua cum cavisatione portavit me ex illa regione.
> Tunc cogitavi ire, et ab illis poétis venire."

Finally this wanderer in search of "poets" comes back to Cologne:

> "Sic ivi ad Coloniam, et inveni bonam componiam,
> Quamvis mihi *Buschius* cum suis auditoribus,

---

[1] See *C. R.*, 10 : 472 *et seqq.*, and Rotermund's edition of the *Epistolæ*, pp. 142 *et seqq.*

ULRICH VON HUTTEN.

FROM A CONTEMPORARY WOODCUT.

Et *Joannes Cæsarius*, qui legit ibi Plinius,
Facerent instantias, quia non curavi has:
Sed steti cum Theologis, et vixi in laetitiis,
Und gab nit ein Har auff den Graven von newen **Ar,**
Quamvis sit Poëticus, quia Pepercornus
In suis dictaminibus dicit de nobilibus,
Qui quamvis sunt clari, non possunt excusari,
Et debent sibi solvere, pro sua obscuritate,
Et sic est finis propter honorem Universitatis."

Melanchthon's participation in the controversy brought him more discomfort than praise. The spirit of Tübingen was still mainly subservient to the old learning. The "heresy" of Luther was combated by Jacob Lemp; and humanists and grammarians were viewed with an evil eye. Even Simler and Stadian clung to the old rather than advanced with the new. Melanchthon was satirised and described as a dangerous man. Hence Tübingen was no longer a comfortable place for him. In 1518, he wrote to Bernhard Maurer: "The method of teaching which ought to improve both the understanding and the manners is neglected. What is called philosophy is a weak and empty speculation, which produces strife and contention. The true wisdom come down from Heaven to regulate the affections of men is banished."[1]

There was nothing more for him to learn from Tübingen, and he could not be content to remain where the new learning did not have free course. Moreover, he had already attracted the attention of foreign scholars. Erasmus, then the literary monarch of Europe, in his notes on the New Testament,

---

[1] *C. R.*, 1: 25.

had written the following encomium on him : " Eternal God, what expectation does not Philip Melanchthon raise, who though a youth, yea, rather, scarcely more than a boy, deserves equal esteem for his knowledge of both languages! What sagacity in argument, what purity of style, what comprehension of learned subjects, what varied reading, what delicacy and almost royal elegance of mind!"[1] Wilibald Pirkheimer of Nuremberg, scholar, statesman, humanist, to whom Melanchthon had addressed a Greek ode, had placed him among his most intimate friends " on account of his studious habits, his learning, and his talents."[2] A call to a professorship at Ingolstadt had reached him. This he declined upon the advice of Reuchlin.

Philip Melanchthon, now in his twenty-second year, was beyond question the best humanistic scholar in Germany. He could not longer remain " in a school where it was a capital offence to study polite literature." Greater and better things were in reservation for him elsewhere.

---

[1] *Com. on Thessal.*, p. 555, Basel, 1515.
[2] *C. R.*, 1 : 23.

CHAPTER IV

EARLY WITTENBERG DAYS

Wittenberg—Founding of the University—Luther Called to Wittenberg—The Ninety-five Theses—Melanchthon Called to Wittenberg—Journey to Wittenberg—Personal Appearance—Liberal
Spirit at Wittenberg—Melanchthon's Inaugural—Luther's Delight—Luther and Melanchthon Compared—Increase of Students—Literary Activity.

WITTENBERG, situated on the right bank of
the Elbe, was founded in the twelfth century by Wendish fishermen. Built on a low, sandy
plain, and surrounded for miles by sandy plains and
a rocky, sterile soil, it has never been distinguished
for commerce or manufactures. It owes its fame
entirely to the fact that it was the cradle of the
Reformation. At the beginning of the sixteenth
century it had a population of about three thousand
souls, who were described by Luther as " disoblig-
ing and discourteous, without any regard for the
finer and higher culture, and dwelling on the bord
ers of civilisation." Myconius says: " The houses
were small, old, ugly, low, wooden, more like a vil-
lage than a city." But it was the capital of Electo-

ral Saxony and had a castle to which was attached a
church known as the Church of All Saints, a parish
church, and an Augustinian monastery. When, in
1490, the Saxon territory was divided between the
Ernestine and the Albertine lines, the Electorate
was left without a university. As it soon became
necessary to provide for higher education, Frederick
the Wise, who had himself been liberally educated,
selected Wittenberg as the location of his university.
Here was the Castle Church with five thousand re-
liques, and with provision for ten thousand masses
per annum. Here also was the monastery, which
could furnish a part of the teaching force, and thus
reduce the expenses. Accordingly, October 18,
1502, the University of Wittenberg was opened.
Frederick spared neither pains nor cost to make his
university equal, or even superior, to its rivals at
Leipzig and Erfurt. He called it his daughter, and
sought to bring into its faculties the best scholars
he could find. Dr. Martin Pollich, physician,
jurist, theologian, called *Lux Mundi*, because of
his much learning, was made Rector, and Dr. John
von Staupitz, a Saxon nobleman, Vicar-General of
the Augustinian Monasteries of Germany, was appointed Dean of the theological faculty. The latter
soon fixed his eye on his young friend, Martin
Luther, an Augustinian brother at Erfurt, as a
proper person for a professor. In 1508, Luther was
called to Wittenberg, and began his work by lecturing on the Aristotelian philosophy.

In 1512, he was graduated Doctor of Theology,
and thenceforth devoted himself to the sacred

science.   In his doctor's oath, he obligated himself
to defend the Holy Scriptures against all errors, and
also to obey the Roman Catholic Church.   He
preached much, heard confessions, and said mass as
became a devout Catholic.   Unexpectedly to him
self he woke the theological world out of its slumbers
by the sound of the hammer strokes which fastened
the Ninety-five Theses to the door of the Castle
Church on the thirty-first of October, 1517.   Henceforth Wittenberg was committed to the new learning,
and was now prepared to furnish a fit working-
place for the literary head of the Reformation.
The fame of the university was growing, and it
became necessary to have professors for Greek and
Hebrew.   Frederick, who was becoming proud of
his " high school," inquired of Reuchlin in April,
1518, for suitable persons to fill the proposed chairs.
The old " phœnix of Germany " rejoiced that " the
University of Wittenberg was to rise to the honour
and praise of all Germany by the use of the Latin,
Greek, and Hebrew tongues."   For Hebrew he
suggested Dr. Paul Riccius, a converted Jew, physician to Cardinal von Gurk, or Conrad Pellican, a
Barefoot prior, one of his own pupils, who, in 1507,
had published a Hebrew Grammar.   For the chair
of Greek he proposed his own nephew, " Master
Philip Schwartzerd of Bretten," stipulating only
that if Master Philip should not fill the place accept-
ably he should be returned free of expense.   He
further suggested that Philip's books could be taken
to Saxony in September by the merchants of Frankfort, and he could ride with them, as he " did not

know the way.''[1] In a subsequent letter to the Elector he commended Philip, saying: '' He will serve
the University and your Electoral Grace with honour
and praise.   Of this I have no doubt, for I know no
one among the Germans who surpasses him, except
Erasmus of Rotterdam, who is a Hollander.''[2]   For
a time the decision hung in the balance.   Peter Mo
sellanus, the celebrated Greek scholar of Leipzig, had
sought the place for himself, and had found advocates in Luther and Spalatin.   The latter had spoken
of him as pious, peaceful, upright, and able to translate from Greek into Latin, and had expressed some
scruples against Melanchthon.   It is probable that
regard for the authority of Reuchlin decided the
matter, and sent Melanchthon to Wittenberg, where
he became the companion of Luther and the chief
promoter of his work.   What would Christendom
be to-day had Melanchthon gone to Ingolstadt and
become the companion and supporter of Eck ?

On the twenty-fourth of July, Reuchlin forwarded
the formal call to Melanchthon, saying:

'' Here you have the letter of the pious Prince, signed
with his own hand, in which he promises you his favour
and protection.   I will not address you in the language
of poetry, but will quote the faithful promise of God to
Abraham : ' Get thee out of thy country, and from thy
kindred, and from thy father's house, unto a land that I
will shew thee; and I will make of thee a great nation,
and I will bless and make thy name great, and thou shalt
be a blessing' (Gen. xii., 1, 2). So my mind forecasts,

----

[1] See Reuchlin's letter in *C. R.*, 1 : 27 *et seq.*
[2] *C. R.*, 1 : 34.

LUTHER'S HOUSE, WITTENBERG.

and so I hope it will be with thee, my Philip, my work, and my consolation."

Then after advising him about his effects and his leave-taking of friends at Tübingen, Bretten, and Pforzheim, and inviting him to come to Stuttgart, he adds: " Such is my advice.   Be of good courage. Be not a woman, but a man.   A prophet is not without honour save in his own country.   Farewell." [1]

Thus dismissed with a prophetic anticipation, and with the assurance of the divine blessing, Melanchthon visited his mother and grandmother, and then hastened to Stuttgart to take a final farewell of his illustrious relative, friend, patron, and counsellor, who from " his youth had taught and instructed him in the Greek language," and whom he should never see again in the flesh.

Urged by the Elector, who was at that time attending an imperial diet at Augsburg, to come to him at once " with his books," early in August Melanchthon mounted a horse and set out for Augsburg, which twelve years later was the scene of his greatest achievement, the composition of the first and most widely endorsed Confession of Protestant Christendom.   Here he saluted the Elector, and formed the acquaintance of Spalatin, with whom he travelled into Saxony, and with whom he formed a lasting friendship.   The die was cast, but no human mind could foresee the result.   It could only have been said that Philip Melanchthon, the best product

---

[1] *C. R.*, 1 · 32.

of the German Renaissance, had left his land and
kindred, the fertile fields and balmy climate of the
South, for an academic home among strangers in
the cold and crude North.

But the change was a relief, since he wished not
longer to remain and be tormented in Tübingen,
where his eminent scholarship and rising reputation
had excited the jealousy of the older professors.[1]
Nor was his departure deplored by his colleagues,
because, as Simler said, " though there were many
learned men there, they were not learned enough to
understand how great was the learning of him who
had gone from the midst of them." [2]   Yet our old
account relates that

" in the meanwhile Duke Ulrich of Würtemberg, who
wished to retain Philip in his own country, sent Conrad
von Sickingen, then in his service, to Philip's mother to
inform her that if her son was minded to enter the
priesthood, he should apply to his Princely Grace.   Then
he would provide him with a good benefice on account
of the faithful service of his sainted father.   However,
Philip was not inclined to become a priest; but intended
in accordance with the invitation of the Elector of Saxony
to serve his Electoral Grace and the University; and so
it came to pass."

After tarrying a few days at Augsburg, where
again he declined a call to Ingolstadt, Melanchthon
started directly for Wittenberg.   At Nuremberg he
made the personal acquaintance of Wilibald Pirk-

---

[1] See his letters to Reuchlin in *C. R.*, 1 : 31.
[2] *C. R.*, 10 : 299.

heimer, and of Christopher Scheurl, who from 1505
to 1512 had been a professor of law at Wittenberg.
Both received the young professor with open arms.
August 20th he reached Leipzig, where he met for
the first time Peter Mosellanus, the young professor
of Greek, and Andrew Francis Comitianus, who
afterward became counsellor to several Saxon
dukes. Camerarius, his lifelong friend and bio-
grapher, relates the following anecdote·

" Philip used to tell what occurred at a banquet given
in his honour by the University. The courses were
many, and as each was served, some person would get
up with a prepared speech and address him. Having
observed this for a while and having responded once and
again, Philip said: ' I pray you, illustrious sirs, allow me
to respond once for all to your speeches, for I am not
prepared to speak so often with the proper variety.' " [1]

Schmidt remarks that Melanchthon was not so
lusty a drinker as the Leipzig professors were.

In addition to this good cheer, the Leipzig professors sought, more earnestly than honourably, to
retain him in the service of their own university.
They spoke disparagingly of Wittenberg, and offered
larger pay than had been promised him—one hundred florins—by the Elector. But, though fearing
lest his salary might not be adequate for his maintenance, he nevertheless stood firmly by his promise,
and on the morning of the 24th pushed on toward
the end of his journey. He passed the night at
Düben, and on the next day, August 25, 1518, at

[1] *Vita Melanchthonis*, p. 26.

one o'clock in the afternoon, he entered "the white city" by the Elbe, where he was destined to labour for forty-two years, and where his body, worn out by toil and suffering, was to find its last resting-place.

Melanchthon's fame had preceded him to Wittenberg, but his appearance disappointed expectation. He was young, below middle size, diffident, hesitating, of frail body and stammering tongue, and carried one shoulder higher than the other. As he passed along the street it may have been said with a wink of the eye and a wag of the head, "There goes Melanchthon, the new professor"; but those who took a closer look, and judged not by the outward appearance only, remarked the high forehead, the large, clear, blue eyes, the thoughtful face, the animated gesture,—all of which gave intimations of the lofty intellect which used that frail body as its instrument. August 26th, under the rectorate of Nicholas Gingelm, Master of Arts, "Philip Melanchthon of Bretten, a Tübingen Master of Arts, was registered as the first professor of the Greek language." So runs the record in the *Codex Bavari*, t. i., p. 1003.

Melanchthon is now installed a professor at the new University of Wittenberg. No restrictions are imposed on his teaching. He came as a pronounced humanist, but a humanist of a loftier purpose, who is to use humanistic learning in the service of religion; and Wittenberg is exactly the place for the execution of such a purpose. From its very beginning a liberal spirit had prevailed in the Saxon university on the Elbe. The first rector had favoured classical studies in opposition to the current subtleties of the scholastic method. The first dean of the theological faculty had laid more stress on practical piety than on the dogmas of the Church. Luther had already raged against Aristotle and the scholastics, and by his lectures on the Psalms and Romans had carried the study of Theology back towards its sources. John Rhagius and Otto Beckman were lecturing on the Latin classics. Jerome Schurf, from Tübingen, lectured on Law. Caspar Borner taught Astronomy. These friends of advanced methods were more than odds for the few remaining Thom ists and Scotists who taught physics and logic in the old way. In addition there was in the theological faculty Andrew Bodenstein, a man of ample learning, and of controversial spirit, but with his eye to the future rather than on the past. Surely no university in Germany furnished at that time such an opportunity and such congenial companionship for the young humanist as Wittenberg. All had awaited his coming with anxious expectation, and all had been disappointed in his appearance But the disappointment was of short duration. August 29th, four days after his arrival, the new professor ascended the rostrum in the presence of the as sembled University and delivered his Inaugural. His subject was " The Improvement of the Studies of Youth " (*De corrigendis adolescentiæ studiis*). He said:

Only regard for the proper studies and the du ties of my office, illustrious Rector and Heads of the University, could induce me to commend to you the study of classical literature, which is so much opposed by rude and uncultured men, who declare that classical studies are more difficult than useful; that Greek is studied only by disordered intellects, and that, too, for display ; and that Hebrew is of little account. To contend with such teachers one needs to be a Hercules or a Theseus. Even before me I see those who are annoyed by this innovation. But hear me patiently, as my relation to you and the dignity of literature require.

In the Middle Ages Roman literature went down with the Roman Empire. Only in England and Ireland did learning flourish, as with the Venerable Bede, who was master of all the knowledge of his times. The Germans were better acquainted with war than with literature. Charlemagne revived the study of literature. He called Alcuin from England to France. Under his leadership Paris became distinguished for culture. Then came a period of relapse, and Aristotle, mutilated and translated into bad Latin, became more obscure than a sibylline oracle. This was followed by the race of scholastics, more numerous than the seed of Cadmus. Law, Medicine, and Theology alike suffered from the decline of classical study. Good literature was supplanted by the bad; the pristine piety was exchanged for ceremonies, human traditions, constitutions, capitularies, pilgrimages, and glosses.

There are three kinds of studies: Logic, Physics, and Oratory. Logic teaches the force and differences of words, and also the limits, origin, and course of things. But the science has been corrupted by many of its modern teachers; and endless disputes arise, as between Nominalism and Realism. Yet Logic is of great service. There is also great confusion among theologians. The Philosophers, Orators, Poets, Theologians, and Historians of antiquity must be studied. All public and private life is profited by the study of history. Homer is the source of all learning among the Greeks, and Virgil and Horace among the Latins. Theology must be studied by the aid of the Greek and Hebrew. When we go to the sources, then are we led to Christ. I shall begin my work with Homer and the Epistle to Titus. Cultivate the old Latins and embrace the Greeks. To the inculcation of such studies I now devote myself.

This oration, of which we have given a brief synopsis, at once points out the relation of Melanchthon to the great intellectual and religious movement of the age. No similar programme had ever been exhibited to the professors and students of a German university. What had lain in the author's mind at Tübingen as a fruitful seed, now in the congenial atmosphere of Wittenberg blossomed out in strength and beauty. In the face of remnants of obscurantism which may have lingered in this newest university, the young professor announces the mission of classical studies. He conceives that they are to regenerate society, and to lead to a better theology. The Erasmian thought that the Church must be reformed by means of classical study takes a step forward, and joins Homer and Paul. It does not

have that deeper knowledge of the Scripture into
which its author was yet to be led, nor that living
relation to the saving doctrine which alone can free
the Church from its Babylonian captivity; but it
points significantly and positively in the right direction, and marks the inauguration of a new era in
culture and religion. In Italy the Renaissance
brought in scepticism and Epicureanism. In Germany it was to bring faith and a higher morality.
The difference in results lay in the fact that in Italy
culture was sought as an end in itself. In Germany
it was used as a means for the cultivation of theology
and for the advancement of piety. And this different use of a revived antiquity has been one of the
most potent factors in making Protestant peoples so
much superior to their Roman Catholic neighbours,
both in theology and in religion. For very much
of this superiority the world is indebted to Melanchthon. His Inaugural is an open declaration of war
against the " men of darkness," and a protest
against the traditional methods in theology. It
enunciates distinctly the evangelical principle: the
Bible as the means and Christ as the goal of truth
and wisdom.

The impression made by the oration was extraordinarily great. A new star, destined to shed its
light wide over the world, had risen in the North.
Luther was in ecstasy. Two days later he wrote to
Spalatin:

" As regards our Philip Melanchthon everything shall
be done as you suggest. On the fourth day after his
arrival he delivered a most learned and chaste oration to

the delight and admiration of all. It is not now necessary for you to commend him. We quickly retracted the opinion which we had formed when we first saw him. Now we laud and admire the reality in him, and thank the most illustrious Prince and your kindness. Be at pains to commend him most heartily to the Prince. I desire no other Greek teacher so long as we have him. But I fear that his delicate constitution may not bear the mode of life in this country. Also, I hear that because of the smallness of his salary the boastful Leipzig professors hope soon to take him from us. They solicited him before he came here." [1]

Luther then exhorts Spalatin not to despise Melanchthon's appearance and age, " for he is worthy of all honour." Two days later he wrote again: " I most heartily commend Philip. He is a most thorough Greek scholar, very learned and highly cultured. His lecture-room is filled with students. All the theological students, the highest, middle, and lowest classes, study Greek." [2]

The two great men were at once drawn to each other. Luther's clear understanding, deep feeling, pious spirit, heroic courage, overwhelmed Melanchthon with wonder, so that he reverenced him as a father. Melanchthon's great learning, fine culture, philosophical clearness, his beautiful character and tender heart, acted as a charm upon Luther. Each found the complement of his own nature in the other. God had joined the two with marvellous adaptation. If Luther was a physician severer than

[1] De W. (De Wette's *Luther's Briefe*). 1 : 134, 135.
[2] De W., 1 : 140.

the diseases of the Church could bear, Melanchthon was too gentle for the hurt of the declining Church, which could not easily bear either her diseases or the remedies required to heal them. Together they achieved what neither could have done without the other. Hence they are entitled to share equal honours for the work of the Reformation. Without Melanchthon the nailing up of the Ninety-five Theses had ended in a monkish squabble, to be followed perhaps by a new school of theology in the old Church. Without Luther the teaching of Greek at Wittenberg would have ended in a higher and purer humanistic culture. Their combined labours produced the Protestant Church, changed the course of history, and introduced the modern era. Luther by his fiery eloquence, genial humour, and commanding personality commended the Reformation to the people. Melanchthon by his moderation, his love of order, his profound scholarship, won for it the support of the learned. Luther himself has put their gifts in happy juxtaposition:

"I am rough, boisterous, stormy, and altogether warlike. I am born to fight against innumerable monsters and devils. I must remove stumps and stones, cut away thistles, and thorns, and clear the wild forests; but Master Philip comes along softly and gently, sowing and watering with joy, according to the gifts which God has abundantly bestowed upon him." [1]

The sowing was just as useful and indispensable as the removal of the stumps and stones. The

---

[1] Preface to Melanchthon's *Com. on Colossians.*

work of the one, especially at the beginning, was
predominantly the work of destruction; that of the
other, as predominantly the work of construction.
Luther tore down the idols of the Roman Catholic
Church. Melanchthon laid the foundation of the
dogmatic system of Protestant theology, and wrote
the first Confession of the Protestant Church. Their
combined labours brought into existence the Evangelical Lutheran Church. Also the friendship established between these great men forms one of the
most pleasing features of the religious drama of
the sixteenth century. Luther loved Melanchthon
as a son, and yet he often sat at his feet as a pupil,
and preferred the opinions of Master Philip to his
own. Melanchthon learned his theology and his
spiritual apprehension of divine truth from Luther.
Each esteemed the other better than himself. Each
saw in the other a wonderful instrument of Providence, and each had the consciousness that he had
been providentially joined to the other for the execution of a common commission. At one time the
ardour of their friendship was slightly damped, but
the warmth of earlier attachment was soon rekin-
dled, and then it endured to the end. Lovely and
pleasant in their lives, they toiled, prayed, and suffered for the same great cause, and in their death
they are not divided, since they sleep together under
the same roof in the Castle Church at Wittenberg,
on whose door Luther nailed the first battle-cry of
the Reformation.

A new era in academic culture had now begun at
Wittenberg. For some years theology had been

taught in an independent and liberal way; but Melanchthon was the first to lead the students to the original sources of theology and to train them by means of logic and classical literature to systematic thinking and to the clear expression of their thoughts. The result was that from all parts of Germany, and from foreign lands, students flocked to Wittenberg, chiefly to hear Melanchthon. In the winter semester of 1518–19, there were only one hundred and twenty students. The next semester the number was doubled. In the summer semester of 1520 there were three hundred and thirty-three; and in the autumn of the same year Spalatin saw six hundred present at one of Philip's lectures.

"Sometimes he had nearly two thousand hearers, among whom were princes, counts, barons, and other persons of rank. He taught over a wide range of subjects, including Hebrew, Latin, and Greek Grammar, rhetoric, physics, and philosophy; thus serving the common weal of Church and State, and in teaching accomplishing as much in all his subjects as other professors did in one subject."[1]

So splendid was his success that Luther exclaimed:

"Whoever does not recognise Philip as his instructor, is a stolid, stupid donkey, carried away by his own vanity and self-conceit. Whatever we know in the arts and in true philosophy, Philip has taught us. He has only the humble title of Master, but he excels all the Doctors. There is no one living adorned with such gifts. He

[1] *C. R.*, 10: 301.

must be held in honour. Whoever despises this man, him will God despise."[1]

Melanchthon also continued his literary activity. In the year 1518 he edited and published the Epistle to Titus, and wrote to Spalatin that he was ready to publish, among other things, a Greek dictionary, two treatises of Plutarch, a Greek hymn, Athenagoras, Plato's *Symposium*, and three books on Rhetoric.[2] He was body and soul devoted to Wittenberg, with the double purpose of bringing honour to the university and of disseminating knowledge. He declared that he should be wanting neither in faithfulness, nor in study, nor in zeal, nor in labour, to increase the splendour of Wittenberg, and to meet the expectations of the Elector.[3]

Thus with his hands full of work, and with his reputation as a scholar and teacher fully established, Melanchthon closed the year 1518.

---

[1] *C. R.*, 10 : 302.
[2] *C. R.*, 1 : 44, 50, 52.
[3] *Ibidem.*

CHAPTER V

PROGRESS OF THE REFORMATION

Effects of Luther s Theses—Progress of the Reformation—John Eck—Controversy—Leipzig Disputation—Eck, Carlstadt, and Luther—Melanchthon Attends the Leipzig Disputation—Controversy with Eck.

LUTHER'S Theses had excited great commotion throughout Christendom. Those who felt themselves oppressed and scandalised by the papal corruptions, hailed the Saxon monk as the coming deliverer of the Church. Those who were content with the existing order of things proclaimed him a heretic, schismatic, babbler, and blasphemer. The Dominicans complained that their order had been insulted, and yet they rejoiced that the Augustinians were about to be brought into disgrace. The Pope, Leo X., who at first thought the commotion was only an insignificant quarrel between the monks, soon learned that it threatened the stability of his throne. Early in February, 1518, he had called on the General of the Augustinian Order to extinguish the fire which Luther had kindled. He then cited Luther to appear in Rome within sixty days to have his case tried before three judges. And when through the good offices of the Elector it was decided to have the case tried in Germany, Luther was ordered to appear before Cardinal Cajetan without delay. The order was promptly obeyed, and, October 7, 1518, Luther arrived at the cloister of the Augustinians in Augsburg. The interview was continued through several days, but without results. Fearing violence, Luther left Augsburg secretly, and October 31st he was again in Wittenberg. Melanchthon had attended his friend on the dangerous journey with his best wishes and prayers; and now he rejoiced at his safe return. Luther had written him to play the man, and to teach the young men properly, as he himself was going to the sacrifice, if it pleased God, and adds: "I'd rather perish, and, what is more grievous to me than all, be deprived forever of your delightful companionship, than to recant things fitly spoken, and be the occasion of putting an end to profitable studies."[1] A few days later he wrote to Carlstadt that he would rather die, be burnt, expelled, and anathematised than recant. He begs all his friends to pray for him; "yea for yourselves, since your own cause is at stake here, viz., faith in Christ the Lord, and the grace of God."[2]

Luther's danger and his courage drew the young scholar still more closely to him, and helped to identify him with the new movement. Hence when, on the twenty-eighth of November, 1518, Luther pub-

---

[1] De W., 1: 146.
[2] De W., 1: 161.

lished his Appeal to the Pope for a general council,
Melanchthon sent a copy of it to Spalatin, saying:

"I send you Martin's Apology. There is no reason
why you should dread the rage of the Romanists. That
is what such men are wont to do. Unless they play the
tyrant they do not think they rule; though in the name of
God what a difference there ought to be between ruling
and being stewards! But ambition and avarice are seen
in everything. Martin defends himself so well that they
are not able to invent a new accusation against him."[1]

Luther and Melanchthon, though fully convinced
of the corruptions of the Church, and of the righteousness of what had now become their common
cause, had no intention of separating from Rome,
or of changing the constitution of the Church or her
order of worship. They hoped that the ecclesiastical
authorities could be led to see the errors and abuses
which prevailed everywhere, and could be induced
to correct them. The old institutions and orders
might remain. They only needed purification.
Melanchthon even praised Frederick for having provided for the priests, built new monasteries, and
restored old ones.[2] But the two Wittenberg professors, who had been so powerfully drawn together,
were not allowed to rest. They had begun an irrepressible conflict. The truth itself was now fighting.
Every day "the Pope's crown and the monks'
bellies," to use the words of Erasmus, were incurring
greater danger. The threats and denunciations of

---

[1] C. R., 1 : 58.
[2] C. R., 1 : 47.

Cajetan had not silenced " that child of Satan and son of perdition," as the Pope had called Luther. Another method must be tried. Miltitz, the papal chamberlain, was despatched to Altenburg to flatter and conjure the bold monk into silence. He succeeded, but with the distinct understanding, on the part of the monk, that he would observe silence provided that his enemies would also do the same. Here, it was thought, the whole matter would rest. But a new actor now came on the stage. Dr. John Eck, Pro-chancellor of the University of Ingolstadt, was one of the most learned men and eminent theologians of his age. He had studied at Heidelberg and Tübingen, had visited other celebrated universities in Germany, and had made the acquaintance of the most illustrious scholars then living. Wherever he went he gained applause as a debater. At the age of twenty he began to lecture on Occam and Biel, on Aristotle's philosophy, on dogmatics, and on the nominalistic morality. He sought to master every subject and to surpass every other scholar. To increase his reputation as a disputant he visited Vienna and Bologna. He was as vain as he was learned, and delighted in recounting his victories. He saw in the Ninety-five Theses, which had been sent him by Luther, a subject for a new debate and a chance for an additional triumph. Against the Theses he published animadversions under the title of *Oelisce*. These were answered by Carlstadt in 406 theses, in which both the learning and the orthodoxy of the Ingolstadt professor were boldly assailed. Luther himself finally replied

in the *Asterisci.* The result was a challenge to Carlstadt for a public disputation.   Over the shoulders of
Carlstadt Eck wished to chastise Luther.   He chose
Leipzig as the place for the disputation, and June 27,
1519, as the time for beginning it.   But already in
February he had published thirteen theses which he
proposed to defend.   Some of these were directed
against Luther.   As his enemies had now broken
the peace, Luther was no longer bound by his
promise to keep the peace.   Hence he began to prepare to meet the challenge, with the declaration that
he feared "neither the Pope, nor the name of the
Pope, nor popelings, nor puppets."   Eck came to
Leipzig early, and made a great display of himself,
so as to attract attention.   On June 24th the Wittenbergers entered the city   Besides the two
champions, Carlstadt and Luther, there came Dr.
John Lange, Vicar of the Augustinians, Philip
Melanchthon, Nicholas Amsdorf, John Agricola,
three doctors of law, and about two hundred students.   Eck disputed with Carlstadt four days on
the freedom of the will; then with Luther on the
Pope's primacy, purgatory, penance, absolution, and
satisfaction.   Luther drew his arguments against
the Pope's primacy from the Scriptures and from the
fact that the Greek Church had never acknowledged
the Pope's primacy.   These were his strong points;
and in this part of the discussion he evinced his
superiority.   He went so far as to declare that a
General Council could not create an article of faith,
and could give no guarantee against error.   Eck
now proclaimed him a heathen and a publican

Natus 2 April. 1490
Denatus peste
22 Sept.
A? 1566.

28

IOHAN AGRICOLA ISLEBIVS THEOLOGVS
BRANDEBVRGICVS ET GENERALIS MARCHIÆ
SVPERINTENDENS.

JOHN AGRICOLA.

AFTER A CONTEMPORARY COPPER PLATE.

The disputation was continued for some days on other subjects, and then brought to a close. Eck claimed the victory, was applauded by his friends, and rewarded by Duke George, in whose Castle of the Pleissenburg the disputation had taken place. Luther departed for home displeased, exclaiming that Eck and his friends had not sought the truth, but fame. Yet the disputation was helpful to Luther. He had now reached the sublime conclusion that in matters of faith the authority of the Roman Church was not to be recognised. He had also discovered that henceforth his chief weapon must be the Word of God, which alone can make articles of faith.

Melanchthon describes himself as "an idle spectator" of the Leipzig disputation. But he was more than that. He did not indeed take public part in the debate, but he furnished his fellow-professors with arguments in the intervals of the discussion, and made suggestions *sotto voce* while the debate was in actual progress. This displeased Eck, who cried out, " Keep silent, Philip; mind your own studies, and don't disturb me."

Eck was already displeased with Melanchthon, because in his Inaugural Melanchthon had classed him with the perverters of Logic. He now describes Melanchthon as a " nephew of Reuchlin, *very arrogant*." But for Melanchthon the Leipzig disputation was a turning-point in life. It marks the real beginning of his active participation in the work of the Reformation. His faith in the authority of the existing Church is now completely shaken, and his studies henceforth take a more decidedly theological direction. The personality of each of the disputants, and the great questions of the debate, awaken in him the liveliest interest.

Four days after the disputation had closed, that is, July 21st, Melanchthon published a letter to his friend Œcolampadius, then preacher at Augsburg, in which he gave an account of the debate, but refrained from expressing a judgment on the result, or on the direction matters were taking. He says that the object of the discussion was to state the difference between the old theology of Christ and the Aristotelian innovations. He also relates that in the dispute about the Pope's primacy, Eck had spoken with bitterness and rudeness, and had sought to prejudice Luther in the eyes of the people. Of the disputants he says:

" They displayed talents, varied erudition, and much learning in the debate, from which I hope religion will be well served. Eck was greatly admired by many among us on account of his varied and splendid gifts. Carlstadt you know from what he has written. He is a good man, having rare and unquestioned learning. In Martin, with whom I have long been well acquainted, I admire the quick intellect, learning, and eloquence, the sincere and excellent Christian spirit. I cannot help loving him." [1]

This letter falling under the eye of Eck, so excited his ire that on the 25th he sent forth from Leipzig a reply against " the Wittenberg Grammarian, who

---

[1] *C. R.*, 1 : 87 *et seq.*

knows some Greek and Latin." He calls him "the literalist," "the bold little man who assumed to play the rôle of the judge." Once he addresses him as "thou dusty schoolmaster," and tells him that he might have gained some reputation had he minded his own business, but that now he has "consigned himself to obscurity." Finally he says:

"Though Philip is not a person whom a theologian should meet in a matter of theology, yet had I kept silent I should have seemed to acknowledge what he has charged me with. Hence I resolved to meet him, just as Augustine did not hesitate to write against Crescon, the grammarian." [1]

The letter as a whole exhibits a spirit of proud contempt for the Wittenberg Grammarian, who is regarded as incapable of expressing an opinion on subjects of theology. But Eck had mistaken his man. In August, Melanchthon sent forth a reply "from the renowned Wittenberg of Saxony," "dedicated to the candid reader." He makes no reference to the personal indignities heaped upon him by Eck, further than to say that he does not mean to return evil for evil, and railing for railing. He then reviews the Leipzig disputation in a way that evinces a clear insight into the questions at issue, and shows that the writer is a master of trenchant logic. He not only sustains and justifies the positions of Carlstadt and Luther, but what is of far greater significance, he declares that the Church Fathers on whom Eck relied in his interpretation of

---

[1] *C. R.*, 1 : 103.

Scripture and in his defence of the Pope's primacy, can have no binding authority.   He says:

" Far be it from me to detract from the authority of anyone.   I revere and honour those lights of the Church, those illustrious defenders of Christian doctrine.   Inasmuch as the Fathers differ in opinion they are to be judged by the Scripture.   The Scripture is not to be wrenched by their different opinions.   The meaning of the Scripture is one and simple; and as the revealed truth is very simple anyone can understand it by following the text and context.   To this end we are bidden to study the Scripture, viz., that to it as to a Lydian stone, we may apply the doctrine and opinions of men.   If the Fathers are to be employed in judging the Scripture, it were better to take their opinion from those passages in which they simply narrate, than from those in which they orate and give way to their feelings.   We know that we ourselves understand the Scripture differently, accordingly as we are differently affected.   Every person is led by his own feelings, and as the polyp reflects the colour of the stone to which it clings, so we strive with all our might to reproduce what we have studied, as we are led by inclination.   Often we get the right meaning and pursue a proper method, such as we cannot afterward recall. So with the Fathers.   Often when led away by feeling they abuse the Scripture by giving a meaning, not exactly bad, but inappropriate."

He then goes on to say that the scholastics, by their allegorical, tropological, anagogical, literal, grammatical, and historical interpretation, have turned the sacred Scripture into a very Proteus. He asks :

" How often did Jerome, Augustine, Ambrose fall into error ? I am not so ignorant of them that I may not venture thus to speak. I am perhaps better acquainted with them than Eck is with his Aristotle. How often do they differ from each other and retract their errors ? But why say more ? The canonical Scripture alone is inspired, is true and pure in all things." [1]

This reply, in which the Ingolstadt professor is so thoroughly refuted, shows not only that Melanchthon was profoundly acquainted with the Fathers, but that he based the study of theology on the sure foundation of the Word of God, and understood the correct principle of Hermeneutics, viz., *that the Scripture has only one sense.* Eck made no reply, but hastened off to Italy to seek aid and comfort from the Holy Father.

Melanchthon's tractate was received with loud applause by the friends of evangelical truth. He was recognised at once as worthy to stand with the theologians of the first rank. On the fifteenth of August Luther wrote an account of the Leipzig disputation to Spalatin, in which he declares that Melanchthon is three or four times more learned in the Scriptures than all the Ecks. He says expressly :

" I return to Philip, whom no Eck can make me dislike, since in all my teaching I know of nothing better than his approval. His opinion and authority have more weight with me than many thousand miserable Ecks. Though a Master of arts, of philosophy, and of theology, and adorned with nearly all of Eck's titles, I should not

---

[1] *C. R.*, 1 : 108 *et seq.*

hesitate to yield my opinion to that of this Grammarian, should he dissent from me. This I have often done, and I do it daily on account of the divine gift which God with his bountiful blessing has deposited in this frail vessel, though it be contemptible to Eck. I do not praise Philip. He is a creature of God. I revere in him the work of my God." [1]

---

[1] De W., 1 : 305.

CHAPTER VI

HIS THESES AND MARRIAGE

Becomes Bachelor of Theology—Doubts the Doctrines of the Church —Writes Theses—His Marriage—Family—Salary.

MELANCHTHON was rapidly growing in the love of the Scriptures, and was devoting more and more of his time to their exposition, especially as since the beginning of the year 1519 he had also taught Hebrew, and had expounded portions of the Old Testament. On the twenty-fifth of January, 1519, Luther had written to Spalatin: " Our Philip is engaged on the Hebrew with greater fidelity and also with better results than that John [1] who left us. The faithfulness and diligence of the man are so great that he scarcely takes any leisure." [2]

On the nineteenth of December Melanchthon himself wrote to John Schwebel that during the summer he had expounded the Epistle to the Romans, and that he was then engaged in expounding Matthew,

---

[1] Luther means John Böschenstein, who came to Wittenberg as professor of Hebrew in November, 1518, and left after a few months.

[2] De W., I : 214.

57

and meant to publish a commentary on Matthew.
He adds: " I am wholly engaged on the Holy
Scriptures, and wish you would also devote yourself
wholly to them.   There is a wonderful charm in
them; yea, a heavenly ambrosia nourishes the soul
which is engaged on them." [1]   The estimate which
Luther placed on these lectures on Matthew is
shown in a letter which he wrote to Lange on the
eighteenth of December: "I am sorry that I cannot
send all the brethren to Philip's theological lectures
on Matthew at six o'clock in the morning.   The
little Grecian surpasses me also in theology." [2]

Melanchthon was now in the theological faculty.
On the nineteenth of September, 1519, in company
with John Agricola, he was made Bachelor of Theology.   This was the only theological degree he ever
accepted, not because he affected to despise higher
degrees, as we learn from one of his letters, but partly
because he thought they ought to be conferred with
great discrimination, and partly because he did not
wish to be responsible for what was involved in the
theological doctorate, though Luther pronounced him
a doctor above all doctors; and he certainly was the
doctor of the German Evangelical Church,[3] *though
he was never ordained to the office of the ministry.*

---

[1] *C. R.*, 1 : 128.

[2] De W., 1 : 380.

[3] In 1542, Melanchthon wrote : " Titulus aliquid habet oneris.
Vides meum exemplum: nemo perpellere potuit, ut illum quemlibet
honorificum titulum Doctoris mihi sinerem.   Nec ego gradus illos
parvifacio ; sed ideo, quia judico esse magna ornamenta et necessaria
Reipublicæ, verecunde petendos esse, et conferendos, sentio."—*C.
R.*, 4 : 811.

Among the subjects which he discussed at his promotion, were: "*That the Catholic Christian needs no articles of faith except those furnished by the Scripture. That the authority of councils is inferior to the authority of the Scripture. Whence it follows that it is not a heresy not to believe Transubstantiation and the like.*" [1]

Luther wrote to his old teacher, Staupitz:

"You have seen, or will see, Philip's theses. They are bold, but they certainly are true. He defended them in such a way that he seemed to us all a veritable wonder, and such he is. Christ willing, he will surpass many Martins and will be a mighty foe of the devil and of the scholastic theology. He knows their tricks and also the Rock Christ. He will powerfully prevail." [2]

The admiration which Luther constantly expresses for his young friend does not rise out of the dark and dubious region of sentiment, but from the firm belief that Melanchthon is a chosen instrument of God for carrying on the work of reforming the Church. In a letter to Lange he describes himself as the forerunner, come in the spirit and power of Elijah, but says that Philip will overthrow Israel and the followers of Ahab.[3] And not less deep and sincere was the admiration which Melanchthon had for Luther: "Martin is too great and too wonderful for me to describe in words," he writes to Schwebel; and again: "You know with what as-

---

[1] *C. R.*, 1 : 138.
[2] De W., 1 : 341.
[3] De W., 1 : 478.

tonishment Alcibiades regarded Socrates.   Much in
the same way, but in a Christian sense, I regard
Martin.   The more I contemplate him, the greater
I judge him to be." [1]

Of the relation which they sustained to each other
at this time, and indeed during most of the time
they lived together, it may be said that Luther relied
on Melanchthon, and used his great learning for the
promotion of the cause with which he had identified
himself body and soul; while Melanchthon by contact with Luther grew in courage against Rome, and
in that spiritual perception of the essential quality
of Christianity which brought him to sharper antithesis with the doctrines and practices of the Church.
In the same letter to Schwebel he says: " We do
not fear the dregs of Rome.   If God be for us who
can be against us ? "   His letter of February, 1520,
to John Hess, of Nuremberg, is taken up largely
with doubts about Transubstantiation and the teaching of the Scholastics, and with an exposition of the
teaching of Paul in opposition to the teaching of
the councils.   He is not willing to number Transubstantiation among the articles of faith; or to say
that anything is an article of faith which cannot be
proved by the Scriptures; or to allow that the
authority of councils is equal to that of the Scriptures.   Nor is he willing to confess that it is a heresy
not to concede both swords to the Pope; nor not to
agree with Peter Lombard touching the number of
the sacraments; nor to withstand the bulls of Indul-

---

[1] *C. R.*, 1 : 264.

gence.[1] But at the same time that he was expressing his doubt in regard to many doctrines of the
Church, he was advancing to clearer conceptions of
the scriptural doctrine of faith; of the sacraments;
of the keys; of eternal life. In July of this year,
perhaps earlier, he wrote eighteen theses for academic discussion. They are as follows·

" Justification takes place through faith; love is the
work of faith; there is no difference between *fides
formata* and *fides informis ; fides informis*, as it is called,
is not faith, but a vain opinion; love necessarily follows
faith; faith and love are works of God, not of nature;
Christianity is a Sabbath and perfect. freedom; satisfaction is not a part of penance; there is no external
sacrifice in Christianity; the Mass is not a work the
benefit of which avails for another; Baptism benefits only
him who is baptised, and the Mass only him who par-
takes. Baptism and the Mass are sacramental signs by
which the Lord witnesses that he will pardon sins; inasmuch as the sum of our justification is faith, no work
can be called meritorious; hence all human works are
only sins; the keys are given to all Christians alike, nor
can the Primacy be allowed to Peter by divine right;
Aristotle's notion of blessedness agrees neither with
Christian teaching nor with the common sense of men;
it is better to derive our notion of blessedness and like
things from the Holy Scripture than from the nonsense
of the vain sophists." [2]

In these theses on justification by faith, the sac-

---

[1] *C. R.*, 1 : 138 *et seq.*

[2] *C. R.*, 1 : 126. For a discussion of the date of these theses, see
ibid., 1 : 126.

rament, the keys, the Pope's primacy, *et cetera*, we have the central doctrines, both material and formal, of the Great Reformation. The rapid advance made by Melanchthon in evangelical conceptions is doubtless due mainly to his study of the Scriptures.

In the years 1519 and 1520, Melanchthon was very active with his pen. At the beginning of the latter year he published two treatises on the doctrines of Paul, and a handbook on Dialectics. In April he is engaged in writing a commentary on Matthew. He published for the students the Greek text of Paul's Epistle to the Romans, an edition of the Clouds of Aristophanes, and a new edition of his Greek Grammar, besides other treatises, some of greater, others of less, importance. His industry was amazing. He began his work at two o'clock in the morning and continued it until evening. Luther and others feared for his life. Even the Elector wrote him to take care of his health.[1] Luther felt that with his hard work and the poor comforts provided by his meagre salary, together with the severity of that northern climate, Melanchthon could not long remain at Wittenberg. Consequently he not only begged the Elector through Spalatin for an increase in Melanchthon's salary, but urged him to get married, in order that he might have someone to take care of his weak body. Melanchthon at first rebelled at the suggestion of marriage; not because he hated women, or esteemed marriage lightly, but

---

[1] *C. R.*, 10 : 193.

because he loved study more.[1]   At length he gave
a reluctant consent, saying, " I am robbing myself
of study and of pleasure in order to follow the
counsel and subserve the pleasure of others."[2]

Luther does not deny that he made the match.
He wishes to do the best he can for his friend, and
invokes God's blessing upon him.[3]   Finally, on the
fifteenth of August, Philip announces to Lange that
he is going to marry Katharine Krapp, daughter of
Hieronimus Krapp, Mayor of Wittenberg.   He declares that she is a young lady possessing such manners and qualities of mind as he should desire from
the immortal gods.[4]   Soon gossips were busy, as
ever they are, and the marriage was hastened.   On
the twenty-fifth of November, 1520, Melanchthon
posted the following verses on the bulletin board :

> " A studiis hodie facit otia grata Philippus,
>   Nec verbis Pauli dogmata sacra leget."

> " Rest from your studies, Philip says you may,
>   He 'll read no lecture on St. Paul to-day."

This was the day of his marriage.   Luther's father,
mother, and two sisters, and other persons, some of
whom were illustrious and learned, attended the
nuptials.

---

[1] In 1540 he wrote to Veit Dietrich : " I am really indignant at
those misanthropes who regard it as a special mark of wisdom to
despise women, and to sneer at marriage.   Women may have their
own infirmities, but men also have vices."—C. R., 3 : 1172.

[2] C. R., 1 : 265.

[3] De W., 1 : 478.

[4] C. R., 1 : 212.

Melanchthon in his four-and-twentieth year is a
married man, and begins to experience the trials and
pleasures of married life, though the latter greatly
preponderated.   He declares that his wife is worthy
of a better man.   She is described by Camerarius
as " a most pious woman, ardently devoted to her
husband, liberal and kind to all."

The happy pair lived together thirty-seven years,
and became the parents of two sons and as many
daughters: Anna, born probably in 1522, was highly
accomplished and very dear to her father.   Luther
calls her " Melanchthon's elegant daughter."   At
the age of fourteen she was married to George Sabinus, a gifted but wayward poet, who neglected
her and her children.   She died at Königsberg in
1547, and was buried in the cathedral there.   Philip
was born January 13, 1525.   He was good-natured,
but " weak in body and mind."   He lived to be
eighty years old, and died as notary of the University of Wittenberg.   George was born November
25, 1527, and died when two years old.   He had
already begun to display extraordinary talents.   His
death brought Melanchthon inexpressible sorrow.
Magdalena was born July 18, 1533.   She was married to Caspar Peucer, who was a professor of medicine in the university, and afterwards became court
physician.   She died at Rochlitz, July 18, 1576,
through excess of grief for her husband, who was
cruelly kept a prisoner for twelve years by the
Elector of Saxony.

To Melanchthon's family belonged, also, John
Koch, a Swabian, who entered his master's service

MELANCHTHON'S HOUSE, WITTENBERG.

in 1519.   He was a man of some culture, " chaste
and a lover of chastity."   He trained the children
and managed the affairs of the house as a steward.
When he died, in 1553, Melanchthon invited the
academicians to his funeral, and delivered an oration
over his grave.   Afterwards he wrote an epitaph for
his tomb.

The house in which Melanchthon lived in Wittenberg is still standing.   A tablet high up on the
front bears the following inscription:

Hier wohnte, lehrte und starb PHILIPP MELANCHTHON.

That is:

" Here lived, taught, and died PHILIP MELANCHTHON."

The front room on the second story was Melanchthon's study, and finally the place of his death, as
we learn from two Latin inscriptions:

Ad Boream versis oculis hac sede Melanchthon Scripta
dedit, quæ nunc præcipua orbis habet.

That is:

" At this place Melanchthon, with his eyes turned
towards the North, wrote those works which the world
now holds in high esteem."

Siste viator

Ad hunc parietem stetit lectulus in quo pie et placide
expiravit vir réverendus PHILIPPUS MELANCHTHON.

Die XIX. April. dodrante horæ post VII. Anno
MDLX.

That is:

" Stop traveller!
" Against this wall stood the couch on which the
venerable PHILIP MELANCHTHON piously and peacefully
died, April 19, 1560, at a quarter past seven o'clock."

The study, the dining-room, the nursery, the
school-room, and the chambers have all, until recently, been preserved in their original condition.
The entire house is now " the Melanchthon Mu-
seum."

In this house Melanchthon dispensed a liberal
hospitality.   Exiles, wandering scholars, comers
and goers of every age, sex, and condition, were invited to his house, or imposed themselves upon him.
One day at dinner he heard eleven or twelve languages spoken at his table.   At first his salary was
one hundred florins, equal to about four hundred
dollars; in 1526 it was raised to two hundred ; in
1536 it was increased to three hundred; and from
1541 it was four hundred, which at that time was
regarded as a very large academic salary.   He received many presents from the city council and an
eighth interest in the water company.   He also
received frequent gratuities from princes whom he
had in some way served, or to whom he dedicated
editions of his works.

By his marriage, Melanchthon became firmly anchored at Wittenberg.   Every attempt to drive or to
draw him away failed.   The first effort in the direction of his removal came from Reuchlin, who in
1519 had accepted a professorship at Ingolstadt.

Desiring to have his nephew with him, and wishing doubtless to detach him from Luther's influence, he wrote him to come to Ingolstadt, and promised him the forgiveness of Eck.   But the young man was now too ardently devoted to Luther and the Elector, and was too closely identified with the Wittenberg move- ment to be influenced by the claims of friendship, or by the love of country.   He wrote to his uncle:

" I have been brought to Saxony.   Here I will do my duty until the Holy Spirit to whom I shall commit my- self shall call me away.   I have such a love for my native land as the gods might envy; but in all things I must consider the call of Christ, rather than my own inclina- tion." [1]

This letter settled the matter, but it cost Mel- anchthon the love and devotion of his uncle.   The aged Reuchlin, who was simply a Catholic humanist, fearing lest he should be suspected of sympathy with his heretical relative, requested Melanchthon not again to write him; and despite his promise, made in the presence of witnesses, to give his splen- did library to Melanchthon, he gave it to the monks at Pforzheim.   Thus, like Erasmus, he drew back from the Reformation which by humanistic studies he had helped to introduce, and, like Erasmus, he died in the bosom of the Roman Catholic Church; while Melanchthon, " his work and his consolation," became one of the chief actors in exposing the cor- ruptions of that Church, and in showing the more excellent way of the Reformation.

----

[1] *C. R.*, 1 : 151.

CHAPTER VII

MELANCHTHON THE ALLY OF LUTHER

Luther Burns the Pope's Bull, and Writes two of his Most Important Works—Melanchthon Approves Luther's Course—Controversy with Rhadinus, and with the Sorbonne—Luther Praises Melanchthon's Apology—Fanaticism at Wittenberg—Melanchthon's Distress.

IN the year 1520, affairs reached a crisis at Wittenberg. Eck had returned from Rome with a papal bull which he sought to have executed against Luther at once. But on the morning of November 11th, just outside the Elster gate, Luther burned the Pope's bull, together with certain books of the canon law, with the bold declaration, " Because thou hast vexed the Holy One of the Lord, be thou consumed with everlasting fire." This was the most courageous act of his life, and it completely cut him off from hope of papal clemency. For this he had already prepared himself by one of his most powerful and influential writings, *The Address to the Christian Nobility of the German Nation concerning the Reformation of the Christian Estate.* In this book he demolishes the walls with which the Romanists had surrounded themselves, and calls upon the temporal Christian power to exercise its office without let or hindrance, or without considering whether it may strike pope, bishop, or priest. In a word, he seeks to make the Church and the Empire free from the dominion of the Pope. In the accomplishment of this object he had the support of Melanchthon, who wrote to John Lange, who thought that Luther had done better had he kept quiet:

" The purpose of writing the letter to the German nobility 1 approved from the beginning. Luther was encouraged in it by those on whom we both rely. Besides, it is of a nature to glorify God. I was not willing to have it delayed. I did not want to curb the spirit of Martin in a matter to which he seems to have been divinely appointed. The book is now published and circulated, and cannot be recalled." [1]

In October of the same year Luther published his *Babylonian Captivity of the Church*, in which he attacks and overthrows the Romish sacramental system. About the same time he wrote the book entitled, *Against the Execrable Bull of Anti-Christ*. In a letter to Spalatin, Melanchthon said: " Martin seems to me to be impelled by a spirit. He accomplishes more by prayer than we do by counsel. Nothing worse could befall us than to be deprived of him." [2]

Luther's publications of this year threw all Germany into a ferment. The people thought they

[1] *C. R.*, 1 : 211.
[2] *C. R.*, 1 : 269.

heard the tocsin of war. But the excitement was increased by the *Oration of Thomas Rhadinus against the Heretic Martin Luther, who is destroy-ing the Glory of the German Nation*, published at Leipzig in October, 1520. Its author was Thomas Rhadinus Todiscus, born at Placentia. The *Oration* had been published at Rome in August. Luther and Melanchthon, who knew nothing of the author, nor of the Roman edition, thought it had proceeded from Jerome Emser, a Leipzig canon. It is ad-dressed to the princes and people of Germany, and covers forty pages in the *Corpus Reformatorum*.[1] It is full of falsehoods, and of coarse abuse of Luther, whom it calls the pest of theology, the disgrace of the Augustinian family, the destroyer of Germany, the bane of the Christian state, the tainted wether which has infected the entire flock. It charges him with resisting the Turkish war, with opposing phi-losophy, and with setting at naught the teaching of Christian antiquity, the decrees and laws of the Church. It classes him with the apostates, schis-matics, and heretics of all ages, and closes by calling on all the gods and goddesses, on whose temples and rites this Luther, ignorant of philosophy and of sacred letters, has declared sacrilegious war, to drive away this enormous mass of wickedness, and pre-serve intact the glory of the Christian name in Ger-many.

Melanchthon, under the name of Didymus Faven-tinus, now took up his pen to defend his friend and colleague. He wrote, and in February, 1521, pub-

---

[1] *C. R.*, 1 : 212 *et seqq.*

lished, an *Oration* which covers nearly seventy-one pages of the *Corpus Reformatorum*.[1] It is learned in form and matter, but bitter and sarcastic in tone. It is directed against Emser, whom it never wearies of calling the he-goat. It declares that Luther has sought only to remove the abuses in the Church; that he is not opposed to the Turkish war, nor hostile to all philosophy; but only to that philosophy which treats falsely of the origin of things; and to such ethics of Aristotle and of other ancient philosophers as disturb the consciences of men. It shows that Luther asserts the authority of the Gospel over against the authority of councils and popes. The Pope is called a tyrant, and his primacy is disproved both from history and Scripture. An appeal is made to the princes to remember that they are Christians and rulers of the Christian people, and are to rescue the miserable remnants of Christianity from the tyranny of Antichrist. The *Oration* is a fit companion to the *Address to the German Nobility*, and to *The Babylonian Captivity of the Church*, with the difference that whereas Luther's pieces are addressed chiefly to the unlearned, this is addressed to scholars.

By this time the danger to the Pope's crown had grown so great that the Wittenberg arch-heretic, who had resisted admonition and defied threats, and had burned the sentence of excommunication, must be summarily dealt with. On the third of January, 1521, the Pope issued another bull against Luther, and urged the Emperor to enforce it. March 6th

---

[1] *C. R.*, I : 286 *et seqq.*

an imperial mandate ordered Luther to appear at
Worms by April 16th " to give information concerning his doctrines and books." On the second
of April, attended by Nicholas Amsdorf and a few
other friends, he set out for Worms. When parting
from Melanchthon he said:

" If I should not return, and my enemies should kill
me at Worms, as may very easily come to pass, I conjure
you, dear brother, not to neglect teaching, nor to fail to
stand by the truth. In the meantime also do my work,
because I cannot be here. You can do it better than I
can. Therefore it will not be a great loss, provided you
remain. The Lord still finds a learned champion in
you."

Of Luther's heroic stand at Worms; of the imperial edict hurled against him; of the sojourn at
the Wartburg; and of the many things done and
suffered by him during the next eleven months,
this is not the place to speak. Gladly would Melanchthon have accompanied his friend to the South,
but permission to do so was denied him. His place
was at Wittenberg, as a part of Luther's labours
had fallen on his shoulders, and his advice and
help were needed in starting Aurogallus, the new
professor of Hebrew, in his work. He also rendered
valuable assistance to Justus Jonas, who in June
came as Provost of the Castle Church and as professor of canon law. And most of all did he serve
the common cause by taking up his pen again in
defence of Luther.

The theologians of Cologne and Louvain had

already condemned the doctrines of Luther. Now on the fifteenth of April, while he was on the way to Worms, the theological faculty of Paris issued a *Determination on the Lutheran Doctrine*.[1] This celebrated faculty, known as the Sorbonne, was the theological oracle of the age. Its judgment of a theological question was supposed to be final. In the plenitude of its wisdom it calls Luther an archheretic; a virulent renewer of the ancient heresies; a pernicious enemy of Christ; an execrable restorer of old blasphemies, who has approved, commended, and extolled the madness of the Bohemians, the Albigensians, the Waldensians, the Heracleans, the Pepucians, the Arians, the Lamperians, the Jovinians, the Artotyrians, and other like monsters. It then extracts twenty-four propositions from Luther's writings. These are treated one at a time, and are summarily declared false, schismatic, impious, heretical. Not a word of proof is offered from the Sacred Scriptures. The condemnation is dogmatic and oracular.

The *Determination* is an out-and-out defence of the old Scholasticism, of which the Sorbonne was now the chief representative. Well did Luther say on reading it: "I have seen the Decree of the Paris sophists, and am heartily glad for it. The Lord would not have smitten them with such blindness, had he not intended to make an end of their tyranny."[2]

The bitterness and ignorance shown in the *Deter-*

---

[1] *C. R.*, 1 : 366 *et seqq.*
[2] De W., 2 : 30

mination might have been its condemnation, had not the authority of the Sorbonne been so great, and had not Eck translated it into German and circulated it among the people.   The Sorbonne Decree had to be answered.

Now it is that the courage of Melanchthon reaches its highest tide.   Undismayed by papal bulls and imperial edict, he enters the lists alone against the Paris corporation.   He advances to the battle not with the arrogance of youth, but with the confidence of the experienced warrior who knows that he has his quarrel just, and knows, too, that he stands on the sure foundation of truth.   In June, 1521, the answer was ready, entitled, *Apology for Luther against the Furious Decree of the Parisian Theologasters*.[1]   It begins by asserting that these Paris theologians have prefixed a bloody letter to their Decree and have added impious and atrocious notes on single sentences taken from Luther's writings and perversely distorted.   It then declares that instead of theologians, sophists, instead of Christian doctors, calumniators seem to rule at Paris where formerly were men like Gerson, full of the Christian spirit.

" It is evident that a profane Scholasticism has sprung up at Paris, which is called theology, but which leaves nothing salutary to the Church.   The Gospel is obscured; faith is extinguished; a doctrine of works is introduced· instead of a Christian people we are a people not subject to law, but to the ethics of Aristotle, and instead of Christianity, a kind of philosophical mode of life has been introduced in opposition to the whole mind of the Spirit."

[1] *C. R.*, 1 : 398 *et seqq.*

Luther, it says, is accused of heresy, not because he departs from the Scriptures, but because he opposes the universities, the Fathers, and the councils. But these have erred, and cannot make articles of faith.   In very many things Luther agrees with the ancients.   The Parisian theologians themselves are in many things directly opposed to the Fathers, as in the doctrines of sin and human ability.   But antiquity did not have the tyrannical laws of the popes, nor the Parisian masters, nor the Parisian articles, which obscure the Gospel.

"Let us now look at the councils.   By which councils is *Luther* condemned?   You make out of Luther a Montanist, a Manichæan, an Ebionite, and the like, and want to have it appear that his doctrine has been condemned by the councils of the ancients.   Unless the author of the Epistle wishes to play the orator here, there is nothing so malignant, so impudent, as the Paris Sorbonne.   It is easy to discover why they wish to associate Luther with the ancient heretics.   It is that his name may become odious.   The Parisian theologians are blind in that they see no difference between the doctrines of Luther and those of the Manichæans.   The Manichæans denied freedom to the human will in such a way as to deny that there is any substance which can be renewed, and therefore it is incapable of liberty.   Luther denies freedom in such a way as to maintain that there is a substance which when it is renewed by the Spirit, is freed from bondage."

They also think that **because** Luther has condemned the councils and the holy Fathers, he is a

Montanist, a Manichæan, an Ebionite, an Artotyrite *et hoc genus aliis.*

"There have been several papal councils during the reign of the Roman antichrists, which Luther confessedly does oppose; but in this he follows the plain Scripture. And why should he not oppose them, since so many things were done in them contrary to the Gospel? The Council of Vienne denied that the keys of the Church are common to all. The Council of Constance denied that the Church consists of the whole body of the predestinated. It also decided that there are some good works apart from grace. Such doctrines are directly opposed to the Gospel. These councils Luther has opposed, following the lead of Christ. They who decide against him are not Christians, but antichrists.

"The Sorbonnists blame Luther because he has not followed the Church. What do you call the Church? The French Sorbonne? But how can that be the Church which is hostile to the Word of Christ, who declares that his sheep hear his voice? We call that the Church which is based on the Word of God, which is fed, nourished, sustained, ruled by the Word of God; in fine, which derives everything from the Gospel."

Luther, who was now at the Wartburg, was greatly delighted with Melanchthon's *Apology.* As a mark of his approval he translated it into German, and added to it a translation of the Paris Decree, and published the two together, with a preface and an appendix, as the best means of opening the eyes of the people. He says that "although my beloved Philip has answered these sophists so well, he has touched them too gently, and has run over them with a light plane. I see I must come down upon them with the farmer's axe, otherwise they 'll think they 've not been hurt."[1] ⅃

Besides much hard work, this year 1521 brought great anxiety to Melanchthon. He felt that he could not take the place of Luther. He could teach, and could write more learned controversial tracts than Luther could; but he could not lead in the work which Luther had begun. Hence, when he learned that Luther had been outlawed, and had disappeared after leaving Worms, his soul was filled with sadness. Great was his joy when he received Luther's letter from the Wartburg, May 12th.[2] He wrote to Link, "Our most dear father still lives."[3]

But Luther's letter must have filled him with forebodings:

"Be thou a minister of the Word. Defend the walls and towers of Jerusalem until they also attack you. I pray for you, and I doubt not that my prayer avails. Do thou likewise, and let us bear the burden together. Hitherto I have stood alone in the battle. After me they will attack you."

Melanchthon longs for the companionship of Luther. To Spalatin he writes that all things go well at the university, except that Luther is wanting. He then exclaims: "Oh happy day, when I shall be permitted to embrace him again!"[4]

---

[1] Erlangen ed., 27 : 408.
[2] De W., 2 : 1.
[3] C. R., 1 : 389.
[4] C. R., 1 : 396.

Still greater troubles were in store for the tender-hearted Melanchthon.   The man who was instant and fearless in controversy, was hesitant and timid in action.   Hitherto the Reformation at Wittenberg had been a war of words, though many of the words were half battles.   Luther had preached, and Melanchthon had taught, that the authority of popes and councils must yield to the Word of God; that vows of celibacy are not binding; that the sacraments do not justify *ex opere operato;* that faith alone justifies; that the cup ought to be given to the laity; that private masses ought to be abolished; that the Lord's Supper ought to be administered according to primitive simplicity.   Men were beginning to demand the practice of what had been preached.   The monks knew that celibacy had been one of the greatest curses to the Church.   The question arose: Is celibacy better than marriage ?   It was answered: It can be better only when one has the gift for it.   Many now felt that they did not have this gift: Then it were better to marry than to burn.   Acting on this principle, Jacob Seidler, pastor at Glasshütte, in Meissen, Bartholomew Bernhard, of Feldkirch, provost at Kemberg, and a Mansfeld pastor had married.   They held that marriage was not forbidden by their vows of ordination.   In Meissen the vow required the observance of chastity only in so far as human weakness should permit. Seidler held it more honourable to explain this in the sense of marriage than in that of unchastity.[1] Bernhard had pledged himself to follow the tradi-

---

[1] *C. R.,* 1 : 420.

tions of the Fathers; and these had not bound them-selves by the law of celibacy. Hence marriage is permitted, he argued. Seidler and the Mansfeld pastor were imprisoned.

Melanchthon, Carlstadt, and Agricola sent a letter of intercession for Seidler to the bishop of Meissen,[1] but without effect. Duke George, to whose domin-ion Seidler belonged, was an implacable foe of the reformers. He had a great personal dislike for Luther, called Carlstadt " a loose, frivolous man," saw in Melanchthon only " a young fellow who ap-plied himself to things beyond his power." Seidler was executed in prison, one of the first of the German evangelical martyrs.

What became of the Mansfeld pastor is not known. For Bernhard, Melanchthon wrote an *Apology*[2] in the name of the Wittenberg doctors of law, in which he showed that neither the law nor the Gospel for-bids marriage to layman or to priest; and that Bernhard had not perjured himself by taking a wife. Melanchthon also wrote to the Elector in the interest of Bernhard. As a result, the matter was dropped, and Bernhard remained an evangelical pastor. This *Apology* of Melanchthon, translated into German, was widely scattered. It awakened thought. The abolition of celibacy, one of the chief supports of the hierarchy, was a long step in the direction of practical reformation.

The leaven of sound doctrine was also working in other directions. In October, the Augustinian

[1] *C. R.*, I : 418.
[2] *C. R.*, I : 421 *et seqq.*

monks in Wittenberg, under the advice and leadership of Gabriel Zwilling, their preacher, conceived
the purpose of abolishing private masses, and of
restoring the cup to the laity.   When this came to
the knowledge of the Elector at Lochau, he directed
his chancellor, Brück, to inquire into the matter, and
to report to him.   On the eleventh of October the
chancellor reported that Zwilling had declared in a
sermon that the adoration of the sacrament is idolatry; that private masses should not be held; and
that the sacrament should be received in both kinds.
It was also discovered that the theologians were in
sympathy with these movements toward practical
reform.   A committee was appointed to take advise-
ment of the matter.   On the twentieth of October
a report,[1] signed by Jonas, Carlstadt, Melanchthon
Pletner, Amsdorf, Doltsk, and Schurf, was sent to
the Elector.   It recites: (1) that the Mass has been
abused and changed into a good work for the purpose of reconciling God.   Hence the Augustinians
desire to hold no more such masses, but to introduce
such as Christ and the apostles held; (2) that the
masses as they are now held are contrary to the
usages of Christ, and of the apostles, who always
communicated to a company, and never to a single
person; (3) that Christ had appointed both forms to
be used.   The report then appeals to the Elector
to abolish the abuses connected with the Mass, even
though he should be called a Bohemian and a heretic, since all who would obey the Word of God must
bear reproach, lest they be cast off by Christ in the

---

[1] *C. R.*, 1 : 466.

FREDERICK THE WISE, ELECTOR OF SAXONY.

FROM A PAINTING BY ALBRECHT DÜRER, 1524.

last day. Though it would not be a sin to hold private masses, if they be not abused.

The Elector was not wholly pleased with the report of the committee, and preferred to advance with caution. He communicated his mind to the committee through Dr. Baier, insisting that in so grave a matter they should proceed with great deliberation, since they were the smaller party; otherwise serious consequences might follow, as the Mass had existed for hundreds of years, and the churches and cloisters had been founded for holding masses.[1] The committee replied with that joyful courage which only the Gospel can inspire:

" That though they are the smaller party they could not despise the truth of the Divine Word, which is above all angels and creatures, and is clearly revealed in the Gospel. Besides, the smaller and despised party has always preached and accepted the truth, and so will it be to the end of the world. Christ sent into the world the despised, poor, simple, unlearned people, to preach the truth; and he has revealed to them the divine truth which he has concealed from the great, the high, the wise of this world."

They proceed to show that the Mass as then held, especially masses for the dead, and with one form, is an innovation, for which they are not responsible. Finally they say: " Let no one hesitate because this will bring great offence; for Christ came into the world, and was given to those who believe on him

[1] *C. R.*, 1 : 471.

and his Word, that they might be benefited in him and have everlasting life."[1]

Nearly all the professors favoured reform in the Mass. But the chapter, Jonas, the Provost, excepted, opposed the reform. The canons wrote to the Elector, and begged him not to change the Mass in the churches and cloisters.[2] As opinion was thus divided, Frederick wisely recommended that they should continue to discuss the matter and further instruct the people before changes were introduced.

Meanwhile the excitement had spread through Meissen and Thuringia. On December[3] 20th of this year the Augustinians of these districts held a provincial convention at Wittenberg, at which they resolved formally to abolish private masses, cloisteral coercion, and other unchristian customs. Melanchthon was especially anxious to have the Mass changed, since he thought that the priests were destroying legions of souls by their masses.[4] But Melanchthon was not the man to introduce the desired changes, though the times were ripe for a reformation. He was not a minister. He could not preach, nor serve at the altar. He must naturally give place to his older colleague, Carlstadt. This man, violent, eccentric, and ambitious of leadership, smarting no doubt under the conscious-

---

[1] C. R., 1 : 494.

[2] C. R., 1 : 503.

[3] This is the date given by Matthes in *Melanchthon's Leben*, p. 48 ; and by Schmidt in *Philipp Melanchthon*, p. 82. See Seckendorf, 1 : p. 214. Köstlin places it in January, 1522, Luther's *Leben*, 1 : 503.

[4] C. R., 1 : 477. 478.

ness of his ill-success in the Leipzig disputation, undertook to revolutionise everything.

He not only made a complete change in the order of worship, by seeking to return to original simplic. ity, but he tried to bring all learned studies into contempt, and advised the students to leave their books and learn trades. He announced in a ser. mon that on the first of January he would administer the Communion, both kinds, and would omit the Canon. Though warned by the Electoral counsel- lors, he did as he said he would do, and also pub- lished a treatise on the abolition of pictures and begging among Christians. So matters stood at the close of the year 1521. Melanchthon had urged the changes in the Mass, but, as the representative of order and science, he could not approve Carl- stadt's revolutionary violence. With Schurf he threw the whole weight of his authority against the dissolution of the university and the abolition of learned studies. In this he succeeded fairly well. But he did not have the age and experience to take command in practical matters against the chief agi tator, between whom and himself strained relations had for some time already existed. His place was the professor's chair, not the pulpit; the instrument of his power was the pen, not the voice. In a storm the pen is impotent, the voice omnipotent; the chair is silent, the pulpit is heard.[1] That he did

---

[1] Melanchthon once said : "I cannot preach. I am a logician, Bugenhagen is a linguist, Jonas is an orator, Luther is all in all. I can write in the presence of the whole Roman Empire, but I am dumb in the presence of an audience."—Planck's *Melanchthon*, pp.

not quiet the storm, nor guide it to salutary results, was his misfortune rather than his fault. Even Luther at Melanchthon's age and with Melanchthon's environment could scarcely have controlled the wild passions of students and populace, which burst forth now that the burden of centuries had been lifted.

62, 63.   After 1540 Melanchthon delivered lectures in Latin, Sunday afternoons, to those foreign students who did not understand German.

CHAPTER VIII

THE REVOLUTIONARY MOVEMENT

The Zwickau Prophets — Increased Confusion at Wittenberg —
Luther's Return—His Eight Sermons—Quiet Restored—New
Order of Service—Translation and Publication of the New
Testament.

THE revolutionary movement at Wittenberg was
reënforced at Christmas, 1521, by the arrival
of three of the Zwickau prophets, Nicholas Storch,
a weaver, another weaver, and Marcus Thomas
Stübner, who had been a student at Wittenberg.
They were soon joined by Thomas Münzer, an eloquent demagogue who subsequently figured in the
Peasants' War. One of their first disciples in Wittenberg was Martin Cellarius, a private teacher.
These prophets were more radical than Carlstadt.
They rejected the written Word, the regular ministry, and infant baptism; boasted of dreams and
special revelations, and of communications with God
and the angel Gabriel; and predicted the overthrow
of the existing civil government.

In the new government Storch was to be God's
vicegerent, for the angel had told him, "Thou
shalt sit on his throne."

The prophets sought and obtained an interview
with Melanchthon, who listened with astonishment
to their claims of inspiration and of interviews with
God, and was much moved by their arguments
against infant baptism. He regarded faith as a
personal act; he did not see how baptism could
benefit without faith. Children cannot exercise
faith; a foreign faith cannot benefit them. Then,
too, he remembered that Augustine and others of
his time had disputed much over infant baptism, and
that Augustine had rejected the doctrine of infant
faith, and had fallen back on the doctrine of original
sin, and on custom.[1] He also discovered that the
prophets had the correct sense of the Scripture in
many of the chief articles of faith[2] This only increased his confusion. That they had a spirit, he
was certain, but whether it was the Spirit of God,
or the spirit of the Devil, who spoke through them,
he could not discern. In his perplexity he wrote
the Elector, December 27th·

"You know that certain dangerous dissensions have
arisen in Zwickau concerning the Word of God. Some
of the innovators have been cast into prison. Three of
the authors of these commotions have come hither, two
unlettered weavers, and one man of education. I have
heard them. They relate marvellous things of themselves, as, that they have been sent by a loud voice of
God to teach; that they have familiar converse with
God; that they foresee the future: in a word, that they
are prophets and apostles. I can scarcely tell how I am

[1] *C. R.*, 1 : 534.
[2] *C. R.*, 1 : 533.

moved by these things. For certain strong reasons I cannot bring myself to condemn them. That there are spirits in them is very apparent. But no one can easily judge concerning them except Martin. Since the Gospel and the glory and peace of the Church are endangered, there is the greatest need that *Martin* should meet these men, for they appeal to him. I would not write to your Electoral Highness about this matter, did not the magnitude of the case require that it should be considered in time. It is needful for us to be on our guard lest we be entrapped by Satan." [1]

The same day he wrote to Spalatin declaring that unless Luther should interfere, things would go to ruin. He asks: "Whither shall I turn in this great difficulty? Assist in this thing in whatever way you can." [2]

Amsdorf also wrote the Elector on the same subject; whereupon the latter summoned both Amsdorf and Melanchthon to Prettin, and inquired of them through Haubold von Einsiedel and Spalatin why they had written him so excitedly about this matter. Each wrote his opinion and sent it to the Elector. Melanchthon's letter is the same in substance as his former one to the Elector. He insists that Luther's opinion is necessary, as only he can judge of the questions raised by these men. [3]

Amsdorf thought that the prophets should be neither wholly believed nor wholly rejected until after they had been heard. [4]

[1] *C. R.*, 1: 513.
[2] *C. R.*, 1: 514.
[3] *C. R.*, 1: 535.
[4] *C. R.*, 1: 534.

The Elector, as a layman, refused to pass judgment, and so turned the matter over to the theologians with the counsel that there be no public disputation, since no good could come out of public discussion.   He also refused to recall Luther, who was under the imperial ban, and whom he did not feel able to protect.[1]

Everything was now confusion and uncertainty. But Melanchthon soon became convinced that these men did not have the good Spirit.   He took Stübner into the house with him that he might have the better opportunity to test him.   One day as they sat together while Melanchthon was writing, Stübner dropped his head on the table and slept.   After a while he awoke and suddenly asked Melanchthon what he thought of John Chrysostom.   Melanchthon replied that he thought well of him, though he did not approve his verbosity.   Then Stübner said: " I have just seen him in Purgatory in a sad plight." At first Melanchthon laughed; but he soon discovered with sadness the man's inconsistency, since on other occasions he had stoutly rejected the notion of Purgatory.[2]

At Wittenberg things were going from bad to worse.   Not only were ecclesiastical vestments abolished, and the pictures removed from the church, and the people admitted to the communion without confession, but the preaching was fanatical, pastoral oversight was omitted, the hospitals and prisons were neglected   Melanchthon was opposed to such

---

[1] *C. R.*, 1 : 535.
[2] Camerarius, p. 51.

violent innovations, but felt himself powerless to check them.

We have no letter from Melanchthon to Luther concerning the advent of the prophets; but in some way Luther learned of their doings and claims, and of his friend's timidity and hesitation. On the thirteenth of January he wrote him a letter of reproof, telling him that he must not rely on what these men say of themselves, but he must try the spirits, as St. John commanded; he himself has not learned of their having done anything that Satan might not do. They must be required to prove their vocation. God sends no one without credentials, and does not speak in the old man except he first be purified as by fire. As to the matter of faith in infants, he cuts the knot by asserting that they are benefited by the faith of others. Finally he could no longer stand it that " Satan was wasting his fold at Wittenberg." He was once heard to exclaim, " Oh that I were at Wittenberg!" Breaking away from his prison, March 1st, despite the Elector's earnest dissuasion, he appeared on the scene of storm and confusion, March 6, 1522.

His letter to the Elector, sent from Borna, south of Leipzig, is written in the loftiest strain of faith and courage. He tells his " most gracious lord " that he goes to Wittenberg under far higher protection than that of the Elector, affirming even that he could protect his Electoral Highness far better than his Electoral Highness could protect him. He is the best protection who has most faith. Inasmuch as the Elector lacked faith, he could not be a protector. If need were he would go to Leipzig even though it rained Duke Georges for nine days, and each Duke George was nine times as fierce as the present one.[1] Riding right across the territory of his implacable foe, he entered the city of his friends on Thursday evening. Two days were spent in learning the situation. The next Sunday he ascended the pulpit of the parish church before a congregation of citizens and students, and began a series of eight sermons, preached in so many consecutive days, by which he brought order out of confusion. These sermons are splendid specimens of pulpit eloquence, full of fervour and Christian faith, and full of moderation and love. Nowhere, and at no time, did Luther appear to better advantage in the pulpit. The ruling ideas of his sermons are those of freedom and charity, which will resist as well the coercion of radicalism as the tyranny of the Pope. The things that the Bible has left free, such as marriage, cloister-life, private confession, images in the churches, may be tolerated. Only things which contradict the Word of God, as private masses and enforced confession, must be abolished. But all changes must be made in a decent and orderly way. Paul preached against idols in Athens, and they fell in consequence, though he never touched one of them.[2]

The victory was complete. It was the triumph

---

[1] De W., 2: 137-141.

[2] Erlangen ed., 28: 202-260. A good *résumé* of those sermons in German is given in Köstlin's *Martin Luther*, 1: 437-445; in English in Meurer's *Life of Luther*, translated, pp. 245-253.

of wisdom, truth, and love over ignorance, error, and passion.   The professors, the town council, and all peace-loving citizens were delighted.   Zwilling confessed his mistake; Carlstadt was silenced; and Jerome Schurf wrote to the Elector, after the sixth sermon, that Luther was leading the poor deluded people back to the way of truth.   " It is plain and manifest," says he, " that the Spirit of God is in him.   And I doubt not at all that he has come to Wittenberg at this time through the special providence of God."[1]

Luther admitted Stübner and Cellarius to an interview.   Stübner affecting to know Luther's thoughts, the latter exclaimed, " The Lord rebuke thee, Satan!"   When they boasted of the power to work miracles, Luther charged their god not to perform miracles against the will of his God.   " So we parted," says Luther.   The same day the fanatics left town, and from Kemberg they wrote Luther a letter full of reproaches and imprecations.

Many of the changes which had been introduced during the commotion were in themselves of the nature of true reform, and were retained after order had been restored.

On the twenty-fifth of January, 1522, Dr. Baier had reported the following to Von Einsiedel:

" The University and council have agreed that in the parish church, to which we all belong, the Mass shall be held as follows: First, singing with the Introit and Gloria in Excelsis, the Epistle, Gospel, and Sanctus;

---

[1] Meurer's *Life of Luther*, p. 253.

then preaching. Then the Mass is begun as God our Lord Jesus instituted it. Then the priest speaks publicly the words of consecration in German, admonishes the people who hunger and thirst after the grace of God, and communicates to them the body and blood of the Lord. The Communion ended, the Agnus Dei, a hymn, and the Benedicamus Domino are sung."

He says further that the Canon has been abolished and begging forbidden among the monks; that the poor are to be served from a common treasury; that a pious man has been appointed for every street to look after the poor, to restrain open transgression, and to have transgressors punished by the university and the council.[1]

Thus the fanaticism of Carlstadt and the Zwickau prophets, under the powerful guiding hand of Luther, was turned to good account, though some of the things that had been abolished were restored for a time. But the Canon, or that part of the service of the Mass in which the priest is thought to offer the body of Christ in sacrifice, was not restored; and henceforth no more private masses were said in the parish church. When the time came for further changes and for the introduction of the Lutheran principles of worship, the way was, in part at least, prepared.

Now that order was restored, Luther took up his abode in the cloister, and wore the habit of his fraternity. In this he had the approbation of Melanchthon, who, in matters of form and in externals, remained more conservative than Luther.

---

[1] *C. R.*, 1: 540.

The recent events had convinced both of them that changes should not be made before knowledge and faith had taught the lesson of true evangelical freedom.   The Reformation could now go on in the development of its fundamental principle *that the Word must do everything*.   And it was in harmony with this principle that Melanchthon had insisted that Luther should translate the Bible.   In compliance with the urgent demand of his friend, Luther had begun the work of translating the New Testament at the Wartburg, and had brought the finished draft with him to Wittenberg.   He and Melanchthon at once began the revision, and by September 21st an edition of three thousand copies was printed. The book sold so rapidly at a florin and a half a copy—equal to about six dollars in our money— that in December another edition was required.

The translation of the Old Testament was immediately commenced.   The finished work is called Luther's translation, and sometimes Luther's Bible, because he was the leading spirit in the little Bible Club that met once a week in his house.   It is his greatest and most important work.   It introduced the Reformation to the people.

CHAPTER IX

THE "LOCI COMMUNES"

The "Loci Communes" or "Theological Common Places"—The
Commentaries on the Epistles of Paul—Luther's Preface.

WHILE Luther was contending with the Pope's
bull at Wittenberg, confessing Christ at
Worms, and writing his Postils at the Wartburg,
Melanchthon was engaged in a work which was destined to exert a powerful influence on the Reformation, and which marks an epoch in the history of
theology; it was the composition and publication
of his *Loci Communes*, or *Theological Common Places*,
which commended the Reformation to the learned.
The purpose conceived by the author was to set
forth in condensed form the leading doctrines of the
Christian religion in opposition to the Aristotelian
subtleties. The book, written amid the stirring
scenes and conflicts of the years 1520 and 1521, was
finished some time in April of the latter year, and
published soon thereafter. It owes its appearance at
this time to a happy accident. On the seventeenth
of April, 1520, Melanchthon wrote John Hess, of
Breslau, saying that while preparing notes on the

Epistle to the Romans, the work had so grown in his hands that he was going to write *Loci Communes* on the law, sin, grace, the sacraments, and other mysteries.[1] These *Loci* were merely the heads of argument, on which Melanchthon proposed to lecture.   They were written down by one of his hearers it is supposed, and printed without the knowledge of the author. Melanchthon was dissatisfied with the little book, and tried to suppress the edition. A few copies, however, survived, one of which is found in the ducal library at Gotha.   Though merely the heads of discourse, intended to set forth systematically the Pauline argument, and called *Lucubratiuncula*, the work covers pages 11–48 in the *Corpus Reformatorum*, and is supplemented by a *Theological Institute on the Epistle of Paul to the Romans*, which covers ten pages.[2] These two works, revised, expanded, and rendered more systematic, became the *Loci Communes Rerum Theologicarum*, sive *Hypotyposes Theologicæ*, which extends from page 82 to page 227 in the *Corpus Reformatorum*," vol. xxi. This, without doubt, is Melanchthon's most important theological work. It systematises what he and Luther had taught, and lays the foundation for the *Evangelical Dogmatic*.   For the time being it was the Wittenberg Confession of Faith, and was the forerunner of the Confession of Augsburg.   Unlike the *Sentences* of Peter Lombard, it is not based on the scholastic philosophy, and developed through thesis and anti

---

[1] *C. R.*, 1: 138.
[2] *C. R.*, 21: 11–58,

thesis; but it is drawn directly from the Holy Scripture, more particularly from the Epistle of Paul to the Romans. And yet it makes a proper use of history, and connects its expositions with the teaching of the Church fathers.

Passing lightly over the metaphysical and philosophical doctrines of theology, it treats chiefly what seemed to its author to be the fundamental doctrines. Its aim is to lead students to a profitable knowledge of theology, not to perplex and confuse them with doubtful disputations. " Yet I desire nothing so much," says Melanchthon in the preface, " as to make all Christians thoroughly conversant with the Holy Scripture alone, and to transform them into the image of the same."

The order of the book is in part inherited from John of Damascus. It begins with the Trinity; but, in harmony with its purely practical aim, it quickly passes to Man, and treats of Sin, the Law, the Gospel, the Fruits of Grace, Faith, the Sacraments, then of the Magistracy, Church Government, Condemnation, and Blessedness.

A few notes will indicate its characteristic features: The mysteries of the Trinity are to be adored rather than investigated. Indeed, they cannot be treated without great peril. There is no need of devoting much time to God, the Unity, the Trinity, the mysteries of creation and of the incarnation. The scholastic theologists have been engaged on these subjects for ages without having accomplished anything. In regard to human powers there is a wide difference between the teaching of the Sacred

Scripture and that of philosophy. In man there are two powers: the power of intellect, by which we understand and reason, and the power of the affections, by which we are rendered favourable or adverse to things known. The reason in itself is neither good nor evil; it serves the will. Freedom is the power to do or not to do, to do thus or so. But there is no freedom. "All things that occur, occur necessarily according to the divine predestination. Our will has no freedom."

Here the author quotes several passages from the Scriptures in support of *absolute predestination*, as Romans xi., 36; Eph. i., 11; Matt. x., 29. This doctrine is contradicted by the reason, but is em braced by the spiritual judgment. To believe that all things are done by God is profitable for repressing and condemning the wisdom and prudence of human reason. In things external there is freedom of will, as the power to put on or off a garment; but we have no power over the inward affections, and no power by which we can seriously oppose the affections.

Original sin is a native impulse or energy, which impels us to commit sin. God created the first man without sin, but he fell, and God's Spirit ceased to rule him. Self-love is the root of all sin, and leads to contempt of God. Original sin is not only the want of original righteousness; it is the flesh, impiety, contempt of spiritual things. What is law? It is that by which the good is enjoined, or the evil forbidden. There are natural, divine, and human laws. Neither theologians nor lawyers have to do with the laws of nature. The divine laws are contained in the Decalogue. The first commandment requires faith; the second the praise of God's name; the third, the upholding of God's work in us. The other commandments are explained by Christ, as loving thy neighbour as thyself (Matt. v.). The Gospel is the promise of grace, or of the mercy of God, and hence the testimony of God's good-will towards us. God revealed the Gospel at once after the fall of Adam, and then more fully in Christ. The Law brings a knowledge of sin. It is the voice of death. The Gospel is the voice of peace and life. Whosoever is comforted by the voice of God, and believes God, is justified.

" Grace signifies favour, that favour in God by which he comprehends the saints. In a word, Grace is nothing but the remission of sins, the gift of the Holy Spirit who regenerates and sanctifies the heart. We are justified, when, mortified by the Law, we are raised up by the word of Grace, which is promised in Christ, or in the Gospel, which forgives sin, and when we cling to Christ nothing doubting that the righteousness of Christ is our righteousness, that his satisfaction is our expiation, his resurrection, ours. In a word, nothing doubting that our sins are forgiven, and that God loves and cherishes us. Hence our works, however good they may seem or be, are not our righteousness. FAITH alone in the mercy·and grace of God in Jesus Christ is RIGHTEOUSNESS. This is what Paul means when he says, the just live by faith, and righteousness is by the faith of Jesus Christ."

The sacraments are signs of promises and testimonies of God's will towards us. They have no power to justify. Faith alone justifies. Circumcision, Baptism, the Lord's Supper, are only witnesses and seals of the divine will in our behalf. Two signs, Baptism and the Lord's Supper, are given by Christ in the Gospel. We call them sacramental signs. Baptism is the washing of regeneration, the passing from death unto life. It is the sacrament of repentance. Penitence is not a sacrament. Rather is it the Chrisitan life itself, which must be constantly renewed. Private Confession is retained. Private Absolution is as necessary as Baptism. Only he dare comfort himself with the Absolution who desires it and believes.

There is no satisfaction apart from the death of Christ. The Lord's Supper is a sign of grace. It consists in eating Christ's body and drinking his blood. This Sacrament is intended to strengthen us as often as our consciences are troubled, and doubt of God's will toward us. It is not a sacrifice. Confirmation and Unction are not sacraments. Matrimony is not a sacrament. Order is only the selection by the Church of those who are to teach, baptise, and administer the Supper. Such is the duty of bishops, presbyters, and deacons. "The Mass-priests are the prophets of Jezebel, that is, of Rome."

For the maintenance of discipline in the State and in the Church, the magistracy is necessary. The civil magistrate bears the sword and guards the public peace. To him Christians should be obedient. Bishops are servants, not lords of the Church.

They cannot make civil laws, nor dare they do anything against the Scriptures.

These notes can give only a faint idea of the contents of the *Loci*.   Yet they may serve to indicate
its practical aim as well as its positive and aggressive
thought.   It may be said that the book is at once a
faithful exhibition and defence of the doctrines
taught in Wittenberg at that time, and a refutation
and rejection of the leading errors of Rome.   Its
tendency is decidedly polemical, and this is its chief
blemish.   It does not have that calmness and that
purely didactic quality which may be expected in a
hand-book of theology.   But it is a genuine product
of its age, which was one of strife and violent contention.   Its author, while preparing it, had in mind
the coarse invectives of Thomas Rhadinus, and the
scholastic sophistries of the Cologne, Louvain, and
Paris theologists, who had issued judgments and
decrees against the teaching of Luther.   Even its
polemic tendency may have been a feature of value
in that first period of the Reformation, when it
was as necessary to refute error as to establish the
truth.

Taken as a whole, the *Loci* must be regarded as
the most remarkable theological work ever produced
by a young man of twenty-four years.   It is emphatically something new—a system of theology
based on Christ and the Word of God.   As over
against Scholasticism it is the theology of a living
principle, and is well illustrated by the words with
which the book closes: "The kingdom of God is
not in word, but in power."

A distinguished theologian of the Reformed Church has described it as follows:

" The book marks an epoch in the history of theology. It grew out of exegetical lectures on the Epistle to the Romans, the Magna Charta of the evangelical system. It is an exposition of the leading doctrines of sin and grace, repentance and salvation.   It is clean, fresh, thoroughly biblical and practical.   Its main object is to show that man can not be saved by works of the law, or by his own merits, but only by the free grace of God in Christ as revealed in the Gospel.   It presents the living soul of divinity in striking contrast to the dry bones of degenerate scholasticism, with its endless thesis, antithesis, definitions, divisions, and subdivisions." [1]

The *Loci* met with extraordinary favour.   Two editions appeared at Wittenberg [2] and one at Basel in the year 1521.   The next year it was reprinted at Augsburg, Strassburg, and Hagenau.   From 1521 to 1525 not less than seventeen editions appeared, besides several reprints of the German translation made by Spalatin.   A Wittenberg student took a copy to Strassburg and showed it to Nicholas Gerbel, who wrote to John Schwebel:

" This young man tells me marvellous things about Wittenberg.   He has shown me the notes dictated by Melanchthon on Paul and Matthew, and also the *Loci*, a divine book, which in my opinion no one studying theology can miss without the greatest loss.   It has so laid

---

[1] Schaff's *Hist. Christ. Ch.*, 6: 369.
[2] Schmidt's *Philipp Melanchthon*, p. 74.

hold of me that day and night I cannot think of anything except Wittenberg.'' [1]

In 1524, an edition was published at Augsburg by
Sigismund Grim, with a picture of Hercules destroy-
ing Cerberus, surrounded by the legend, '' Hercules
the Destroyer of Monsters.''   Luther, in his reply to
Erasmus, calls the *Loci* '' an invincible book, worthy
not only of immortality, but of being placed in the
Canon.''   John Cochlæus called it a new Koran,
more pernicious than Luther's *Babylon*, and both
Eck and he wrote *Loci* against it.   An Italian translation bearing the title, *I principii della Theologia
di Ippofilo da Terra negra*, published at Venice, was
sold in large numbers in Rome, and was read '' with
the greatest applause '' until a Franciscan monk
discovered that it was '' Lutheran,'' whereupon all
the copies were seized and burned.

Under the improving hand of its author, the *Loci*
subsequently underwent great changes.   It became
more calm and dignified, and was extended over a
wider field of discussion.   In the later editions the
polemical bearing towards Scholasticism was almost
completely abandoned, and a still more respectful
relation was assumed towards the Fathers ; but the
book never abandoned its Scriptural basis nor its
practical character.   The changes of later editions
represent Melanchthon's growth in the knowledge
of Scripture and of history.   He also learned to dis-
criminate between a true and a false Scholasticism,
between the idolising of Aristotle then current in

---

[1] *Centuria Epist. Theol. ad Schwebelium Zweibrücken* (1597), p. 24.

the universities, and the proper application of philosophy to the investigation of sacred truth.

The different editions of the *Loci* are classified in three periods. The first form extends from 1521 to 1535; the second form, from 1535 to 1544, and contains fourteen editions; the third form, from 1544 to 1559, and contains thirty-four editions. The characteristic changes made in the second and third forms will be considered at the proper time and place. Suffice it to say here that these changes resulted from continuous study of the Bible and of the Fathers, from the criticisms of his opponents, from the reading of Erasmus, from contact with Catholic and Reformed theologians at the various diets and conferences which he attended, and from the growing independence of his own judgment.

The *Loci* continued to be published after the death of its author, and for fifty years more held the first place as a text-book of theology in the universities. Victorin Strigel and Martin Chemnitz, pupils of Melanchthon, wrote each a commentary on it. Leonhard Hutter followed it in his own *Loci;* but in 1610 Hutter published a *Compend*, drawn chiefly from the Symbolical Books, which threw Melanchthon's *Loci* in the shade during the seventeenth century.

It has been noticed already that from time to time Melanchthon expounded the Epistles of Paul. While he and Luther were engaged in revising the German translation of the New Testament, Luther insisted that Melanchthon should publish his lectures on the Epistles to the Romans and Corinthians.

This he refused to do, his extreme modesty leading
him to say that the Scripture should be allowed to
do its work without the word of man.   Luther
thought that a man who expounded the Scripture
as Master Philip did, rendered an invaluable service
to the Church.[1]   Accordingly he obtained a copy of
the lectures secretly and published them without
the knowledge of the author, writing the following
Preface[2] in the form of a letter to Melanchthon:

" Grace and Peace in Christ.
" *Be angry and sin not.   Speak upon thy bed*, and *be
silent*.   It is I who publish these annotations of yours,
and send you to yourself.   If you do not please yourself,
very good; it is enough that you please me.   The sin is
on your side, if there be any sin here.   Why did not you
yourself publish ?   Why did you suffer me to ask, command, and urge you so often to publish ?   This is my
defence against you: I am willing to be, and to be called,
a thief, fearing neither your complaints nor accusation.
But to those who, you think, will turn up their noses, or
will not be satisfied, I shall say: Publish something
better.   What the impious Thomists falsely claim for
their Thomas, viz., that no one has written better on
Saint Paul, that I truthfully assign to you.   Satan per-
suades them to boast thus of their Thomas, that his impious and poisonous doctrines may be the more widely
propagated.   I know with what spirit and judgment I
declare this of you.   What is it to you if those famous
mighty men turn up their noses at this opinion of mine ?
Mine is the peril.   That I may the more provoke these

---

[1] De W., 2: 303,
[2] De W., 2: 238.

fastidious gentlemen, I say further that the commentaries
of Jerome and Origen are mere trifles and absurdities as
compared with your annotations. Wherefore, you will
say, provoke the ill will of men of the highest talents?
Be modest.   Let me be proud of you.   Who prohibits
the men of highest talents from publishing something
better and exposing the rashness of my judgment?
Would that there were those who could do better.
Finally, I threaten you, that I will steal and publish
what you have written on Genesis, Matthew, and John,
unless you shall anticipate me.   The Scripture, you say,
must be read without commentaries.   You say this correctly about Jerome, Origen, Thomas, and the like.
They wrote commentaries in which they give their own
teaching, not that of Paul and of Christ.   Nobody should
call your annotations a commentary, but a guide to
reading the Scripture and learning Christ—something
which no commentary has hitherto presented.   When
you plead that your notes are not in all respects satisfactory to you, I am forced to believe you; but behold,
I believe you will not satisfy yourself.   This is neither
asked nor sought from you without regard for the honour
of Paul; nor will anyone boast that Philip is superior or
equal to Paul.   It is enough that he is next to Paul.
We envy no one if he should come nearer.   We know
you are nothing.   Christ is all in all.   If he speaks by
the mouth of an ass we shall be satisfied.   Why should
we be dissatisfied if he speaks by the mouth of a man?
Art thou not a man?   Art thou not of Christ?   Is not
his mind in you?   But if you wish to adorn the book
with a more polished diction, and with ampler learning,
and to increase its size, all right; and it will also be
agreeable that we have the matter and the mind of Paul
through your assistance.   I do not beg your pardon, if I

offend yðu in doing this. Cease to be offended, that you may not rather offend us, and have need of our pardon. The Lord enlarge and keep thee forever.

" Wittenberg, July 29th, Anno M.D.XXII.

" Yours,   MARTINUS LUTHERUS."

Very soon the commentary was published at Nuremberg, disfigured by numerous errors. Then Melanchthon laughed, and said to Luther, " he hoped that, made wiser by experience, he would commit no more such thefts."

The book, notwithstanding its many errors, was soon published at Strassburg and Basel, and at Augsburg translated into German. It at once made its author famous as an expounder of the Scripture. Early in the next year Luther obtained Melanchthon's lectures on the Gospel of St. John and sent them to Basel for publication.

In these commentaries, as in his *Loci*, Melanchthon avoids all philosophical and speculative questions, and confines himself to a practical exposition of the text. Christ, Faith, and Justification occupy the chief places.

CHAPTER X

PRIVATE LIFE DURING 1522–1525

Melanchthon Wishes to Relinquish Theology and to Teach Greek and Literature Only—Luther Interferes—A Compromise—Melanchthon Opens a School in his own House—Visits his Mother Honoured by the University of Heidelberg—Cardinal Campeggius—Controversy Between Luther and Erasmus on the Will Melanchthon Meets Philip, Landgrave of Hesse.

AFTER Luther's return from the Wartburg to Wittenberg, Melanchthon began to think seriously of abandoning theology, and of devoting himself wholly to giving instruction in languages and literature. He was influenced in this direction partly by the disorders created by Carlstadt and the Zwickau prophets, and partly by the feeling that he could best serve the cause of the Reformation by preparing young men properly for the study of theology. During the temporary reign of iconoclastic confusion at Wittenberg he wrote to Spalatin:

"Oh that with pious hearts we might recognise the divine goodness, and show our gratitude by better manners! If I mistake not, Christ is about to avenge the contempt of the Gospel by new darkness. He is blinding the minds of those who, under cover of the name of Christ are now confounding things divine and human, sacred and profane.   In a word, I fear that this light which a little while ago appeared in the world, will be taken from us." [1]

He thought that classical culture was the best means for preparing young men for the study of theology, and for overcoming the spirit of disorder This thought he expressed in several letters of the year 1522.   To Spalatin he wrote:

" I hear that Dr. Martin wants me to commit the Greek teaching to another.   This I do not wish to do. I would rather discontinue theology, which, according to custom, I began to teach on account of the bachelor's degree.   Hitherto my work was only a substitute for that of Martin, when he was absent, or otherwise engaged.   I see the need of many earnest teachers of the classics, which at present, not less than in the age of sophistry, are neglected." [2]

A little later also to the same: " It is a very bad condition of affairs that in so large a number of professors here, scarcely one can be found who really cultivates the classics.   If these be not faithfully studied what kind of theologians shall we have ? " [3] In April of the next year he wrote to Eoban Hess that those who despise classical studies think scarcely better of theology.   He exclaims· " Good God! how absurdly they pursue the study of theology

[1] C. R., 1 : 547.
[2] C. R., 1 : 575.
[3] C. R., 1 : 576.

who want to seem wise by despising all that is good!
What is this else than a new sophistry more foolish
and impious than the old ?"[1] ·

About the same time he delivered an oration entitled, " The Praise of Eloquence " He deplores
the neglect of classical studies, and wishes for the
power of Pericles to recall into the right way the
foolish young men who think that classical studies
are not profitable for other disciplines, or who neglect
them out of laziness.   He insists on the thorough
study of the Greek and Latin classics as the proper
preparation for the study of theology.[2]

It is thus evident from his letters and from public
deliverances that at this time Melanchthon felt that
his calling was to teach the classics, and to prepare
young men for the study of theology.   But Luther
was of a different opinion.   On the fourth of July,
1522, he wrote to Spalatin:

" How I wish you would see that Philip be relieved
from Grammar, that he may devote himself to Theology!
It is utterly shameful, as I wrote some time ago, that he
should receive one hundred gulden for teaching Grammar, when his theological lectures are beyond price.
There are plenty of masters who can teach Grammar as
well as Philip, who, because of him, are forced to be
idle.   May God destroy that Bethaven,[3] so that the
revenues taken away from the howling priests may be
transferred to the support of good teachers."[4]

---

[1] *C. R.*, 1 : 613.
[2] *C. R.*, 11 ; 50.
[3] The Wittenberg chapter.
[4] De W., 2 : 217.

When he saw that nothing could be accomplished
through Spalatin, he wrote to the Elector on the
twenty-third of March, 1524:

"Your Princely Grace undoubtedly knows that
through God's grace there are many excellent young
men here from foreign countries eager for the blessed
Word. Some are so poor that they live on bread and
water. Now I have recourse to Master Philip, because,
by the special grace of God, he is splendidly qualified to
teach the Holy Scriptures, even better than I myself.
If I should do it, I must neglect the translation of the
Bible. Instead of teaching Greek, let him devote himself to teaching the Holy Scriptures. The whole school
and we all, earnestly desire this. He resists on the sole
ground that he is appointed and paid by your Princely
Grace to teach Greek, and so can not omit this. Hence
I humbly entreat your Princely Grace, for the good of
the young men and for the sake of the Gospel of God,
to appoint him a salary for teaching the Holy Scriptures.
There are other young men who are qualified to teach
Greek, and it is not right that he should be forever engaged on this juvenile teaching, while the better kind is
neglected, in which he can furnish such results as cannot be acquired for wages."[1]

No immediate action was taken by the Elector;
and Melanchthon still insisted, partly out of regard
for his health, on devoting himself exclusively to
teaching languages.[2]

Finally it was determined at the beginning of the
year 1526, that his salary should be increased one

---

[1] De W., 2: 490.
[2] C. R., 1 : 677.

SPALATIN.

hundred gulden, on the condition that besides lecturing on Greek, he should deliver one lecture daily on
theology.   Now Melanchthon's conscience rebelled.
He did not see how he could do all his other work
and lecture once a day on theology.   Hence he did
not wish to accept the increase in salary.   Luther
again took the matter in hand, and wrote the
Elector John, February 9, 1526, requesting that he
should be satisfied to have Philip lecture once a
week on theology, or as often as he could.   He was
deserving of the increase in salary, as he had lectured for two years on the Scriptures without pay.[1]

The matter was now settled to the satisfaction of
all concerned.   The Elector did not insist that he
should lecture daily on theology.   Henceforth to
the end of his life Melanchthon remained ordinary
Professor of Theology and Greek, and taught theology, classical literature, and philosophy.   Thus he
was a member of two faculties.

We now turn back two years.   In the spring of
1524, we find Melanchthon with greatly impaired
health.   Nor are we surprised at this, when we recall the superabundance of his labours, trials, and
conflicts.   Besides the duties incident to his public
position, already, in 1519, he had opened " a private
school " in which young men and boys should be
prepared for the university.   In 1522, he wrote a
Latin Grammar for his pupils, and sought in many
ways to promote their advancement.   The most
diligent scholar was placed in charge of the others
as a reward, and named house-king.   He who had

[1] De W., 3 : 91.

composed the best essay in prose or poetry, was
crowned with the ivy, or heard his praises sung by
Melanchthon in a festive poem.   From time to time
he allowed his pupils to render dialogues and comedies from Seneca, Plautus, and Terence, and thus
incited them to higher diligence.   In this private
school he taught Greek, Latin, Rhetoric, Logic,
Mathematics, and Physics.   His personal influen
over the young men was extraordinarily great.   No
one now dared to make sport of the young and un-
gainly Magister.   He had conquered the respect and
won the confidence of colleagues and of pupils by
his massive learning, his devotion to science, and his
affection for the young.   John Kessler, who afterward became a reformer in Switzerland, wrote thus
of him in 1523 :

" In size he is a small, unattractive person. You would
think he was only a boy not above eighteen years old,
when he walks by the side of Luther. Because of their
sincere love for each other they are almost always together. Martin is much taller than he, but in understanding, learning, and culture, Philip is a great stalwart
giant and hero. One wonders that in so small a body
there can lie concealed such a great and lofty mountain
of wisdom and culture." [1]

By this time his fame as a scholar and teacher had
spread far beyond the boundaries of Saxony. Dis-
tant lands were beginning to regard Wittenberg as
the home of the most profound learning. Leipzig

[1] Quoted in Schwartz's *Darstellungen aus dem Gebiet der P æt-
gogik*, 1 : 98.

had grown jealous, and had announced that Erasmus would take a chair in that renowned university. Even some Roman Catholic scholars spoke the praises of Melanchthon, and esteemed him a restorer of learning.   At the University of Freiburg his writings drove out the old scholastic text-books, and kindled a new zeal for the study of theology.

Melanchthon now needed rest, and thought of a journey to his native land as the best means of restoring his broken health.   He hesitated to ask permission from the Court to be absent.   But Luther encouraged him by saying:

" Go, dear Philip, go in God's name.   Our Lord was not always engaged in preaching and teaching.   Sometimes he turned aside and visited his friends and relatives. Only one thing I ask of you: Come back soon.   I will pray for you day and night.   Now go." [1]

On the fourth of April he ventured to inform Spalatin that he needed rest, as he was suffering from insomnia, and that he " greatly desired to visit his dear mother and the rest of the family " He asks of the Elector through him for a vacation of five weeks, as the university will not miss him for such a length of time, he thinks.[2]   In a few days he writes again, thanking " his patron " for his good offices in procuring him the desired leave of absence.

On the sixteenth or seventeenth of April, with William Nesen, of Frankfort-on-the-Main, Francis Burkhard, of Weimar, John Silverborn, of Worms,

---

[1] Schmidt, p. 103.
[2] C. R., 1 : 652.
8

and Joachim Camerarius, of Bamberg, he began the
journey on horseback   The travellers arrived at
Leipzig on the eighteenth, just in time for Melanchthon and Camerarius to visit Peter Mosellanus, who
on that day breathed his last.   In his death Melanchthon mourned the loss of a friend, and Camerarius the loss of a former teacher.[1]   In July,
Melanchthon wrote an epitaph in Latin and Greek,
of which the following is a translation:[2]

> " Beneath this tomb that meets the stranger's eye
> The dear remains of Mosellanus lie ;
> In vain might friends protracted life implore,
> The lovely rhetorician speaks no more ;
> But in the records of eternal fame,
> Ages to come shall find inscribed his name,
> While from this transient life of tears and sighs,
> God has removed him to yon fairer skies."

From Leipzig the party proceeded to Fulda,
where they were entertained by Crotus Rubianus
and Adam Kraft, and where they learned of the
death of Ulric von Hutten, who had been a valiant
champion of the Reformation.   Three days later
they reached Frankfort, where Nesen remained.
The others went on to Bretten to the house of Melanchthon's mother.

When Melanchthon caught sight of his native city
he dismounted from his horse, and, kneeling on the
ground, exclaimed: " Oh my fatherland! How I
thank thee, Lord, that I am again permitted to
enter it."

---

[1] *C. R.*, 1 : 654.
[2] *C. R.*, 10: 491.

In 1520, his mother had married Christopher
Kolbe, a citizen of Bretten. In 1526, she was
married to her third husband, Melchior Höchel.[1]
She lived and died a Catholic. There is no evidence
that either at this time or during a subsequent
visit Melanchthon sought to have her change her
faith.

During this visit Philip enjoyed much pleasant
converse with his mother and with his brother
George. The days sped swiftly by, and soon it was
time for him to turn his face again toward the north.

While sojourning at Bretten, Melanchthon received
two visits that were of peculiar significance. The
philosophical faculty of the University of Heidelberg, as if to make amends for the slight of ten years
before, when it refused to enter him as a candidate
for the master's degree, sent a deputation to present
him with a handsome silver goblet. The aged Hermann Busch, professor of Latin, Simon Grynæus,
professor of Greek, and the Dean, performed this
pleasant duty in recognition of Melanchthon's
scholarship, and of his services to science. In his
letter of thanks Melanchthon declares himself un
worthy of such a gift, but promises to show that it
has not been bestowed on an ungrateful recipient,
since he would ever strive to deserve well in regard
to learned studies.[2]

The other visit was also from Heidelberg, but was
of a very different kind. Lorenzo Campeggius, the
papal legate for Germany, had gone to Heidelberg

[1] Matthes, p. 61.
[2] C. R., 1 : 656.

after the close of the Diet of Nuremberg. Hearing that Melanchthon was at Bretten, he sent thither his private secretary, the learned Frederick Nausea, to hold an interview with the Wittenberg professor on the religious dissensions.

The secretary, as if acting on his own motion, characterised Luther as a disturber of the peace, who sought only to revolutionise the Church, and held out to Melanchthon the vision of a brilliant future if he would become reconciled to the Church. The latter answered :

" When I have ascertained that a thing is true I embrace and defend it without the fear or favour of any mortal and without regard for profit or honour; neither will I separate myself from those who first taught and now defend these things. As hitherto I have defended the pure doctrine without strife and abuse, so shall I continue to exhort all who in this matter of common interest wish for peace and safety, to heal the wounds which can no longer be concealed, and to restrain the rage of those who with hostile hands do not cease to tear open the wounds. If they will not do this, let them look out lest they themselves be the first to fall." [1]

When he found out that Nausea had come as the agent of the Cardinal, he sent to the latter a brief account of Luther's doctrine ·

" Luther does not abolish public ceremonies, but distinguishes between human righteousness and the divine and employs the Scriptures for fortifying the conscience against the gates of hell. Human rites and ceremonies

---

[1] Camerarius, p. 97.

do not constitute the righteousness of God; but out of love they may be observed where they do no harm. In the Mass and in celibacy there is great corruption.

" Many who are by no means Lutherans attach themselves to Luther, and thus mislead the people. It is madness to threaten all with destruction who name the name of Luther. It is impious to think that the essence of religion consists either in despising or in observing ceremonies." [1]

While Melanchthon tarried with his mother and brother at Bretten his companions in travel, Camerarius, Burkhard, and Silverborn, went on to Basel to visit Erasmus. Melanchthon would gladly have gone with them, but was restrained out of considerations of prudence. Even before the party had set out from Wittenberg, it had been known there that " the sage of Rotterdam " was writing a refutation of Luther's doctrine of the Will. Melanchthon foresaw that the controversy would be bitter, inasmuch as Luther had written of Erasmus in a way that wounded the vain man's pride.[2]

Also Melanchthon himself, by classing Erasmus with the heathen philosophers, and explaining, " However, I would not hesitate to prefer Erasmus to all the ancients," [3] had bestowed doubtful praise. But Erasmus, so he wrote to Pirkheimer, would have been glad to see Melanchthon, since he still wished to retain this " young man of purest soul " among his admirers.

---

[1] *C. R.*, 1 : 657.
[2] De W., 2 : 199.
[3] *C. R.*, 20 : 700.

Soon the controversy broke out which was destined to make a complete separation of Erasmus from Luther, to alienate the former from the Reformation, to modify Melanchthon's view of the Will, and to damp the warmth of friendship between the two greatest humanists of the sixteenth century. Seldom has a controversy between two men had a more powerful influence.   In September, 1524, Erasmus published his book on the Freedom of the Will, entitled *De Libero Arbitrio Diatribe sive Collatio*.   The book is not to be despised.   It contains many strong arguments against Luther's doctrine of the absolute bondage of the Will; but it lacks deep insight into the principles of the Reformation. Melanchthon praises it for its moderation, " albeit it is sprinkled with black salt," and says that it was received at Wittenberg with impartiality.[1]

At the same time, September 6, 1524, Erasmus wrote an apologetic and explanatory letter to Mel anchthon.   He tells him why he had written the *Diatribe*.   Had he published nothing against Luther, " the theologians, monks, and Romish minions would have charged him with cowardice or with conversion to Luther, and thus would have compassed his ruin."   He also takes occasion in this letter to deliver his opinion of Melanchthon's *Loci*. He praises the candid and happy genius of the author and

" the array of doctrines admirably constructed in opposition to the Pharisaic tyranny.   But there are some

[1] *C. R.*, 1 : 675.

things which, to speak frankly, I cannot accept.   There
are some things which, even though it were safe, I would
not teach for conscience sake.   There are some things
that I might teach, but without profit." [1]

Melanchthon was evidently influenced by Erasmus's book.   He sent it to Spalatin, and expresses
the earnest desire that

" this subject, which is the most important in the Christian religion, should be carefully examined.   For this
reason I rejoice that Erasmus has entered the lists.   For
a long time I have desired that some prudent person
should oppose Luther in this matter.   Erasmus is the
man, or I am deceived." [2]

Here we have the beginning of that change in Melanchthon's doctrine of the Will which subsequently
exerted an important influence in Lutheran theology, for it is due to Melanchthon that no article on
Predestination was placed in the fundamental Lutheran Confession.

Deeply concerned as Melanchthon was for a
thorough discussion of the great question, he
sought chiefly at that time, though in vain, to restrain the contestants from violence.   To Erasmus
he wrote that Luther was not so irritable that
he could not bear anything, and said that he
promised to reply with a moderation equal to that
shown by Erasmus.[3]   But Erasmus himself soon be-

[1] *C. R.*, 1 : 667.
[2] *C. R.*, 1 : 673.
[3] *C. R.*, 1 : 675.

came irritated, and wrote sharp words against the Reformation, and complained of Luther's teaching as not pleasing him. He deplores the many disorders which are following in the wake of the Reformation, and predicts that Luther will not reply with moderation.[1]   In this he was not mistaken. In December, 1525, Luther published his book *On the Bondage of the Will—De Servo Arbitrio.*   It is one of his most powerful polemic writings; but it is so sharp and bitter that Erasmus complained that he was treated worse than a Turk.   The next year Erasmus replied in the first part of the *Hyperaspistes*, not less sharply and bitterly than Luther had written.   Melanchthon became almost frantic, and was equally displeased with both disputants. He wrote to Camerarius:

" Did you ever read anything more bitter than Erasmus's *Hyperaspistes?*   It is almost venomous.   How Luther takes it, I do not know.   But I have again besought him by all that is sacred, if he replies, to do so briefly, simply, and without abuse.   At once after Luther published his book, I said this controversy would end in the most cruel alienation.   It has come, and yet I think Erasmus has reserved something more offensive for the second part of his work.   He does me great wrong in imputing to me a part, and that, too, the most offensive part, of the work.   I have decided to bear this injury in silence.   Oh that Luther would keep silent! I did hope that with age, experience, and so many troubles, he would grow more moderate; but I see he becomes the more violent as the contests and the oppon-

---

[1] *C. R.*, 1 : 688.

ents exhibit the same characteristics. This matter
grievously vexes my soul.'' [1]

In 1527, Erasmus published the second part of the
Hyperaspistes.   Melanchthon begged Luther not to
reply, since it had become a tedious and intricate
discussion which the people could not understand.
He also continued the good offices of pacificator
with Erasmus; but it was now too late.   The two
disputants became irreconcilably hostile towards
each other.   Luther saw in Erasmus only an enemy
of all religion, an atheist, a follower of Lucian and
Epicurus; and Erasmus declared that wherever Lutheranism prevailed, there learning declined.

After this Melanchthon and Erasmus exchanged
letters from time to time, but ceased to discuss
theological questions.

Having presented in its connection a brief report
of the Erasmian episode in the history of the Reformation, and in the life of Melanchthon, we go
back to Bretten to complete the account of the visit
to the south.   On the return of his three friends
from Basel, Melanchthon set out with them for
Saxony.   Not far from Frankfort he had an adven
ture which in the sequel brought important results
to the Reformation.   The Landgrave of Hesse was
on his way to Heidelberg with his retainers to attend
a gathering of the princes.   He had heard that Melanchthon was in those parts.   Meeting " a cavalcade
of wretched cavaliers,'' he rode up to one of them
and inquired whether he was Philip Melanchthon.

---

[1] *C. R.*, 1 : 793.

The person addressed responded, " I am he," and
prepared to dismount as a mark of respect. The
Prince bade him remain on his horse, to be of
good courage, and not to fear, as he wished to speak
with him about certain things. Melanchthon answered that he was not afraid, and that he was a
very unimportant person. The Landgrave replied,
smiling: " But if I should deliver you up to Campeggius, I think he would be very glad." The
two then rode together for some distance, the Landgrave asking questions and Melanchthon briefly and
pertinently replying. At length they separated with
the understanding that Melanchthon, when he returned home, should send the Landgrave a written
statement concerning the religious innovations.

The Landgrave gave the party a safe conduct
through his dominion and bade them adieu.[1]

The promise made to the Landgrave was not forgotten. In the following autumn, 1524, Melanchthon sent him " A Summary of the Renovated
Christian Doctrine."[2] He says that many princes
and bishops support the Pope out of regard to their
secular interests, but the people follow Luther as
the promoter of freedom. Two subjects agitate the
Church: The one is Christian righteousness, and
the other has reference to human ceremonies.
Christian righteousness is the preaching of repentance, and the remission of sins. The Holy Spirit
uncovers the sin of the heart, alarms the conscience,
and incites to faith in the promises of Christ, who

---

[1] Camerarius, p. 98.
  C. R., 1 : 703.

satisfies for our sins and graciously pardons them. The Holy Spirit begets faith in the heart, the fear of God, humility, chastity, and other good fruits. We teach that repentance is required, which calls us from evil works. This righteousness Christ requires, not ceremonies. The kingdom of God is within.

There are traditions which may be observed without sin, as those things which have been appointed in regard to food, vestments, and similar adiaphora. There are others which cannot be observed without sin, as celibacy, which has been cruelly and impiously imposed by the Pope. No human tradition can stand against the Word of God. Neither are doctrines obligatory which cannot be followed without sin. It is a sin to suppose that monasticism can justify anyone. Paul calls those lying spirits who forbid marriage. The princes who support the law of the Pope are the satellites and the executors of such spirits. It is the duty of princes to have the Gospel preached, and to restrain the violence of the rabble, which, under pretence of the Gospel, creates confusion and threatens the safety of others.

He closes the letter by commending the cause of religion to the Landgrave's conscience, and by praying that Christ would supply him with the Spirit, and give him the disposition to provide well for the public safety, and not to delay the cause of the Gospel, nor persecute those whom necessity and conscience compel to renounce the authority of the Pope.

The effect of the letter was most salutary. The Landgrave had been a violent enemy of the Reformation, and had punished those preachers of his land who had embraced it, some with banishment and others with imprisonment.   On the twenty-fifth of February, 1525, he declared for the Reformation. He was often humourously called Philip's disciple. Young, spirited, brave, aggressive, and well in-structed in theology, he was a valiant champion of " the renewed Christian doctrine "; but, rash, im-pulsive, and immoral, he often brought reproach upon the same.

CHAPTER XI

AS PRECEPTOR OF GERMANY

Death of Nesen—Melanchthon's Discomforts—Call to Nuremberg—
Oration on Education—Services in the Cause of Education.

CAMERARIUS relates that while passing through Hesse on their return from the visit to the South, in 1524, it chanced that he, Melanchthon and Nesen stopped to water their horses while the others rode on. Nesen called attention to three crows on a neighbouring hill, cawing and making strange gestures with their wings, and asked Melanchthon what that portended. The latter answered: " What, but that death is very near one of us three ? "

Nesen laughed and rode on. Camerarius was greatly agitated, and feared to ask Melanchthon what he meant. But he recalled the augury and the prophecy very vividly when, on the fifth of July, 1524, William Nesen was drowned in the Elbe. He says he does not mention this incident because either he or Melanchthon attributed anything to the flight of birds, but to show that things sometimes occur in a marvellous way, which ought not to be

laughed at, and which, when they occur, start
strange thoughts in our minds.[1]

But Melanchthon, still depressed through insomnia and wretched health, saw in the sad death
of his friend the forerunner of catastrophe, and
at the same time suffered " the most poignant
grief." Months afterward he wrote, " The lament-
able fate of Nesen so troubles me at times that I
tremble all over."[2] And this grief and trouble
changed into melancholy when in August his friend
Camerarius returned to his native city of Bamberg.
In October he wrote him · " I am living here as in
a wilderness. There is no society except that of
the uncultured, in which I find no pleasure. I sit
at home like a lame cobbler. In my state of health
this is distressing to me."[3] He doubtless alludes
to those of the professors who opposed the Reformation and classical studies. He says that Luther is
not well, and that he is, he thinks, annoyed by the
public scandals, meaning, probably, Carlstadt's agitations at Orlamünde and in the South.

Evidently Melanchthon was at this time in a very
uncongenial environment. Things were not going
smoothly at Wittenberg. He was probably beginning to feel some of the effects of that imperiousness
in Luther's nature, and of that love of controversy,
of which later in life he complains, and which came
near rending their friendship. He writes Camerarius
that there are some things which it is not safe to

---

[1] Camerarius, p. 100.
[2] C. R., 1 : 684.
[3] C. R., 1 : 683.

communicate by letter.[1]   He has discovered that
Luther is too violent in controversy, and yields too
much to his feelings in discussing matters of public
interest.   He says he is miserably tormented and
almost killed when he thinks of the theological
controversies that are going on.[2]   But the personal
relations of the two were not at that time disturbed.
When he complains to Camerarius that he has no
friends and companions at Wittenberg with whom
he can pleasantly converse, he especially excepts
Luther, "who alone," he says, "is my friend; but
he is so troubled and harassed that whenever we
converse together, I have to grieve over his affairs.
The others either have no use for me or are vulgar."[3]
It is evident that also Bugenhagen and Jonas must
be excepted.   For in August, 1524, Melanchthon
wrote a Preface to Bugenhagen's commentary on
the Psalms, and in the year 1525 he addressed Jonas
in several beautiful Latin poems.

Among the many causes of Melanchthon's melancholy in the years 1524–25, were "the public
evils," "the domestic cares," and "the implacable
insomnia" of which he writes, together with the
conviction that the Elector is slow to make proper
provision for the improvement of the university.
But there is a silver lining to the dark cloud that
overhangs his life.   He finds solace in his little
daughter, his infant son, and his wife.[4]   Often was

---

[1] C. R., 1 : 683.
[2] C. R., 1 : 648.
[3] C. R., 1 : 729.
[4] C. R., 1 : 729.

he seen rocking the cradle with one hand, and holding a book in the other.

It was during this period of gloom and despondency that Melanchthon's gifts began to be called into
requisition in that work which more than any other
procured for him the title of *Preceptor of Germany.*
It was the work of reorganising and directing the
higher education of his country.

At the close of the Middle Ages nearly every
town in Germany had one or more schools. The
cathedral schools mostly cared for the training of
the clergy. The parochial schools prepared the
young for the duties of Church membership. In
the manufacturing and commercial cities secular
education was conducted in relative independence
of the Church. The knightly and burgher classes,
both male and female, were generally well instructed
in Grammar, Rhetoric, Dialectic, History, Geo-
graphy, and Arithmetic, and in many cases in the
Latin language.

The printing-press helped to diffuse knowledge,
and increased the desire to read. That in the first
half of the sixteenth century vast numbers of persons could read, is evidenced by the enormous sales
of Luther's New Testament, of his sermons and
books. It is said that five thousand copies of his
*Address to the Christian Nobility of the German Na-
tion* were sold in five days.[1] His most powerful
books, his sermons, hymns, and pamphlets, composed in the vernacular, were placed on sale at the
book-stalls and at the commercial fairs. Peddlers

---

[1] Putnam, *Books and their Makers*, ii., 221.

and colporteurs[1] carried them by the thousands to
the people, who read them, or listened while others
read them aloud.

It is not strange that under these circumstances
Luther should promptly recognise the value of the
printing-press as an instrument for promoting Reform, and should see that if the war against Rome
was to be carried on with success, the masses of the
people as well as the classes must be educated; for,
notwithstanding the general intelligence of the
higher, middle, and knightly classes, dark and dense
ignorance prevailed among the people, so that they
have been described as " barbarous " and " bestial."

Now it was that Luther, in 1524, seized his pen
and wrote his appeal to the Aldermen of all the
German cities in behalf of Christian schools.[2] He
declares: " For the maintenance of civil order and
the proper regulation of the home, society needs
accomplished and well-trained men and women.
Such men are to come from boys, and such women
from girls." He lays great stress on the languages,
calling them " the scabbard in which the Word of
God is sheathed; the casket in which this jewel is
enshrined; the cask in which this wine is kept; the
chamber in which this food is stored."

This little book marks Luther as the father and
founder of popular education, and the development
and application of the principles of this book have
made the land of Luther the land of libraries and of
schools. In this book Luther says that men must

---

[1] Putnam, *Books and their Makers*, ii., 219.
[2] Erl. Ed., 22 : 168 *et seqq.*

be specially trained for the higher duties of life, for teaching, for expounding the Scriptures, and for ruling in the State, " since it is irrational and barbarous to permit ignoramuses and blockheads to rule, when we can prevent it."

A Latin translation of Luther's appeal, adorned with a Preface by Melanchthon, appeared at Hagenau the same year. This shows that Melanchthon and Luther were at one on the subject of popular, as well as of higher, education. What Luther suggested and urged, that Melanchthon formulated and carried into effect.

Among the first, if not the very first, of the German cities to heed Luther's appeal and to make provision for the higher education of her youth, was Nuremberg. This imperial city, celebrated for its strong walls, its ancient castle, its rich monasteries, its noble churches, its splendid schools of art, so far surpassed all other German cities in intelligence and refinement at the close of the fifteenth, and at the beginning of the sixteenth century as to be called " the eye of Germany." It was the home of Albrecht Dürer, the most renowned of the German painters; of Adam Kraft, whose ciborium in the St. Lorenz is almost a miracle in stone; of Peter Vischer, whose monument of St. Sebaldus in the St. Sebaldus Church is reckoned " the most exquisite gem of German art"; of Hans Sachs, the cobbler-poet, " the prince and patriarch of all master-singers." It had four Latin schools, and had long been a centre of industry, politics, and commerce. Among its scholars and patricians were Wilibald Pirkheimer,

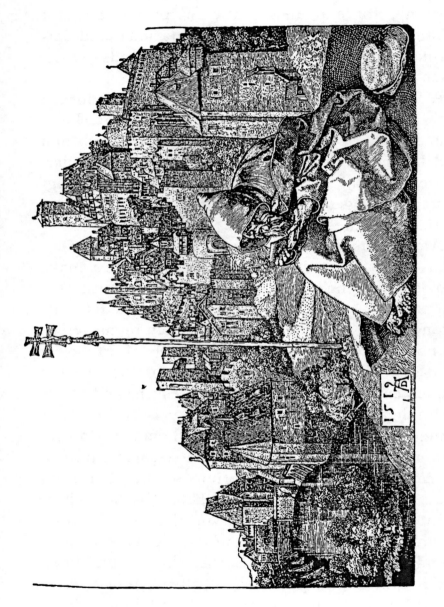

NUREMBERG IN 1519.

AFTER A PAINTING BY ALBRECHT DÜRER.

Casper Nützel, Hieronimus Ebner, Lazarus Spengler, and Hieronimus Baumgartner. It was only natural that the city should seek to add Melanchthon to this galaxy of illustrious men. When now, at the special instance of Spengler and Baumgartner, it was decided to establish a gymnasium, on the seventeenth of October, 1524, Melanchthon, "because of his extraordinary fitness and culture," was invited to become Rector and Professor of Rhetoric.[1] But, dissatisfied as he was with the condition of affairs at Wittenberg, and poorly as he was then paid for his services, he declined the invitation. He could not desert the Elector and incur the imputation of ingratitude. Besides, he distrusted his fitness for the position offered, since such a school needed not only a lecturer, but also an orator, who should serve as a model for the students. His style was poor, dry, and without ornament.[2] That he was perfectly sincere in this self-depreciation is evident from what he wrote on the same day to Camerarius, viz., that he wanted Nuremberg to have a professor more competent and more opulent in speech than he was.[3]

But the Nurembergers still pressed the matter upon him, and wrote that it was his fault that the opening of the school was delayed.[4] On the third of December, 1524, he declined in the most emphatic manner, and urged the selection of a

---

[1] Hartfelder's *Melanch. Pædagogica*, p. 6.
[2] *C. R.*, 1 . 678.
[3] *C. R.*, 1 : 682.
[4] *C. R.*, 1 : 686.

professor equal to the magnitude of the work. In the autumn of the next year he went to Nuremberg, accompanied by Camerarius, and gave directions for organising the school and for the selection of suitable professors.[1]

In the spring of 1526, the gymnasium was formally opened. Melanchthon was invited to be present, and went personally before the Elector in Torgau to obtain the necessary leave of absence.

On the sixth of May, in company with several friends, he arrived in Nuremberg, and gave the Senate the benefit of his counsel and experience. Camerarius was chosen Rector and Professor of Greek; Eoban Hess was appointed Professor of Rhetoric; Michael Roting, Professor of Latin, and John Schoner, Professor of Mathematics. The Senate, the ministers, and all the cultured people joined in the ceremonies of inauguration. On the twenty-third of May, Melanchthon delivered a brief Latin oration in praise of learning. He began by apologising for his youth and inexperience. He did not take this honour upon himself. Others had imposed it upon him. It is an evidence of divine favour that the Nurembergers have determined in this time of great peril to preserve and promote learning. No art, no industry, no production of the earth, not even the light of the sun, is of more

---

[1] The Nuremberg "School-Order," *Ratio Scholæ*, which undoubtedly proceeded from the pen of Melanchthon, "since its characteristic thoughts and maxims agree with numerous expressions of Melanchthon," is given in Hartfelder's *Melanch. Pædagogica*, p. 7 *et seq.*

value than learning, for by it good laws, courts, and religion are maintained.   As evidence of this, look at the Scythians, who are ignorant of letters.   They have no laws and no courts of justice.   They live by violence and robbery.   Without learning there can be no good men, no love of virtue, no refinement, no proper notions of religion and of the will of God.   It is the duty of rulers to foster schools. But there are some who do not know the value of learning, and others are so wicked as to think that their tyranny would be promoted by the abolition of all laws, religion, and discipline.

"What shall I say of the bishops who have been appointed by the emperors to superintend learning?   The colleges of priests were scholars to whom leisure and endowments were given that they might serve as teachers. Nor did it appear unfortunate that letters should be cultivated by this class of persons.   But now we behold none more hostile to the liberal arts than the sacerdotal fraternity."

He praises the Nurembergers for having furnished an asylum to learning, which had strayed into exile. He closed with an invocation: " I will pray Christ to bless this most important work and to crown your counsels and the diligence of those who study here with His favour." [1]

This eloquent oration shows that Melanchthon had a genius for higher education.   His countrymen were not slow to avail themselves of his wisdom, and posterity has named him the *Creator of the*

[1] *C. R.*, 11 : 106 *et seqq.*

Protestant Educational System of Germany. Nearly
all of the Protestant Latin schools and gymnasia of
the sixteenth century, and the splendid *Fürstenschulen*, that is, gymnasia established by the prince,
were founded according to directions given by Melanchthon. We still have correspondence between
him and fifty-six cities asking counsel and assistance
in founding and conducting Latin schools and
gymnasia. He wrote the constitutions, arranged
the courses of study, and nominated most of the first
instructors for such schools.

His scheme for a Latin school is given with minute-
ness in the *Saxon Visitation Articles*[1] of 1528. " The
Preachers are to exhort the people to send their
children to school, that they may be qualified to
teach in the Church and to govern." The three
fundamental principles with which he starts are, that

" the teachers shall be careful to teach the children only
Latin, not German, nor Greek, nor Hebrew, as some
have formerly done, who burden the poor children with
a diversity which is not only unprofitable, but harmful.
They shall not burden the children with many books;
and they shall separate them in three classes."

The first class shall study the Primer, which contains the Alphabet, the Lord's Prayer, the Creed,
and other prayers. They shall then read Donatus,
and listen to a daily explanation of a verse or two
from Cato, ·in order to acquire a good vocabulary.

The second class shall learn Grammar, including
Etymology, Syntax, and Prosody. They shall read

---

[1] *C. R.*, 26 : 90.

the Fables of Æsop, the Dialogues of Mosellanus, and the Colloquies of Erasmus, also Terence and Plautus. They are required to recite the Lord's Prayer, the Creed, the Ten Commandments, and to commit a number of psalms. They must study the Gospel of Matthew, the two Pauline Epistles to Timothy, the First Epistle of John, and the Proverbs of Solomon.

The third class shall continue the study of Grammar, shall read Virgil, the Metamorphoses of Ovid the Offices or Letters of Cicero, shall write Latin verse, and study Dialectic and Rhetoric.

" During the first hour in the afternoon all the children, both small and large, shall be trained in music.

" The boys are required to speak Latin, and the teachers, so far as possible, shall speak only Latin with the boys, in order that the latter may be incited to and encouraged in such exercise."

Such is the substance of the so-called " *Stiftungsbrief* " (foundation document) of the German gymnasia. The three classes do not represent so many years of study. Students were advanced from a lower to a higher class only when they had completed the studies of the lower class. Several years were occupied in completing the threefold course.

From the Latin schools boys were sent to the gymnasia proper, and to the *Fürstenschulen*, which latter were founded in the fifth decade of the sixteenth century. The gymnasia formed the connecting link between the Latin schools and the university. Their scheme of study included the

Latin, Greek, and Hebrew languages, Dialectic, Rhetoric, Mathematics, and Cosmology. Only a fair beginning was made in Hebrew; but in Greek the writings of Isocrates, Xenophon, Plutarch, Hesiod, Theognis, and Phocylides were read and studied.

This scheme for gymnasial instruction remained essentially unchanged to the beginning of the nineteenth century. But it was chiefly through his text-books that Melanchthon exerted the greatest influence on the schools of his day. He wrote text books on Latin and Greek Grammar, Dialectic, Rhetoric, Psychology, Physics, Ethics, History, and Religion. From 1518 to 1544 his Greek Grammar passed through seventeen editions, and from 1545 to 1622, twenty-six editions were published. Fifty-one editions of his Latin Grammar were published from 1525 to 1737, and to the year 1737 it was used in all the Saxon schools. His Elements of Rhetoric and Dialectic passed through numerous editions and reprints. Several of his text-books were long used in Roman Catholic schools.

Also the most distinguished rectors of the century, Camerarius, John Sturm, Trotzendorf, Neander, Wolf, and others, were his friends or scholars, and were imbued with his spirit. Those who had sat at his feet carried with them the lofty ideals of " the dear master," used his text-books, and adhered to his methods. When a prince wanted a professor for his university, or a town wanted a rector or a teacher for its school, the first thought was to confer with Melanchthon. Hence, when he died in 1560, there was scarcely a city in Germany that did not have a teacher or a pastor who had been a pupil of Melanchthon.

According to the Melanchthonian scheme, the Latin and Greek authors were studied with the greatest avidity, and with the most salutary results. The seeds of classical culture which Petrarch and his followers had revived in Italy, not without injury to Christianity, Melanchthon and his pupils scattered on the fruitful soil prepared by the Reformation, in order that " posterity might have seminaries of the churches." That for three hundred and fifty years Germany has had the best " seminaries of the churches," is due primarily to Melanchthon; and that the Reformation was enabled to utilise the vast treasures of classical culture, and to commend itself to the learned, is due to the same person, whom a great Roman Catholic historian, Dr. Döllinger, calls

" the most brilliant phenomenon which proceeded from the Erasmian school, equal to his master in many respects, superior to him in others. Riches of knowledge, the choicest classical culture, facility of expression, versatility of composition, rhetorical fulness, and improvisation, united to untiring industry—this rare combination of excellences fitted him above all others for the literary headship of the mighty movement." [1]

This " literary headship," in the highest sense of the phrase, and in its most lasting influence, was exercised by Melanchthon mainly through the universities, which were organised, or reformed, accord-

[1] *Die Reformation*, i., 349.

ing to his ideas.   In a literary sense he was the soul
of the University of Wittenberg, and gave inspiration to all of its literary movements.   He lectured
on almost every subjĕct, and prepared lectures and
declamations for others to deliver.   In 1533, he
wrote the statutes for the reorganisation of the
theological faculty,[1] whereby a scriptural and exegetical theology took the place of a philosophical and
scholastic theology.   In 1545, he wrote the laws
and statutes for the government of the faculty of
theology and the faculty of the liberal arts.[2]   The
latter faculty is to have ten professors, who are to
lecture on Latin, Greek, and Hebrew literature; on
Ethics, Mathematics, Physics, Philosophy, Dialectic, and Rhetoric.

In the prominence given to these literary and
philosophical studies, we have an illustration of
Melanchthon's fundamental principle, viz., that all
thorough training in theology must rest on a philo-
logical and philosophical foundation.   He was accustomed to say, " Every good theologian and
faithful interpreter of the heavenly doctrine, must
be first a linguist, then a dialectician, and finally a
witness."

In a large sense the University of Wittenberg became the model for the other Protestant universities.
The " Order of Lectures " in the Marburg statutes
of 1529 is essentially the same as that of Wittenberg
in 1536. " There is no doubt," says Paulsen, " that
it was composed under the direct or indirect influ-

---

[1] In Förstemann's *Liber Decanorum.*
[2] *C. R.*, 10 : 992.

MARBURG IN THE 16TH CENTURY.

ence of Melanchthon."[1]   Königsberg was founded
in 1544 almost exclusively according to directions
given by Melanchthon, as was Jena in 1548.   His
counsel was sought and his plans were adopted in
the reorganisation of the universities of Tübingen,
Leipzig, and Heidelberg, as will be seen hereafter.
Frankfort-on-the-Oder and Rostock were reformed
and reorganised mainly by Melanchthon's scholars.
Greifswald, in 1545, took Wittenberg as its model,
named Melanchthon " our highly esteemed and
venerated teacher," a‚ d adopted his text-books as
the basis of the lectures.[2]

The universities were all institutions of the State,
and their professors were bound by the Confessions
of the Church.   All the sciences, theology, philo-
logy, law, and medicine were studied in these universities according to the Melanchthonian n.ethod, with
the Melanchthonian thoroughness, and with the
Melanchthonian view of honouring God and of
carrying on an irrepressible conflict with an opposing ecclesiastical principle of higher education.
Without these universities thus anchored to the
State and to the Church, Protestantism never could
have passed safely through its many conflicts with
sect and doubt and armed foe.   Without these universities—in their fundamental idea essentially the
creation of Melanchthon—German science would
not to-day be the boast of Germany, and the glory
of the age.   Without these universities, German
theology would not have had a Gerhard, a Spener,

---

[1] *Geschichte des Gelehrten Unterrichts*, i., 226.
[2] Paulsen, i., 237.

a Schleiermacher, a Dorner; nor German philo-
sophy a Leibnitz, a Kant, a Hegel, a Lotze; nor
German poetry a Gellert, a Klopstock, a Goethe, a
Schiller.

The ideal of these great scholars has been the
union of classical antiquity and of all sciences and
philosophy with the religious and moral powers of
Christianity and of the German people. Protestant
Germany is still building on the educational founda-
tions laid by Melanchthon more than three hundred
and fifty years ago.

During his sojourn of nearly a month at Nuremberg, Melanchthon was entertained at the St. Ægidius
Convent, and often enjoyed the hospitality of Pirkheimer. The most distinguished citizens did him
honour. He made the acquaintance of the learned
Osiander, preacher at the St. Lorenz Church; and
of Albrecht Dürer, who painted his picture, and then
engraved it on copper.

On the fourth of June, 1526, he set out for home,
via Coburg, where he had " a discussion with a
supercilious priest about the Holy Supper." By
the middle of June he was again in Wittenberg,
strengthened in body and cheered in spirit by his
visit among congenial friends in Nuremberg. On
the fourth of July he wrote to Camerarius that he
would gladly have spent the entire summer at Nuremberg, both on account of his health and for other
reasons which he could not write about. He declares
that no slave in a mill is more incessantly occupied
than he is, and yet he seems to accomplish nothing. .

He laments the absence of his friend and says:
" You have Mica [Michael Roting].   I have no one
like him.   But, as Plato says, there are λυκοφιλιάι,
full of cares and anxiety."[1]   What these λυκοφιλιάι
(wolf-friendships) were, we are not prepared to say,
but it is certain that Melanchthon was still far from
being happy.

Indeed the hindrances which had stood in the way
of the Reformation and of learning, and the public
evils which had fallen on Germany, were quite
enough to bring despondency upon a person of so
frail a body and so meek a spirit as Melanchthon
possessed.

---

[1] *C. R.*, 1 : 804.

CHAPTER XII

THE PEASANTS' WAR

Death of Frederick the Wise—Melanchthon's Funeral Oration—
Insurrection of the Peasants—Luther's Advice—Melanchthon's
Confutation—Luther's Marriage—Melanchthon's Letter.

ON the fifth of May, 1525, Melanchthon's friend
and patron, Frederick the Wise, died at
Lochau. He was a devout and pious prince. He
protected Luther and Melanchthon from the enemies of the evangelical doctrine. Shortly before
his death he received the communion in both kinds
thus confessing himself a convert to Luther's doctrine in at least one of its most important features.
His body was taken to Wittenberg and buried in
the Castle Church, on whose door Luther had nailed
the Ninety-five Theses. Melanchthon improved the
occasion by delivering a funeral oration in the name
of the university. He magnifies, but not unduly,
the virtues of the illustrious deceased:

" Let others laud the images of their ancestors and
their venerable pedigrees—a distinction in which the
Saxon princes are preëminent. But greater things be-

THE PEASANTS IN ARMS IN 1525.

FROM A CONTEMPORARY WOODCUT.

long to Frederick, as skill in government, and lofty
magnanimity. It is a mistake to suppose that the State
is maintained by arms only, and by power. Of greater
value to this end are the arts of peace, justice, moderation, constancy, care of the public safety, diligence in
proclaiming the law and in settling the disputes of citizens, patience in bearing the faults of the people, vigour
in punishing transgressors, kindness in sparing those
who can be reclaimed. In the popular estimation
military virtues are more splendid, and a soldier is more
admired because of physical prowess, than the modest
and quiet civilian; and civil virtues like other good
things are ignored by the vulgar. Hence they are
faintly praised who are given to the pursuits and arts of
peace.

" In my judgment, he who would promote the welfare
of man must prefer the pursuits of peace to the camp.
Anthony was a great commander, but he was inferior to
Augustus, who promoted peace and quiet. Solon contributed more to Greece than Alcibiades did. The one
ruined his country by wars, the other saved it by laws
and institutions. God endowed Frederick with these
better and more useful virtues. Hence in these turbulent times he was careful to preserve the German people
from wars."[1]

He closes his oration with the prayer—

" that God in his mercy may guard the soul of Frederick,
may prosper the new rule of his brother, may protect the
country in these wretched times, and may give the disposition to cherish the public tranquillity and to reverence those in authority, as the divine precept requires,
with all fidelity and good conscience."

[1] *C. R.*, 11 : 90 *et seqq.*

The " wretched times " of which Melanchthon
speaks in his prayer had been brought about by the
Peasants' War, a sort of communistic rebellion of
the lowest order of society against the civil and
spiritual rulers.   For generations the peasants had
been the victims of injustice, violence, and cruelty.
More than once had they been driven to despera-
tion, and had sought relief through rebellion, as in
1476, 1492, 1493, 1502, 1513, and in Würtemberg
in 1514 against the lawless tyranny of Duke Ulrich.

Hence this popular outbreak cannot be attributed
to the Reformation, but there is no doubt that the
preaching and the teaching of Luther at Wittenberg
gave a new impulse to the desire for freedom, and
to some extent influenced the course taken by the
war at this time.

The peasants, whose condition was little better
than that of beasts of burden, and whose burdens
had been made heavier in recent years by the growing love of luxury among the rulers, were seeking to
do exactly what many of their superiors were doing,
viz., to throw off the oppressive yoke imposed by
those above them.   It is impossible for a humane
person who has inquired into the condition of those
serfs, and who has seen the condition of their descendants in Germany to-day, not to sympathise
with their purpose, at the same time that, as a lover
of order, he must reprehend the violence which they
employed as a means of attaining the desired end.

Carlstadt and Münzer, whose revolutionary methods have been already described, were the chief in-
citers of the insurrection.   The former, in 1524,

settled at Orlemünde and preached communism, and published a new doctrine of the Lord's Supper. From Jena, where he had a small printing-office, he circulated incendiary tracts. Driven from Saxony, he went first to Strassburg and then to Basel, where he excited the theologians against the Wittenberg Reformers, and contributed to the general discontent of the people.

Thomas Münzer, after his expulsion from Zwickau and his failure in Wittenberg, proclaimed a compound of communism and fanaticism at Alstädt, in Thuringia. Forced to leave the country, he travelled through Southern Germany and returned to Thuringia, preaching everywhere against the whole existing social, political, and ecclesiastical order, and especially against infant baptism, the rejection of which became the watchword of the entire party of revolutionists. He signed himself " Münzer with the hammer," and " with the sword of Gideon." He advocated the destruction of all the ungodly, and said: " Look not on the sorrows of the ungodly; let not your sword grow cold from blood. Strike hard on the anvil of Nimrod [the princes]; cast his tower to the ground, because the day is yours." [1]

The result was inevitable. Inspired by the thought that God had created all men equal, the peasants of Southern Germany rose up almost *en masse*, and demanded their rights under the banner of the Gospel. A manifesto of grievances and claims was published in twelve articles:

1. The right to choose their own pastors, who

[1] Walch, xvi., 150.

should preach the Gospel purely and plainly without any additions, doctrines, or ordinances of men.

2.   Exemption from the small tithe.   The tithe of grain they were willing to pay for the support of pastors.

3.   Release from serfdom, since they as well as the princes had been redeemed by the blood of Christ.

4.   The right to fish and hunt, since when God created man he gave him dominion over all animals, over the fowl of the air, and the fish in the waters.

5.   A share in the forests for all domestic uses.

6.   A mitigation of feudal services.

7.   Payment for labour in addition to what the contract requires.

8.   Reduction of rents.

9.   Security against illegal punishment, and a desire to be dealt with according to the old written law.

10.   The restoration of the meadows and of the corn land which at one time belonged to a community.

11.   The abolition of the right of heriot, by which widows and orphans had been shamefully robbed.

12.   The resolution to submit all these articles to the test of Scripture, and to retract one, or all of them, if found not to agree with the Word of God.[1]

It must be conceded that these demands are just and scriptural.   Melanchthon says that Luther approved the articles of the peasants.   This is certainly

---

[1] These articles are given in German by Walch, Strobel, and Gieseler; in English, in Gieseler, translated by Smith, vol. iv., 114-116. For the authorship see note in Ranke, Eng. Trans., iii., vi.

true in the main. In May, 1525, he addressed an exhortation to the *Princes and Lords*, in which he chides the rulers for their severity, and tells them that they themselves are to be thanked for the rebellion, and exhorts them to yield a little to the popular storm.

He declares that some of the articles of the peasants are so remarkable and just that before God and the world they verify Psalm 107: 40: "They pour contempt upon princes."

To the Peasantry he wrote that the princes and lords by forbidding preaching the Gospel, and by oppressing the people intolerably, have right well deserved that God should cast them down from their thrones. He warns them against faction and rebellion, and urges them to give up certain articles which ask too much, and reach too high.[1]

All this was in harmony with Luther's love of order and with his determination that the sword should not be used in the cause of the Gospel. Had his admonition been heeded, Germany would have been spared the slaughter of one hundred and fifty thousand men, the destruction of millions of property, and the other horrors of civil war. But princes and peasants alike were blinded to their true interests; the one party by false notions of liberty, and the other party by equally false notions of authority augmented by the lusts of the flesh and the greed of avarice. The peasants departed from their programme, and aimed at a democratic recon-

---

[1] German in Erlangen ed., 24 : 269 *et seqq*. Summary in English in Gieseler, iv., 116, 117.

struction of Church and State.   The princes rejected
reason, and yielded to passion and the desire for
revenge.   Now it was that Luther, when he witnessed the excesses and disorders of the peasants,
forgetting their grievances and affirming the duty of
absolute obedience to civil rulers, wrote those terrible words against " the rapacious and murderous
peasants "' : " Cut, stab, smite, strangle, as among
mad dogs, who can, and as he can.   A more blessed
death you will never have "—which no admiration
for his love of order, and no respect for his constant
appeal to Rom. xiii. 1, should lead us to approve.
They may be explained, but under no circumstances
can they be justified, however sincere Luther may
have been in his conviction of duty to the civil
magistrate, and however strong his determination
that the Gospel should not be assisted by the sword.

Only too ready were the princes to obey Luther's
advice.   At the decisive battle of Frankenhausen,
May 25, 1525, in Alsace, along the Rhine, in
Franken, in the Tyrol, they wreaked a vengeance
by arms and by treachery, the record of which forms
one of the bloodiest pages of modern history.

But what is more remarkable in the premises is
that the tender-hearted Melanchthon fully agreed
with Luther in his attitude towards the peasants.
He saw portents in the skies, and declared that
Satan was seeking the overthrow of religion, of civil
order, and all that is good.   Asked by the Elector
of the Palatinate, " as one born and brought up in
the Palatinate," to come to Heidelberg the week

---

¹ Erlangen ed., 24 : 308.

OPPOSITION TO THE POPE AND THE MONKS, AND THE
UPRISING OF THE PEASANTS IN 1522.

FROM A CONTEMPORARY WOODCUT.

after Whitsunday, and assist by his counsel in the dangerous affairs, or in case he could not come, to send a written opinion on the Twelve Articles,[1] he wrote his *Confutation of the Articles of the Peasants.*[2] The leading thoughts are as follows·

Since the peasants have appealed to the Scriptures they should be instructed out of the Scriptures, for many of them have sinned through ignorance. If they were properly instructed they might turn from their wantonness. The Christian faith is of the heart, and is the source of love and of all the virtues. Among these virtues is obedience to rulers, and that not from fear of punishment, but for conscience' sake. Even unjust rulers must be borne. If they do wrong, only God is their judge. Were all the articles of the peasants scriptural, which, however, is far from being the case, they would nevertheless sin against God, should they attempt to enforce their rights by violence and insurrection. It is the duty of rulers to have the Gospel preached. Should they neglect it, or persecute preachers of the pure doctrine, vengeance must not be taken on the preachers of error, but they must be shunned. Everyone must confess his faith for himself, or the community must support pastors at their own cost; and should the magistrates forbid this, then the people must bear it with patience. The tithe must be given because the rulers order it. The tithes should be given to pastors and monks so long as the rulers have not provided otherwise. Villeinage should not be thrown

---

[1] *C. R.*, 1 : 742.
[2] *C. R.*, 20 : 641 *et seqq.*

off by violence. The freedom brought by Christ is only internal. Spiritual freedom can be enjoyed even under oppression. The right to hunt and fish can be settled by the courts. The peasants are bound to do Villein service, but the lords should be lenient in the exercise of their rights. Heriot (*Todfall*) belongs to serfdom, but the lords may make concessions for the sake of widows and orphans.

The peasants act against God if they seek by insurrection to free themselves from the lawfully existing condition. Before going to war the princes should attempt compromise, and should concede what is right, for even they have done much wrong.

The best means against insurrection is the purification of the Church. Marriage should be allowed to ministers, and the Church goods should be applied to the maintenance of the poor and of schools. The people should have faithful pastors who can instruct them in the Christian faith. If the princes would treat the people more kindly, commotion might cease. But should any persist in rebellion they should be punished with the utmost severity.

Finally he urges the princes, as the more intelligent, as the wise and powerful, to show pity to the more ignorant people, and to help them, looking to God for their reward. But he declares that " the peasants have no ground of complaint against serfdom. Necessarily, a people so wild and unruly as the Germans, should have still less freedom than they have " He also calls the peasants " murderers " and " liars," who are instigated by the devil.

The *Confutation* is remarkable for its union of

moderation and severity. But severity greatly pre-
ponderates. Not being of the peasant class, and
having never borne burdens like theirs, Melanchthon
was incapable of giving an impartial, much less a
humane judgment. He knew nothing of the rights
of man as man, and recognised only the duty of absolute obedience on the part of subjects. His argu
ment is based chiefly on Rom. xiii. 1, as though
that contained all that the Bible teaches in regard to
submission to authority. The freedom of which the
Bible speaks is understood to be spiritual, not bodily
freedom. Hence he justifies Villeinage, and incul-
cates upon princes only the virtues of kindness and
forbearance. But unlike Luther he does not preach
a crusade, and when he has learned that the war
is practically over, and that the peasants have
been put down, he adds an Appendix to the *Confutation*, in which he says:

"As God has now given the victory, and as the
murderous rabble which would not have peace has been
punished according to the laws of God, the princes
should further be very careful that no harm befall the
innocent, and should show mercy to the poor people,
some of whom sinned through folly."

These words of Christian counsel were not so
readily heeded by the princes as Luther's words of
severity had been. Ranke says: "Wherever the
matter had been decided by arms, the laws of war
were enforced. The most barbarous executions
took place; the severest contributions were exacted,

and in some places, laws more oppressive than ever were imposed." [1]

August 16, 1525, Luther wrote to Brismann:

" The war of the peasants is over.   A hundred thousand have been killed, many orphans have been made, and everything left is in so ruined a condition, that the aspect of Germany has never been more deplorable than now.   The victors so rage as to perfect their iniquity." [2]

In the midst of " these turbulent and perilous commotions," Luther surprised his friends and himself by marrying Katherine von Bora, an escaped nun, June 13, 1525.   Camerarius says " this act gave Philip the greatest pain, not because he disapproved it, but because he saw it would give Luther's numerous and powerful enemies an occasion for persecution and slander." [3]

When Melanchthon discovered that the sudden change and the evil surmises had affected Luther with gloom and perturbation of mind, he did all he could to comfort him, and wrote an apologetic and explanatory letter in Greek to Camerarius.   He regards the marriage as unseasonable, but not in itself wrong. He thinks Luther is " susceptible " and was by nature strongly impelled to marry.   He also says that he was much beset by the machinations of the nuns.   But Luther's life, he says, is humble and devout, and gives the most indubitable evidence of

---

[1] *Hist. Ref.*, iii., vi., **221.**
[2] De W., 3 : 22.
[3] Camerarius, p. **103.**

piety.   The sequel showed that Melanchthon did
not understand the motives which impelled Luther
" to take his Kathe."   Melanchthon misjudged his
friend.   Luther's marriage proceeded from a correct
impulse, and was attended by every circumstance of
honourable conduct.   It proved a great blessing to
the Reformer himself, and laid the foundation for
the beautiful home-life which has mostly characterised the German pastorate.[1]

---

[1] It was fortunate that Melanchthon's letter to Camerarius was not
published during the lifetime of its author.   Only in 1875 was the
original discovered in the Chigi Library at Rome.   Camerarius published the letter with sundry omissions and additions in 1569.   This
edition, with a Latin translation of the same, was reprinted in the
Corpus Reformatorum.   The Melanchthon text is given in the *Reports of the Munich Academv of Sciences for 1876*, Heft V., 601.

CHAPTER XIII

ORGANISATION OF THE SAXON CHURCHES

Melanchthon's Labours in Teaching and Writing—Opinion on the
Reformation of the Churches—Treatise on the Mass and Celibacy
—Melanchthon's Isolation—The *Visitation Articles*.

AFTER his return from Nuremberg in the middle
of June, 1526, Melanchthon applied himself
again to the work of teaching, writing, and reforming, notwithstanding his constant illness. In July
he lectured on Demosthenes and Theocritus, and
translated the Fifth Psalm into Latin. In August
he was so ill that for more than twelve days his life
was despaired of. But in September he was able to
respond to a request from Philip of Hesse for an
Opinion on the reformation of the churches in the
Landgrave's dominions. His chief suggestions were
that one Mass should be celebrated as the Eucharist
in each parish church every festival day, according
to the old rites, and that all the other masses should
be abolished. Quarrels and disputes should be
quelled. The old ceremonies should be retained,
since they cannot be removed without offence.
Christianity does not by any means consist in rites,

but in the fear of God, in faith, in love, and in
obedience to magistrates. These things should be
inculcated by the preachers without regard to the
Pope. And since Christ abstained so long from
vengeance, and of his own will gave himself up as a
lamb to the slaughter, so should your Highness for-
bear, and not fly to arms in the affairs of the Church.[1]

This mild and conservative *Opinion* had little or
no influence on the reforming synod of Homberg,
which, under the lead of the fiery Francis Lambert,
of Avignon, suppressed the cloisters, removed the
pictures, and ordered a form of worship which ob-
literated all traces of Romanism. Yet Melanchthon
remained so much in favour with the Landgrave that
the next year he was invited to a professorship in
the newly founded University of Marburg. But the
Elector would not allow him to leave Wittenberg.

On the thirtieth of September, 1526, Melanchthon
went to Leipzig to attend the commercial fair.
Thence he proceeded to Nordhausan, Mansfeld, and
Eisleben, and returned to Wittenberg in November.
In this year he also wrote his treatise on *The Mass
and Celibacy*.[2] He says there are three opinions
touching the Mass. The first is that of Thomas,
Scotus, and the like, who teach that the Mass is a
work offered to God in order to obtain grace for the
living and the dead. Hence the Mass is regarded
as a meritorious sacrifice, and such an opinion leads
to the multiplication of masses and to the establishment of funeral and other venal masses. This false

---

[1] *C. R.*, 1 : 819.
[2] *C. R.*, 1 : 840.

opinion is refuted by the doctrine of justification by faith.   Righteousness is by faith and not by the work of the Mass.

The second opinion is that of the advocates of Private Masses.   They think that the Mass is a good work which we offer to God as a thanksgiving service.   Hence masses must be celebrated every day, and certain persons have been appointed in the Church, not to preach the Word, but to celebrate Mass.   The body of Christ is not offered in the Lord's Supper, but was offered once for all.   That the body of Christ is not offered in the Supper is proved from the words, *Take, eat*.   Faith alone and confession are the proper thanksgiving.

The third opinion is ours, which alone we judge to be true and consistent with the Scripture, viz., that the Supper was not instituted to be an offering to God, but by it something is offered and given to us, viz., a sacrament by which grace is offered, and by which we are led to believe and have our troubled consciences comforted.   This doctrine can be proved, first by the word *Sacrament*, because a sacrament is a sign of the grace promised us.   Therefore the Supper is a thing which testifies that grace is offered and given us.   It is not a sacrifice, or work, in which we offer something to God.   He also states that remission of sins is offered in the Supper, and that the Supper exhorts us to believe, for, *Do this in remembrance of me* means, believe that Christ gives us his grace.

The question of Celibacy is dismissed with a few observations: It is chiefly a matter of conscience.

Marriage is permitted the deacons by the ancient canons. The Pope has no right and no warrant from the Scripture to take wives from the priests by violence, and synods have no right to forbid marriage. Nothing should be required which is contrary to the Word of God.

This little tract presents more sharply than had hitherto been done the Lutheran doctrine of the Lord's Supper. It is a *Sacrament*, in which grace and remission of sins are offered to us. It is both a means of grace and a sign of the grace promised in the Gospel. Its end is justification, or the impartation of the blessings of the Gospel.

From these views Melanchthon never departed. They recur again and again in his treatment of the Lord's Supper, and are given special prominence in his *Apology* of the Augsburg Confession.

At the beginning of the year 1527, we find Melanchthon hard at work and "living on a slender diet" He is by no means happy. His lamentations are pitiful, and serve to give us a view of his own tender, peace-loving heart, and of the distractions at Wittenberg. To his beloved Camerarius he writes on the twenty-sixth of February:

"Behold me, an exile far from home, far from friends and relatives, among a people with whom I could not converse were I ignorant of Latin. Besides, in this place the greatest envy burns in the bosoms of all. At this time in this city those who have the management of affairs are not very harmonious." [1]

[1] *C. R.*, 1 : 859.

It is easy to conceive that the refined and sensitive nature of Melanchthon must have suffered from an environment where rudeness and strife prevailed. He sought peace and was engaged in the work of peace; but others, even his colleagues—for to these he is supposed to allude in this letter—are engaged in strife. Yet neither his conscience nor his Elector would permit him to leave Wittenberg, and it would have been disastrous, if not fatal, to the new movement, had he left at this time. He was needed to check and to moderate the stormy violence of Luther, to lead in organising an evangelical Luth eran Church, and to write the Magna Charta of its faith.

Up to this time the work of the Reformation had consisted chiefly of attacks on the papacy and its institutions. The result was a general dissolution of the old ecclesiastical system, with the lapse of discipline and the neglect of public worship. If the Reformation is to be a blessing and not a curse, it must proceed to reorganise the churches on an evangelical basis. To this end Luther had already, in 1526, exhorted the Elector to institute a formal visitation of the churches in his dominions. Accordingly the Electoral territory was divided into four parts, each of which was to be visited by several theologians and civil counsellors, who were instructed to examine the ministers and to inquire into the con dition of the churches. The aged and inefficient ministers were to be retired on a pension; the re fractory were to be removed from office; new schools and congregations were to be established where needed; contentions were to be quieted; and better provision was to be made for the administration of the Church goods.

This was the work of reorganisation and of reconstruction. In this, as in almost all of the practical affairs of the Reformation, Melanchthon had to take the lead.

On the fifth of July, 1527, he left Wittenberg for Thuringia, where, in company with Frederick My conius, since 1524 pastor at Gotha, and Justus Menius, pastor at Erfurt, John von Planitz, Erasmus von Haugwitz, and Dr. Jerome Schurf, he visited the schools and churches in and about Kahla, Jena, Neustadt, Weida, and Auma. In this work he was engaged about one month. The condition of the churches was deplorable. Among the ministers, many of whom had been priests or monks, there was much ignorance. More than one was found who knew scarcely anything besides the Decalogue, the Creed, and the Lord's Prayer. One former monk, who was asked, " Do you teach the Ten Commandments ?" replied, " I have n't the book " One pastor preached the evangelical doctrine in the parish church, and read the Roman Catholic Mass in a filial church,—because the people wanted it so. Very few of the pastors had clear ideas of the new doctrines. Some preached justification by faith, or the forgiveness of sins, without saying anything of repentance, or of the way of attaining faith. Some in an Anabaptistic way raged against the civil government, and others chiefly denounced the Pope. Disorder and confusion reigned everywhere. The people also had sunk into the deepest immorality. Many lived in concubinage, and were little better than blank heathen. Luther has graphically described the general condition in the Preface to his *Small Catechism:*

" Eternal God! what distress did I behold! The people, especially those who live in the villages, and even curates, for the most part, possess so little knowledge of the Christian doctrine, that I even blush to tell it. And yet all are called by the sacred name of Christ, and enjoy the sacraments in common with us, while they are not only totally ignorant of the Lord's Prayer, the Apostles' Creed, and the Decalogue, but cannot even repeat the words. Why need I hesitate to say that they differ in nothing at all from the brutes ? "

It will be understood that this is the condition in which the Reformation found the German people, not that into which it had brought them in the ten years of its activity. The Visitation was the beginning of a moral and intellectual transformation of these same people. But it is easy to see how his discovery would affect Melanchthon. He wrote to Camerarius: " I am engaged in a most difficult business, and, so far as I see, without result. Everything is in confusion, partly through the ignorance, and partly through the immorality of the teachers." [1]
And again:

" What can be offered in justification that these poor people have hitherto been left in such great ignorance

[1] *C. R.*, 1 : 881.

and stupidity ? My heart bleeds when I regard this wretchedness. Often when we have completed the visitation of a place, I go aside and pour forth my distress in tears. And who would not mourn to see the faculties of man so utterly neglected, and that his soul which is able to learn and to grasp so much, does not know even anything of its Creator and Lord ? "

As it was designed that this first Visitation should extend to only a few localities, on the ninth of August Melanchthon returned to Jena, whither the university had been transferred, because the plague had broken out in Wittenberg. Here he remained until the eighth or ninth of the following April, lecturing on Demosthenes, the Psalms, and the Proverbs of Solomon. But the most important work done by Melanchthon during that time was the preparation, under commission from the Elector, of the *Visitation Articles*, which were to serve as a guide in the visitation of the other districts, and were to be used by the ministers as a norm of doctrine and a directory of worship. He first made a draft in Latin. This, elaborated and expanded in German, but not changed in substance, was sent to the Elector, who forwarded it to Luther for examination, with instructions to change it as he might see fit. The latter reported to the Elector that he and Bugenhagen had examined it, and had made very few changes in it, " for it pleased us very well, because it is composed in the most simple manner for the people." [1]

---

[1] De W., 3 : 211.

At the beginning of 1528, the German Articles, *Unterricht der Visitatoren*, were published by order of the Elector, adorned with a Preface by Luther, in which it is said:

" We do not publish this as a rigid command as though we would institute a new papal decree, but as a history, a witness, and confession of our faith. Hence we hope that all pious pastors who truly love the Gospel will accept it and hold with us."[1]

This shows the liberal spirit in which the Lutheran Church was organised, and the real design of the first Lutheran Confession of Faith. It was not to be imposed as a decree or law, but to be accepted in the freedom of the Gospel, " until God the Holy Ghost furnish something better."

According to these *Articles* were the other three districts of the Electoral territory visited by Luther, Bugenhagen, Jonas, Spalatin, and others. In the winter of 1528 Melanchthon made a second trip through Thuringia. Churches and schools were reformed, superintendents were appointed, consistories were established, and competent pastors were put in charge. Scarcely two years passed before Luther could report to the Elector that " the Word of God is effective and fruitful in the entire land. Your Grace has more and better pastors than any other country in the world. They preach faithfully and purely and live in entire harmony."

Thus, through the *Visitation Articles*, Melanchthon was the organiser of the Saxon Church, which

[1] *C. R.*, 26: 46

in turn became the model for organisation in other Lutheran lands.   The work was completed by the publication of Luther's two catechisms in the year 1529, and of Melanchthon's *Catechetical Instruction* in the year 1532.[1]

As the *Visitation Articles*[2] are so closely connected with the organisation of the Lutheran Church, and with Melanchthon's personal relations to the same; as they contain at once a confession of faith, a directory of worship, and a school order, they deserve more than a passing notice.   They consist of eighteen articles.   The first thirteen exhibit the Doctrine which is to be preached, the fourteenth treats of the Turkish War, the fifteenth of Divine Worship, the sixteenth and seventeenth of Discipline and Church Orders, the eighteenth of Schools.

They impress the reader at once with their mildness, simplicity, and practical tact.   No attack is made on the Roman Catholic system, but every efforts is made by positive teaching to build up an evangelical system on the basis of pure doctrine. Justification by Faith is made the central governing principle of the series, but this is not to be preached in a one-sided manner, nor to the exclusion of other doctrines.   The article on Doctrine says:

" But how many now only speak of the forgiveness of sins, and nothing or very little of repentance, and yet there is no forgiveness of sins without repentance; and forgiveness of sins cannot be understood without re-

---

[1] *C. R.*, 23 : 104 *et seqq.*

[2] *C. R.*, 26 : 7 *et seqq.*

pentance, and when we preach forgiveness of sins without repentance, it will come to pass that the people will believe that they have already obtained forgiveness of sins, and will become thereby secure and careless. Therefore we have instructed and exhorted the pastors that it will be their duty to preach the *whole* Gospel, and not one part without the other."

The people are to be brought to a knowledge of their sins by the preaching of the Law, and are to be exhorted to repent and to fear God. Repentance and faith go together, so that " where there is no repentance there is a painted faith." As the two first parts of the Christian life are repentance and faith, so is the third part good works. These consist in living a chaste life, in loving one's neighbour, in doing him good, in not lying, nor stealing, nor murdering.

Subtle discussion about the merit of good works is to be avoided, but good works which God has commanded must be done.

Baptism signifies the same thing that circumcision signified. As children were circumcised, so should they now be baptised. Baptism brings the blessing that God is thereby the Protector and Benefactor of the child, and receives it. In the sacrament of the Lord's Supper the people are to be taught three things: First, that the true body of Christ is in the bread and the true blood of Christ in the wine; secondly, both forms should be used, but where the people are weak in faith, or have timid consciences, or have not been sufficiently instructed, they may be allowed to receive the sacrament in one form; that it is a great sin to use the sacrament unworthily. Open transgressors should be excluded, and no one should´ be admitted who has not previously been examined by the pastor.

Repentance is regarded as a sacrament, because all sacraments signify repentance.

It is not advisable to preach much on human ordinances in the Church, but the preachers should labour to awaken repentance, faith, and the fear of God. Nor should there be any dispute about festi val days, should different persons hold different days. It is declared that man has free will to do or to omit to do external works by his own ability. This is the righteousness of the flesh. But man cannot purify his own heart, or effect the divine gifts, such as sorrow for sin, true fear of God, hearty love, chastity, and the like. Therefore we should earnestly pray that God would work these gifts in us. The preachers are not to indulge in invective against the Pope and the bishops, except where it is necessary to warn the people.

Minute directions are given for organising and conducting schools. The children are to be divided into three classes, and are to be taught Latin; not German, Greek, and Hebrew (as Melanchthon ordered in the larger cities, like Nuremberg, Mühl-hausen, and in the Saxon *Fürstenschulen* founded in 1543). Neither are the children to be burdened with many books, nor with too great a variety of studies. Those in the second class shall learn the Lord's Prayer, the Creed, the Decalogue, and some

Psalms by heart.   Those of the third class, besides
Cicero, Ovid, and Virgil, shall be taught Dialectic
and Rhetoric.

It will thus be seen that the *Visitation Articles* are
constructive in their nature, and practical and ethical in their aim.   Without learned discussion of
doctrines little understood, Melanchthon here presents the practical and ethical features of Christianity, as they had never before been attached to the
Augustinian system.   A new application has been
given to the Gospel of free grace.   The Christian is
not only to have pardon of sin, but he is to live an
ethical religious life.   While repentance and faith are
the beginning of a Christian life, good works are its
fruits.   Even the sacraments, which are so immediately connected with the forgiveness of sins, are
made to exert their influence on the entire life of
the Christian in begetting repentance, faith, and
love.   In a word, we have here the beginning of a
science of Evangelical Christian Ethics, and it is
exactly at this point that Melanchthon has most
beneficially influenced Protestant theology.   All his
teaching was dominated by the idea of the ethical
personality, and was directed toward making man
ethically better.   His motto was: '' Ego mihi con-
scius sum non aliam ob causam unquam τεθεολογη-
κέναι nisi ut vitam emendarem.''   That is: '' I am
perfectly certain that I have pursued theology only
that I might bring about a higher morality.''

CHAPTER XIV

DISPUTES AND DANGERS

Controversy with Agricola—Tracts against the Anabaptists—The
Affair of Pack—War Threatened.

THE Latin draft of the *Visitation Articles*, published without the knowledge of the author,
brought on a controversy between Melanchthon and
John Agricola of Eisleben. In the chapters on the
Decalogue and the Law, Melanchthon had taught
that "the law must be preached to terrify consciences, since by the law is the knowledge of sin";
that is, men are thus called to repentance, and by
repentance to faith and righteousness in Christ.
"The preaching of the law incites to repentance."

Agricola, who was ambitious of a theological professorship at Wittenberg, and who had taken offence
at Melanchthon's friendly counsel to bide his time
and remain content for the present with his position
as Rector of the school in his native city,[1] saw an
opportunity to display his theological learning, and
to get on even ground with Melanchthon. He took

---

[1] *C. R.*, 1: 784.

the position that the law had been abolished by the Gospel, and that repentance must come, not from the knowledge of the law, but from the Gospel. He appealed to Melanchthon's *Loci*, and to some of Luther's writings, in which it was taught that by the Gospel we are freed from the law, and that Moses had been given for the Jews, and not for Christians. But this was a one-sided use of his authorities. They had also taught that the law brings the consciousness of sin. Melanchthon wrote Agricola as follows·

" I do not recall that I have ever written or spoken a word which would seem to violate Christian liberty, nor would I knowingly write anything which I should think would corrupt the purity of the Gospel. In regard to *Repentance* I think you will agree with me that fear and alarm and confusion of conscience ought to exist in the mind before vivification and consolation. These feelings are to be called fear of the divine judgment, sometimes also the sense of the divine wrath. But this expression: *the fear of divine judgment*, can be more easily understood by the people. Also, it cannot be denied, that in such a struggle there is the fear of eternal punishment. I do not speak of that fear which men awaken by their own struggle; but of that which God awakens, and I distinctly said 'that God works such terrors.' " [1]

The noise of the controversy at length reached the ears of the Elector, who invited Agricola and Melanchthon together with Luther and Bugenhagen

---

[1] *C. R.*, 1 : 905.

to Torgau, to talk over the matter and to take
further counsel about the Visitation.[1] They came
on the twentieth of November, 1527. Luther and
Bugenhagen were appointed mediators between the
two disputants. Agricola affirmed that repentance
must proceed from the love of righteousness. Melanchthon replied that the soul must be filled with
alarm before justification, and in this state it is not
easy to distinguish the love of righteousness from
the fear of punishment. Agricola contended that
Melanchthon erred in requiring an explanation of
the Decalogue, since we are made free from the law,
and so do not need it, as the moral precepts of the
New Testament are sufficient. Melanchthon explained that the Decalogue is the basis of the moral
precepts of the New Testament, and must be
preached for the reasons which had been given.
Weary of strife, Melanchthon offered the hand of
reconciliation, but Agricola " was as unresponsive
as a statue."[2]

Luther finally made some explanation with which
Agricola seemed satisfied, and henceforth claimed
the victory, but Melanchthon saw in the contentions
of Agricola the beginning of a new sophistry. Luther regarded the dispute as only a war of words,
and wrote to Jonas, " Our famous discussion at
Torgau amounted to scarcely anything."[3] He had
already expressed his approval of Melanchthon's
position in his endorsement of the German Articles,

---

[1] *C. R.*, 1 : 914.
[2] *C. R.*, 1 : 917.
[3] De W., 3 : 215, 243.

which contain the very same teaching, and when, ten years later, Agricola, then a professor in Wittenberg, renewed the strife, Luther powerfully refuted him in six masterly disputations,[1] and forced him to recant.

During his sojourn at Jena, Melanchthon composed two treatises against the Anabaptists, who had created much confusion and disorder in and around Kahla and Orlamünde.

The first, written in 1527, perhaps during the Visitation, is very brief, and was intended to furnish the people with a few arguments in support of Infant Baptism, and in refutation of the Anabaptistic errors.[2] He argues as follows: Children were circumcised in the Old Testament. Therefore they should be baptised in the New. Circumcision and Baptism are signs of promised grace and of eternal life. Christ has commanded: *Suffer the little ones to come unto me.* Therefore infants should be baptised. The Anabaptists say there is no command for the baptism of infants. We reply that though there is no express command, there is example, which ought to prevail, since the Scripture does not contradict itself. The Scripture does not prohibit the baptism of infants, and furnishes the example of circumcision.

They say: Infants do not believe Therefore they ought not to be baptised. The Sacrament ought to be administered to believers only. But children are to be baptised that they may acquire

---

[1] Erlangen ed., *Var. arg.*, 4: 424 *et seqq.*
[2] *C. R.*, 1: 931.

faith, for no one can acquire faith except from the Word of God. In Baptism there is the Word of God.

They say: Children do not understand the Word, therefore Baptism should not be applied to them. This objection is refuted by the example of circumcision. It is asked: How does Baptism benefit infants ? By Baptism they are taught that the remission of sins pertains to them. All to whom the Sacrament is applied acquire remission of sins. The Sacrament is applied to infants, therefore infants acquire the remission of sins.

The second treatise against the Anabaptists, written in April, 1528, is much more elaborate than the first. In it he discusses the Meaning and the Use of Sacraments, Baptism, the Use and Benefit of the Sacrament of Baptism, the Baptism of John, Infant Baptism. He closes this treatise by confuting the views of the Anabaptists on civil government.[1]

On the eighth or ninth of April, 1528, Melanchthon left Jena for Wittenberg, accompanied by his family, which had been increased by the birth of a son, November 25, 1527. But he was not allowed to sit down peacefully in his old haunts. While the Visitation had been going on, suspicion arose that a storm was gathering against the Reformation. The suspicion changed to alarm when in February, 1528, Dr. Otto von Pack, ex-chancellor of Duke George, gave the Landgrave of Hesse, for ten thousand gulden, a copy of an alleged document which bound several Catholic princes and bishops to restore

[1] *C. R.*, 1: 955 *et seqq.*

the old faith, and to divide the Electoral and Hessian territories among themselves.

Philip hastened to Weimar, where he imparted the information to the Elector, and where, March 9, 1528, the two formed a counter-alliance to enter the field with twenty-six thousand men, and to make the attack. But scruples arising in the mind of the Elector, he called Luther and Melanchthon to Torgau, May 15th, and laid the matter before them. They strongly advised against war, especially against making the attack. On the 18th, Melanchthon wrote a letter to the Elector, pleading that, for the sake of his soul's salvation, his children, the poor country, and the people, he should avoid war, otherwise not only men, but God would be his enemy. He also reminded him that they who take the sword, shall also perish by the sword, and said:

" It is the greatest comfort in all trials to have a good conscience, and not to have God as our enemy. If we take the sword first and begin the war, we shall lose this comfort. I write this with great sorrow and anxiety. God knows that I do not prize my life ; but think of the shame that will come upon the Holy Gospel, if you begin the war and do not first seek other ways and means of peace." [1]

The Elector was so influenced by the advice of his theologians, that while he continued to prepare for war, he urged upon the Landgrave the necessity of heeding the admonitions of Luther and Melanchthon.

[1] *C. R.*, 1 : 980.

Finally, ready to begin hostilities, Philip sent a copy of the document obtained from Pack to Duke George, and inquired whether he meant to keep the peace. The Duke at once pronounced the document a forgery, and declared Pack a knave. Other princes denied the existence of a conspiracy to crush the Evangelicals.

Thus war was happily averted by the application of the evangelical principle that the Gospel is not to be promoted by violence. But the cause of the Reformation suffered from the suspicions and growing dissensions among the princes. The Catholics became more and more hostile, and the Evangelicals grew more and more anxious as the political heavens darkened. Melanchthon wrote to Camerarius, " I am almost consumed with anxiety when I think what a scandal has come upon our good cause."

It was doubtless anxiety for the good cause that brought Melanchthon into a condition of wretched health this summer; but he went on with his work, assisting Luther in revising his translation of Isaiah, lecturing on the Proverbs of Solomon, and preparing notes to Aristotle's Ethics, until October 15th, when he set out to complete the Visitation in Thuringia, which occupied him until January 5, 1529.

CHAPTER XV

SPIRES AND MARBURG

Diet of Spires—The Protest and Appeal—Doctrine of the Lord's Supper—Controversy with Zwingli—The Marburg Colloquy—Articles of Agreement—Schwabach Articles.

THE Diet of Spires of 1526 had given the rulers permission to execute the Decree of Worms of 1521, or not, as they were willing to give account to God and the Emperor. This action was very favourable to the Evangelicals, but it increased the hostility of their enemies. The relations of the two parties became more and more strained. The Emperor had conceived the strongest dislike for the followers of Luther, and had resolved to meet them with violence, if necessary. Ferdinand, since 1526 King of Hungary and Bohemia, was as intent upon suppressing Lutheranism as upon the repression of the Turk. The Catholic princes, embittered by the precipitate conduct of the Landgrave, had been excited to greater energy for the defence of the Church. Everything appeared unfavourable for the Evangelicals, and when on November 3, 1528, a diet was proclaimed for February 2, 1529, at Spires, and

CATHEDRAL OF SPIRES

then deferred to February 21st, they had nothing
good to expect for their cause.

Indeed the horoscope seemed very unpropitious
during the first half of the year 1529. In January
a light had appeared in the North. This was followed by a peculiar conjunction of the stars, by great
floods of water, and by other phenomena of nature.
Luther and Melanchthon were filled with alarm.
The latter wrote to Jonas, " I am not a little excited by these things." [1]

It was a time of intense anxiety all around. The
Diet was numerously attended by princes and ec-
clesiastics. The Elector took with him thither Melanchthon and Agricola. This was the first diet
attended by Melanchthon, and was the beginning
of his activity in negotiations and conferences in
which he served the Reformation for more than a
quarter of a century.

As the opening of the Diet was again deferred, he
embraced the opportunity thus afforded to visit his
mother and his brother George at Bretten. Melchior
Adam says that the mother took occasion to ask
her son, now one of the leaders of the Reformation,
what, amid such disputes of the learned, she should
believe. He requested her to say her prayers before
him, and when he perceived that they were free
from superstition, he bade her continue thus to pray
and to believe, and not to be disturbed by the controversies.[2] His brother George, who was Mayor of
Bretten, he found to be a zealous Lutheran.

---

[1] *C. R.*, 1 : 1075.
[2] *Vitæ Theolog.*, 333.

This was the last time that Melanchthon visited his mother, for shortly after his return to Wittenberg he received intelligence of her death.[1]

March 13th, Melanchthon arrived at Spires. Two days later the Diet was opened. The Recess of the Diet of 1526 was nullified, and all innovations in religion were forbidden. This arbitrary action filled the Evangelicals with consternation. Jacob Sturm, of Strassburg, wrote that Christ had fallen again into the hands of Caiaphas and Pilate. Melanchthon wrote to Camerarius:

" To-day the imperial mandate was read. It is simply dreadful. The former Recess of Spires has been abrogated. Many dire punishments are threatened those who will not heed the edict. The rest concerns the Turkish War. You have the sum of what has been done. You can easily see what danger we are in. The attendance of bishops is larger than at any previous diet. Some of them show by their looks how they hate us, and what they are contriving. May Christ look upon and save the poor people, for in the city we are outcasts. You know that I feel the lack of many things on our side; yet nothing is done to remove our faults, but everything to oppress the good cause. May Christ frustrate the counsels of the Gentiles, which mean war." [2]

The mind of the Catholics is well illustrated by the declaration of John Fabri, that the Turks are better than the Lutherans, for the former fast, and the latter do not; and again, " That if the alterna-

---

[1] *C. R.*, 1 : 1083.
[2] *C. R.*, 1 : 1039.

tive were required, he would rather reject the Script-
ures than the venerable errors of the Church."
Melanchthon declared that it would require a long
Iliad to recite all of Fabri's blasphemies.[1]

After a long debate about religion it was decreed
that those who had observed the Diet of Worms
should continue to do so, and oblige their children
to do so, until the meeting of a council, which was
promised; that those who had changed their re
ligion, and could not now retract for fear of troubles
and seditions, should make no more innovations
before the sitting of a council; that the doctrine of
those who dissent from the Church about the Supper of the Lord, should not be received; that the
Mass should not be abolished, and that those who
wished should not be hindered from going to Mass
in those places where a new doctrine was taught;
that ministers should preach according to the sense
of Scripture approved by the Church.[2]

Against this decree, which was enacted by a
majority vote, and was read on Sunday, the Evangelical minority presented their celebrated Protest,
April 19th, on which account they were in derision
called *Protestants* by their enemies.

Ferdinand, who represented the Emperor, refused
the Protest, and adjourned the Diet, April 24th.
The following day the Protestants added an Appeal
to the Emperor, to a national council, or to impartial
judges, and sent both documents to the Emperor.

These two important documents were signed by

---

[1] *C. R.*, I : 1041, 1046.
[2] Sleidan, p. 118, Eng. Trans.

John, Elector of Saxony; Philip, Landgrave of Hesse; George, Margrave of Brandenburg; Ernest, Duke of Brunswick-Lüneburg; Wolfgang, Prince of Anhalt; and by fourteen imperial cities.

What part Melanchthon took in the composition of the Protest, and of the Appeal, is not now known; but it is not likely that the chief theological counsellor of the leading Protestant prince was an idle spectator.

In one other matter, which was now brought into prominence, he did what will forever stand to his honour. The paragraph in the Decree of the Diet about the Lord's Supper was directed against the Zwinglians. The aim of the Romanists was to divide the reforming forces by passing sentence on the Zwinglian doctrine without allowing its adherents a hearing. Here it was that Melanchthon insisted that the Zwinglians should not be condemned until they had been heard. This he did, not because he approved the doctrine of the Zwinglians, but because he regarded it as wrong to condemn them unheard.

It was during the sitting of this Diet that the Evangelicals felt the need of united action. April 22d, the Saxons and Hessians formed a defensive alliance with Strassburg, Ulm, and Nuremberg. The Landgrave wished to include the Swiss. This at once brought up the question of the Swiss teaching on the Lord's Supper, and the bitter controversy which for years had raged between Luther and Zwingli on that subject. The former, after abandoning the doctrine of transubstantiation, and hesi-

tating for some time about the meaning of the words
of institution, had finally settled down in the doctrine
that the body of Christ is really and substantially
present in the bread, and that the blood of Christ is
really and substantially present in the wine, and
that body and blood, without any change in the
material elements, are really given to all who com-
mune in the Lord's Supper.   In controversy he
affirmed the doctrine of *Ubiquity,* as a condition or
prerequisite of the presence of the body of Christ
in the Supper, though it is proper to state that he
never laid much stress on this doctrine, but based
his views chiefly on the words of institution.

Melanchthon was the disciple of Luther in the
doctrine of the Lord's Supper, though not without
many misgivings and some formal deviations.   Already in December, 1527, at Torgau, he expressed
some doubt to Luther about his doctrine of the
Supper; but when the latter assured him that he
did not in the least doubt the correctness of his
doctrine, Melanchthon declared himself satisfied,
and rejoiced in his friend's steadfastness.[1]   His
mind at this time was deeply interested in the subject.   To the preachers of Reutlingen he wrote from
Marburg, " Not without the greatest struggle have
I come to hold that the Lord's body is truly present
in the Supper."[2]   And in 1537 he wrote that " not
a day nor night had passed for ten years in which
he had not thought on the subject."[3]   He declares

[1] *C. R.,* 1 : 913 ; 4 : 964.
[2] *C. R.,* 1 : 1106.
[3] *C. R.,* 3 : 537.

that the doctrine of Luther is very old, and that a
good man will not rashly depart from the teaching
of the ancients.' In this, as in many things, he was
much influenced by his dislike of innovation. April
8, 1529, he wrote to Œcolampadius: " I am not
willing to be the author or defender of a new dogma
in the Church." ' Neither could he endure speculation on this subject, but preferred to treat it as a
mystery, and " without subtlety." The ability of
Christ to be present in the Supper he makes depend-
ent upon the divine appointment, and thus modifies
Luther's doctrine of Ubiquity:

" That Christ gives us his body and blood does not
depend upon the prayers of the priest or of the people,
for that would be magical. I prefer that it should be
referred to the institution of Christ. For as the sun
rises daily by the divine appointment, so the body of
Christ is in the Church wherever the Church is. No
sufficient proof is offered that the body of Christ cannot
be in many places. Christ is exalted above all creatures
and is everywhere." '

It was the *fact* of the real presence and reception
of the body and blood of Christ in the Supper which
Luther emphasised as over against the doctrine of
Zwingli, who denied such presence and reception
except by the contemplation of faith, and · interpreted the words of institution, " This is my body,"
as, " This signifies my body."

---

¹ *C. R.*, 1 : 823, 830.
² *C. R.*, 1 : 1048.
³ *C. R.*, 1 : 948, 949.

Melanchthon was as violent against such a doctrine of the Supper as his mild nature would permit him to be. In May, 1528, he wrote·

" Instead of theologians they [the Zwinglians] seem to me gradually to have become sophists, for I see that they rationalise and philosophise about the doctrines of Christ. It is on this account that I have not mixed in the controversy on the Eucharist. But so soon as I shall have leisure, I will express my view. They represent Christ as sitting in one place, as Homer does his Jove living with the Æthiopians. To deny the presence of Christ in the Eucharist seems to me most contrary to the Scripture." [1]

And in 1530 he wrote: " I would rather die than affirm with them [the Zwinglians] that Christ's body can be in only one place." [2]

Besides the doctrine of the Lord's Supper the Wittenberg theologians held the Zwinglians as errorists in other important doctrines. In 1528, Luther had indeed declared, " I confess that I do not regard Zwingli as a Christian, for he holds and teaches no part of the Christian faith correctly, and has become seven-fold worse than when he was a papist." [3] Melanchthon wrote in March, 1530:

" Justifying faith is not mentioned in any of the books of the Zwinglians. When they speak of faith they do not mean that which believes the remission of sins,

---

[1] C. R., 1: 9;~
[2] C. R., 2: 25.
[3] Erlangen ed., 30 : 225.

which believes that we are received into grace, heard and kept by God, but they mean a historical faith." [1]

It is easy to see that under these circumstances both Luther and Melanchthon would oppose an alliance with the Swiss for the protection of religion. Melanchthon wrote to Baumgartner of Nuremberg urging him to do all in his power to defeat the alliance with the Zwinglians, saying, " It is not right to defend an impious doctrine, or to confirm the power of those who maintain an impious doctrine, lest the poison spread." [2]   The Nurembergers withdrew from the alliance, and at the urgent solicitation of Luther the Elector did the same.   Thus the matter ended for the time being.   But the Landgrave, who was ever ready to form political combinations for the defence of religion, was not easily diverted from his purpose.   He now sought to bring the theologians of both sides together, that they might talk over their differences and come to an understanding.   As early as February, 1529, on the way to Spires, he had spoken to the Elector of the desirability of a colloquy between Luther and Zwingli.   At Spires Melanchthon received a letter from Œcolampadius in which the latter begged that the Swiss be not cast off by the Germans, saying, among other things, " You can certainly affirm that we take it ill when it is said that like Judas, or the cattle, we eat nothing but bread in the Lord's Supper." [3]

---

[1] C. R., 2 : 25.
[2] C. R., 1 : 1070.
[3] Quoted by Schmidt, p. 171.

On his return from Spires, Melanchthon, to whom
the Landgrave had made known his wish, mentioned
the matter to Luther. But Luther did not think
that any good could come from such a colloquy as
was proposed. Nevertheless they agreed to lay the
matter before the Elector, saying, " If your Electoral Grace thinks it would be proper to hold such a
colloquy, there will be no hesitation on our part." [1]

At the same time Melanchthon wrote an Opinion
for the Electoral Prince in which he expresses his
willingness to confer with Œcolampadius on the
Sacrament, but thinks a colloquy with Zwingli
would be unprofitable. He also thinks that " some
honourable and reasonable papists " ought to be
present to hear both sides, otherwise it might be said
that the Lutherans and Zwinglians had met to form
a conspiracy. He declares that he will never agree
with the Strassburgers, and says, " I know that
Zwingli and his followers have written erroneously
of the Sacrament." [2]

The letters of Melanchthon and Luther show conclusively that they both disapproved of the colloquy,
not because they were afraid to meet their opponents, but because they sincerely believed that the
chief disputants were so fully set in their respective
beliefs that no understanding could be reached.
Besides, they were both fundamentally opposed to
defending the Gospel by the sword, and the proposed colloquy was intended to be a step toward
that end.

---

[1] C. R., 1 : 1064.

[2] C. R., 1 : 1067.

Melanchthon became almost frantic as he forecast the probable results of a colloquy. He wrote to Ulrich Wiland, saying:

" There are learned men on the side of the Zwinglians, able disputants, who have many plausible reasons and testimonies from the early Church, which they will so use as to make it appear that the early Church favours their view. But they bring nothing which satisfies the heart, and they find fault with us if we seek greater certainty. There is unspeakable danger in spreading, with a doubting conscience, a new dogma, which may bring a dreadful revolution not only upon the Church, but upon all the states of the Empire."[1]

Says Schmidt:

" It was manifestly a painful time for Melanchthon. In his embarrassment he mingled political apprehensions and theological scruples; personal prejudices against men whom he knew not, and objections to a doctrine which he regarded as a new and unscriptural invention. Though with justice he regarded Zwingli's opinion as unsatisfactory, yet he felt the weight of some of the arguments which had been developed against the view of Luther. He struggled with himself, but he returned to his former convictions, for there seemed to be no other way open to him by which to lift himself above the two extremes."[2]

At length the Elector gave his consent to the

---

[1] *Epist. Judic.*, etc., p. 40.
[2] Schmidt, *Philipp Mel.*, 175.

holding of the colloquy, but wished, for political reasons, that it might take place at Nuremberg.[1]

Luther and Melanchthon both wrote the Landgrave that they were willing to meet the Zwinglians in colloquy, but that they did not expect very favourable results.[2] They say nothing about Nuremberg.

The Landgrave, who had determined that the colloquy should be held in his own dominions, issued invitations to Zwingli of Zurich, Haller of Bern, Œcolampadius of Basel, Hedio and Bucer of Strassburg, Brentz of Swabian Hall, Urban Regius of Augsburg, and Schwebel of Zweibrücken. But no Catholic theologians were invited, as Luther and Melanchthon had suggested. On July 8th, Luther and Melanchthon addressed the Landgrave jointly as follows:

'As your Grace has received our letters and has decided that we should come to Marburg, with the hope that unity will result, we shall cheerfully do our part, and at the time appointed, if alive and well, we will appear in Marburg. The Father of mercy and unity grant his Spirit that we may not meet in vain, but for good, and not for injury. Amen.'' [3]

September 29, 1529, Zwingli, Œcolampadius, Bucer, Hedio, and Jacob Sturm came to Marburg. The next day Luther, Melanchthon, Jonas, Cruciger, Menius, Brentz, Osiander, and Stephen Agri-

---

[1] *C. R.*, i : 1071.
[2] De W., 3 : 473 ; *C. R.*, i : 1078.
[3] *C. R.*, i : 1080.

cola arrived.   They were all entertained with almost
princely hospitality in the castle.   The Landgrave
arranged for a preliminary interview between Luther
and Œcolampadius, and between Zwingli and Melanchthon.   Each pair was closeted separately for
six hours.   On the doctrines of Original Sin, Faith,
and the Trinity a satisfactory conclusion was soon
reached between Zwingli and Melanchthon.   On
the doctrine of the Lord's Supper there was no agreement.   Each stood essentially by his former position.   Melanchthon declared that he would stand
by the simple plain sense of the words of institution.
Zwingli denied that Melanchthon had the true conception of these words.   The conference between
Luther and Œcolampadius likewise was without
effect on the main question.

The two following days the colloquy was conducted more publicly, but chiefly between Luther
on the one side and Zwingli and Œcolampadius on
the other.   Neither side advanced any new arguments, and neither made any impression on the other.
The Zwinglians insisted that a body must be con-
fined to one definite place.   This Luther denied.
The Zwinglians appealed to John vi. 33: "It is the
Spirit that quickeneth; the flesh profiteth nothing."
Luther refused to admit that this passage has anything to do with the Supper.   Finally the Zwinglians declared that there were no persons on earth
with whom they were so anxious to agree as with
Luther and Melanchthon.   Luther replied, "Your
spirit is different from ours."   This practically
ended the colloquy, though both parties agreed that

they would not in the future write so bitterly against each other as they had previously done.

In order to show that the colloquy had not been a complete failure, the Landgrave commissioned Luther, with the assistance of the other theologians, to compose some articles of doctrine. He replied, " I will do the best I can, but they will not receive them." He then immediately wrote fifteen articles, covering the chief doctrines of the Reformation. On fourteen of these, after a few changes in form, there was no dissent. The fifteenth reads as follows:

" We all believe and hold concerning the Supper of our dear Lord Jesus Christ that both forms should be used according to the institution, also that the Mass is not a work, whereby one obtains grace for another, dead and living; also that the sacrament of the altar is a sacrament of the true body and blood of Jesus Christ, and that the spiritual partaking of this body and blood is specially necessary to every true Christian. In like manner, as to the use of the sacrament, that like the Word of God Almighty, it has been given and ordained, in order that weak consciences might be excited by the Holy Ghost to faith and love.

" And although we are not at this time agreed, as to whether the true body and blood of Christ are bodily present in the bread and wine, nevertheless the one party should show to the other Christian love, so far as conscience can permit, and both should fervently pray God Almighty, that by his Spirit he would confirm us in the true understanding."

The fifteen articles were subscribed by Luther, Melanchthon, Jonas, Osiander, Brentz, and Agricola on the one side, and by Œcolampadius, Zwingli, Bucer, and Hedio on the other. The articles are characterised by simplicity, and by greater mildness in statement than might naturally have been expected of Luther at that time. They have no confessional value either in the Lutheran or in the Reformed Church, but are of great historical significance as preliminary to the Lutheran confessional system.

While the Landgrave was trying at Marburg to bring about an understanding between the Saxon and Swiss theologians, the Elector of Saxony and the Margrave of Brandenburg were deliberating at Schleiz on the propriety of forming an alliance with the Landgrave and the cities of Upper Germany for mutual support in case of an attack by the Emperor, which at this time was greatly feared. It was agreed that doctrine should be the first condition of the alliance, since the protection of religion was the chief end in view. Luther was instructed to bring together a summary of the evangelical doctrines, and to have it in readiness. On the basis of the Marburg Articles he and his companions composed seventeen articles, which on the fifth or sixth of October, 1529, were carried to Schleiz. At a convention held at Schwabach, near Nuremberg, October 16th, these articles were presented by representatives of the Elector and the Margrave; but the representatives of Upper Germany refused to sign them, inasmuch as they had not been instructed to that effect. Hence the convention was without consequence.

ANDREW OSIANDER.

Luther tells us that he " helped to compose such articles," and that they were not intended for publication.[1]   His companions in this work were Melanchthon, Jonas, Osiander, Brentz, and Agricola. Yet the articles bear throughout the imprint of Luther's peculiar spirit, and contain a more positive and distinct statement of the Lutheran doctrines than is found in the Marburg Articles. " But the style, language, and expression show unquestionably an influence from the pen of Melanchthon." [2]

At Schwabach these Articles bore the title: " Articles of the Elector of Saxony concerning Faith."   But they are known in history properly as the Schwabach Articles.   They were used by Melanchthon as the foundation of " the first or dogmatic half of the Augustana, whose seventeen fundamental or chief articles agree with the seventeen Schwabach Articles in numbering, and in large part also in arrangement." [3]

---

[1] Erlangen ed., 24 : 337.
[2] Zöckler, *Augs. Con.*, p. 9.
[3] Zöckler, *Ibia.*

CHAPTER XVI

MELANCHTHON AND THE AUGSBURG CONFESSION

The Evil Aspect of Affairs—The Emperor Orders a Diet at Augsburg—Protestant Princes and Theologians Gather at Augsburg Melanchthon Writes the Augsburg Confession.

THE year 1530 opened very inauspiciously for the Protestants. Their efforts of the preceding year to effect a defensive union had failed. The ambassadors, John Eckinger, Alexius Faventraut, and Michael Kaden, who had carried the Protest and Appeal to the Emperor, had been detained as prisoners at Piacenza and Parma, and had been charged under threat of death not to communicate with their principals in Germany. The Emperor and the Pope had composed their differences, and were living in the same palace at Bologna. The former had pledged himself to the latter to bring back the dissidents to the faith, and '' to avenge the insult offered to Christ '' Campeggius was urging the Emperor to try promises, threats, and alliances, and, should these fail, to apply fire and sword. From Italy came only appalling rumours, while in

Germany Ferdinand was playing the hypocrite with the Elector in order to gain time.[1]

January 6, 1530, representatives of the Protestants met at Nuremberg to take counsel for the emergency; but they quarrelled among themselves, and separated without having reached a conclusion. Both Luther and Melanchthon had powerfully insisted that the Emperor should be obeyed, even though he should come with fire and sword, for the Gospel must not be defended by violence. Melanchthon wrote the Elector: "It is not lawful to take arms against the Emperor even though he come with violence. Everyone must profess the Gospel at his own peril."[2] Luther exclaimed, "God is faithful and will not forsake us," and quoted the words of the prophet, "Be still and ye shall be holpen." "Unquestionably this is not prudent, but it is great," says Ranke.

Suddenly this mighty tension in Germany was broken. January 21, 1530, the Emperor issued a mandate from Bologna announcing an Imperial Diet at Augsburg, to begin April 8th. The reference to religion was couched in mild and conciliatory language:

"To consult and decide about the disturbances and dissensions in the Holy Faith and Christian Religion. And in order that all dissensions, differences, and errors may be abolished in a salutary manner, all sentiments and opinions are to be heard, understood, and considered

---

[1] Ranke, v., ix.
[2] *C. R.*, 2 : 20–22.

between us in love and kindness, and are to be composed in sincerity, so as to put away what is not right in both parties, that true religion may be accepted and held by us all, that as we live and serve under one Christ, so we may live in one fellowship, Church, and unity." [1]

The Imperial Rescript reached the Elector at Torgau, March 11th. The pacific tone of the document inspired the hope that the long-desired General Council was about to be held. The Elector, following the advice of his counsellors, decided to attend, and began at once to make the necessary preparations for the journey. Luther, Jonas, Melanchthon, Musa of Jena, Agricola, and Spalatin were to attend " as learned counsellors." The first-named was to remain at Nuremberg and await further decision.

Chancellor Brück then suggested that their party should prepare a written statement of matters in dispute, fortified by ample proof from the Scriptures, and have it in readiness for the Diet. Accordingly the Elector commanded his theologians to compose articles of faith and external ceremonies, that at the opening of the Diet it might be decided what could be done with a good conscience and without offence, and to present themselves at Torgau, Sunday, March 20th. Not appearing at the appointed time, the next day the Elector wrote them to hasten, and to bring their books, as other matters awaited consideration. On the 27th, Melanchthon was at Torgau, but Luther probably did not go. [2]

---

[1] Original in Förstemann's *Urkundenbuch*, i.
[2] Köstlin, ii., 651.

CHANCELLOR BRÜCK.

There is no record in evidence that Melanchthon took any documents with him to Torgau. It is not improbable, however, that for " doctrine " he appealed to the Articles which a few months before had been presented at Schwabach, and which their authors had not yet published. Of specific " Torgau Articles " we have no report from the times. It is the judgment of many scholars that the Schwabach Articles must be included in the common designation, " Torgau Articles." For " external ceremonies " it is highly probable that Melanchthon handed in an essay composed by himself, March 14th–27th.[1] This essay, after a brief introduction, treats: (1) Of the Doctrine and Ordinances of Men, (2) Of the Marriage of Priests, (3) Of Both Forms, (4) Of the Mass, (5) Of Confession, (6) Of Jurisdiction, (7) Of Ordination, (8) Of Vows, (9) Of the Worship of Saints, (10) Of German Singing.

This essay would doubtless be accepted by the Elector, and taken by him to Augsburg, as an important document coming from the pen of one who was held in the highest esteem for learning and moderation.

April 3d, Luther, Melanchthon, and Jonas left Wittenberg to join the Elector at Torgau, who, the next day, after ordering prayer to be offered in all the churches of the land for God's blessing upon the

---

[1] Catalogued " A " in Förstemann's *Urkundenbuch,* pp. 68–84 ; English in Jacobs' *Book of Concord,* ii., 75–86. See Plitt's *Einleitung,* i., 520 ; Breiger, *Kirchenges. Studien,* 267 *et seqq. ;* Knaake, *Luther's Antheil an d. Augs. Conf. ; Real-Encyc.* (3d), ii., 243 ; *C. R.,* 4 : 981, 985.

13

Diet, set out for Augsburg, having in his train, besides "the learned counsellors," his son John Frederick; Francis, Duke of Lüneburg; Wolfgang, Prince
of Anhalt; Albert, Count of Mansfeld; with seventy
other noblemen and their escorts, numbering in all
one hundred and sixty persons. They took with
them three chests of Documents, among which were
the Marburg and the Schwabach Articles, and " The
Opinion (*Bedenken*) of the learned at Wittenberg,
which is to be delivered to his Imperial Majesty
about Ceremonies and What is connected there-
with," which last, the same that is described above
as composed by Melanchthon, is now regarded as
the basis of the second or apologetic part of the
Augsburg Confession.

The Electoral train passed through Grimma, Altenburg, and Isenberg, and arrived at Weimar on
Saturday the 9th. Here Luther preached the next
day, and the Elector partook of the communion.
Coburg was reached on the 15th, where a halt was
made in order to gain intelligence about the Em
peror. Here it was decided that Luther should
remain at Coburg, inasmuch as the Nurembergers
declined to furnish him either a safe-conduct or
hospitality during the Diet.[1] For his better security he was placed in the castle. At Coburg he
would be safe, and could be reached by messenger
from Augsburg in about four days. As he was still
under the imperial ban he would have been outlawed at Augsburg. His life also would have been

---

[1] Kolde in *Kirchengesch. Studien*, p. 255 *et seqq.*

in danger, and his wonted violence in discussion would have been fatal to the Protestant cause.[1]

At Coburg, or on the way thither, Melanchthon was commissioned to write a defensive statement, which at first was called an *Apology*, and which after passing through many changes finally became the *Augsburg Confession*.

How much of the Apology was written at Coburg and subsequently on the way thence to Augsburg, or what was its first form, is not now known. May 4th, two days after the Electoral party arrived at Augsburg, Melanchthon wrote to Luther· '' I have made the exordium of our Apology somewhat more rhetorical than I had written it at Coburg. In a short time I will bring it, or if the Prince will not permit that, I will send it.''[2] It is not supposed that the '' exordium '' mentioned in the letter forms any part of the Augsburg Confession. It was no doubt omitted when it was found that the Emperor would require brevity, and when unexpected conditions forced a change in the method of representation.

Dr. John Eck, at the instance of the dukes of Bavaria, had composed a book of 404 articles, made up chiefly of passages garbled from the writings of Luther, Melanchthon, Zwingli, Carlstadt, John Denck, and Balthaser Hubmeier. This book he sent to the Emperor as an exhibition of the doctrines of those who were disturbing the Church. His object was to identify the Reformers with the ancient heretics and the modern fanatics. These

---

[1] Matthesius, *Ninth Sermon*.
[2] *C. R.*, 2 : 40.

articles had been printed and circulated among the people. The Apology could not meet the demands of the new situation. It was necessary now expressly to disclaim all fellowship with heretics, whether ancient or modern, and to establish the soundness of the Wittenberg teaching by connecting it with the teaching of the primitive Church. In compassing these ends Melanchthon had to keep in view the purpose of the Diet, which was to heal the schism; besides, he had to state the common fundamentals of Christian belief in the mildest possible form consistent with truth, lest new contentions arise. These are the points of view from which Melanchthon now worked, and it is from these points of view alone that we can understand the frequent references to history, and the condemnatory clauses in the Confession. Indeed, this changed purpose is the real beginning of the Augsburg Confession as such. To assist in realising this new purpose, Melanchthon would naturally appropriate the materials at hand. Hence he took the Schwabach Articles, which had already been approved by the Elector, as the *basis* of the doctrinal part of the Confession. His own *Bedenken*, mentioned above, the so-called Torgau Articles, would be retained as the basis of the apologetic part.

He wrought so rapidly that by May 11th he brought the document into a form suitable for presentation to the Diet. On that day it was sent to Luther by the Elector with an explanatory letter from himself, and with the following note from Melanchthon:

" Our Apology is sent to you, though it is more properly a Confession. For the Emperor will not have time to hear prolix discussions. I have said those things which I thought especially profitable or becoming. I brought together almost all the Articles of faith, because Eck has published the most diabolical slanders against us. Against these I wish to oppose a remedy. Do you determine about the whole writing in accordance with your spirit." [1]

May 15th, Luther replied to the Elector's letter in these words: " I have read over Master Philip's Apology. I know not how to improve or change it, nor would it become me, since I cannot move so softly and gently. Christ our Lord help that it may bring forth much fruit, as we hope and pray." [2]

The Confession had now assumed a form known as " the first draft." It was yet very far from what it finally became. It did not contain Article XX., Of Faith and Good Works; nor was Article XXVII., Of Vows, nor Article XXVIII., Of Ecclesiastical Power, laid before Luther in their final form. It is probable that the latter had not yet been written. May 22d, Melanchthon asks the attention of Luther to the doctrinal articles of the Confession in so far as they were then finished, saying:

" In the Apology we change many things daily. The Article on vows, which was too meager, I have supplanted by another discussion of the subject. I am now treating of the power of the keys. I wish you would run

---

[1] C. R., 2 : 45, 47.
[2] De W., 4 : 17.

over the articles of faith.   If you think there is nothing
defective in them, we will treat the rest as best we can,
for they must be changed continually and adapted to the
circumstances." [1]

So far as is known, this is the last time that Luther's attention was directed to the Confession until
after it had been presented before the Diet.   Nor is
the matter again mentioned in the correspondence
between Augsburg and Coburg while the Confession
was in further preparation.   But Melanchthon went
on changing and adapting it to circumstances until
the last hour before the presentation.
He not only polished the style, but he made
changes in the matter.   He aimed to unite perfection of finish with fidelity to truth and history.   To
this end he sought assistance from the theologians
present, and from the civil counsellors.   In his
efforts to conciliate and to preserve the unity of the
faith, he was not a little influenced by the irenic
Bishop Stadion of Augsburg, and by Alphonsus
Valdesius, the Emperor's secretary.   The latter
invited him to an interview, and insisted on mildness and brevity.   He said to Melanchthon· " The
Spaniards have the idea that the Lutherans hold
horrible things about the Trinity, Christ, and the
Mother of God.   Hence they think it is a more
meritorious service to kill a Lutheran than a Turk."
" I know it," replied Melanchthon, " and I have
spoken to several Spaniards on the subject, but I
have not effected much with them."   Valdesius in-

[1] *C. R.*, 2 : 60.

quired, " What do the Lutherans want ?   How can
matters be remedied ? "   " Our contention," said
Melanchthon, " is not so long and ill-advised as has
probably been reported to the Emperor.   The difference consists in the following articles : The Sacrament under both forms ; the marriage of priests and
monks ; and the Mass.   The Lutherans do not
regard private masses as right."   He thought that
if an understanding could be reached on these
articles, there would be no difficulty in regard to
other things.   The Secretary promised to report to
the Emperor.   Later, he again called Melanchthon,
and said that the Emperor, who was favourably disposed in the case, had commanded him to speak
with Cardinal Campeggius on the subject.   The
Cardinal, he declared, was willing to concede both
elements in the Sacrament, and the marriage of the
clergy, but would not yield in the matter of private
masses.

The Secretary also requested a copy of the
Lutheran Articles, in the briefest compass, for the
Emperor, that he might examine them, as " his
Majesty thought it would be best to take up the
subject quietly and not to have a long public discussion." [1]   Melanchthon referred the request to
his principals, but these were not willing to have
their cause disposed of quietly and without a hearing.   They had come to Augsburg to present their
Confession.   They demanded to be heard.[2]   The

---

[1] C. R., 2 : 122, 123.

[2] It is not true, as reported by Cœlestin and others, that Melanchthon sent articles to the Emperor.   See C. R., 2 : 123.

Emperor now appointed June 24th for the presentation of the Protestant Confession.

Prior to June 8th, the Confession on which Melanchthon had been labouring was intended to be
the reply of the Saxon Elector alone.   But from
that time on, at the suggestion of the Margrave of
Brandenburg, seconded by the delegates of Nuremberg, it was so shaped as to be the Confession of all
the princes and cities that had accepted the Lutheran
Reformation.   Consequently, June 23d, the princes,
their counsellors and theologians, and the delegates
from Nuremberg and Reutlingen assembled for consultation.   " The Confession was read, examined,
and considered."   Melanchthon desired that it
should be subscribed by the theologians.   But the
princes chose to confess their own faith and that of
their churches.   The Confession was then solemnly
subscribed by seven princes, and by the representatives of two cities.

Friday, June 24th, was consumed in hearing the
delegates from Austria touching the Turkish War.
Saturday, June 25th, the most memorable day in
Lutheran history, the Diet assembled at three
o'clock in the private chapel of the episcopal palace.
The first hour was consumed with preliminaries.
The Emperor requested the Protestants simply to
hand in their Confession.   This they refused to do,
and expressed the desire to be heard.   Then he
asked that the Latin copy be read.   The Elector
interposed, and said that as they were on German
soil, he hoped his Majesty would permit the reading
of the German copy.   Chancellor Baier then read

DR. JOHN ECK.

TRADITIONAL PORTRAIT.

the German copy with a voice so loud and clear that every word was understood, not only by every person in the chapel, but by the throng assembled in the court beneath.

Both copies—both are to be regarded as originals —were delivered to the Emperor, who gave the German copy to the Imperial Chancellor, the Elector of Mayence, but kept the Latin copy in his own hands. Every effort in later times to recover the originals has failed. It has been thought that the Latin was taken to Spain, and the German to the Council of Trent, and that both have perished.

Thus after more than two months of unremitting toil Melanchthon's most arduous work was brought to a happy conclusion. The Augsburg Confession stands as his loftiest monument, and marks the climax of his usefulness. The most eventful day of the century had dawned. The destiny of the Church and of Civilisation in the West hung trembling in the balance. A single word misplaced, a single sentence wrong, might change the course of history, and shape the career of millions unborn. But the man for the day was there—the only man of the century who could have met the demands of the day. Of all the great men of that century, Philip Melanchthon alone possessed the learning, patience, mildness, literary skill, and diplomatic tact required in the composition of the fundamental Creed of German Protestantism; and it is not too much to say that no similar work ever gave its author so much anxious solitude, so many sleepless nights, so many agonising days. Every word was weighed;

every thought was pondered.   The Confession itself, to-day the Magna Charta of the faith of fifty millions of Evangelical Christians, is the all-sufficient proof of the care bestowed on its composition, and of the eminent qualifications of the author for the work assigned him.   He was not a philosophical genius, nor a speculative thinker, but he was a great theologian, and a master of the art of expression. He could draw truth from the wells of salvation, and could mould it in the most perfect forms of expression; and it is the boast of the Confession itself, and of its adherents, that it is drawn from the Word of God, and not from the speculations of men.

The influence of the Confession was extraordinarily great.   In the consciousness that they had confessed their faith before the Emperor and the Empire, the Protestants felt united and strengthened.   Spalatin exclaimed, " To-day occurred one of the greatest events that ever occurred on earth." Luther rejoiced that he had " lived to see the hour when Christ was confessed by such great confessors in such a glorious Confession." [1]

Even the Emperor is said to have exclaimed, " Would that such doctrine were preached throughout the whole world." [2]   Duke William of Bavaria said to the Elector, " Heretofore we have not been so informed of this matter and doctrine "; and to Eck, " You have assured us that the Lutherans could easily be refuted.   How is it now ?"   Eck answered, "With the Fathers it can be done, but not

[1] De W., 4 : 82.
[2] Luther's *Tischreden*, fol. 346a.

with the Scriptures." "Then," said the Duke, "I understand that the Lutherans stand on the Scriptures, and we Catholics outside of them."[1]

Melanchthon's own account of the composition of the Confession, written a few months before his death, the fullest and most explicit that ever came from his pen, will be read with interest:

"It is very useful and necessary that everybody, and posterity, should know that this Confession, which was delivered to the Emperor Charles V. at Augsburg, in the Diet in the year 1530, did not proceed from individual purpose; nor was it delivered to the Emperor privately and unsolicited. On the contrary this important matter occurred as follows: At that time the Emperor Charles V. earnestly desired to have an orderly General Council held. Hence after his coronation at Bologna he came to Augsburg in the year 1530, and allowed this to take precedence of all other imperial matters, since it was evident that difference in doctrine had arisen in several countries and cities. And since in this difference diverse opinions were current, his Majesty wished to know what the doctrine in the churches was; and since a change had been made, what the Elector and princes rested on. This effort of his Majesty was followed by a variety of opinions and discussions. Also some papal writers had scattered slanders in the Diet, by which abominable falsehoods were heaped upon our churches, as that they had many damnable errors, and, like the Anabaptists, were heretical and seditious.

"Now an answer had to be made before his Imperial Majesty; and those slanders had to be refuted. Hence

---

[1] Walch, xvi., 1046.

all the articles of the Christian doctrine were drawn up
in order that everyone might know that our churches
were unjustly slandered by these papal falsehoods.   But
while there were at the same time several diffuse treatises,
no one wanted to put anything into shape.   Besides, the
forms were different, since for a long time this important
matter had been carefully pondered and arranged by
several distinguished men.   Finally this Confession, so
God ordained and granted, was composed by myself,
which the Reverend Dr. Martin Luther declared pleased
him.   But prior to its being publicly read before the
Emperor, it was laid before the Elector, the princes, and
legates, who subscribed it.   These with their counsellors
and preachers who were present diligently pondered all
the Articles.   As now the Emperor required an answer,
this Confession was read publicly in the presence of the
Emperor and of all the Electors, princes, and counsellors
who were at the Diet.   Then the copy was given to the
Emperor, who had it read again in his own council.

"Then the Confutation was prepared by the Papists,
but not published in print.   This was followed by the
Apology, which I composed, in which several articles
are further explained.   That this was done thus, noble
princes and counts know; and other honourable men,
who by the grace of God still live, can report that this
Confession was not presented to the Emperor unsolicited.
It is necessary for posterity to know this." [1]

The mental agony which Melanchthon endured,
and the opposition he experienced in the composition
of the Confession, are best learned from his own
statements.   To his brother he wrote from Augsburg:

---

[1] *C. R.*, 9: 929.

" I could almost believe I was born under an unlucky star. For what distresses me most has come upon me. Poverty, hunger, contempt, and other misfortunes I could easily bear. But what utterly prostrates me is strife and controversy. I had to compose the Confession which was to be given to the Emperor and the Estates. In spirit I foresaw insults, wars, devastation, battles. And now does it depend upon me to divert such great calamity ? Oh God in whom I trust, help thou me. Thou judgest us as we purpose in heart. Dear brother, I dare not drop the matter so long as I live. But not by my fault shall peace be destroyed. Other theologians wanted to compose the Confession. Would God they had had their way. Perhaps they could have done it better. Now they are dissatisfied with mine, and want it changed. One cries out here, another there. But I must maintain my principle of omitting everything that increases the bitterness. God is my witness that my intentions have been good. My reward is that I shall be hated." [1]

In 1556, he wrote to Flacius: " You find fault because I wrote the Repetition of the Confession [the Saxon]. I also wrote the former [the Augsburg]. Then I had many to assail me, no one to assist me." [2] Melanchthon may have made mistakes in some instances; he may have been inclined to yield too much to Rome for the sake of peace; but it is the verdict of history that no man ever acted with purer motives than he. His mild and conciliatory spirit made the Augsburg Confession a

[1] *Melanch. Pædagogica*, p. 38.
[2] *C. R.*, 8 : 843.

fact in history. While other men clamoured for war, he pleaded for peace.

It will assist in understanding the Augsburg Confession to learn from his own pen the principle that guided the author in its composition, and indeed in all his theological teaching:

" When at Augsburg, in '30 I composed the first Confession; when no one would write a letter, and yet the Emperor demanded a confession; in true sincerity I brought together the summary of the doctrine, and omitted some unnecessary perplexing discussions, that everyone might know what the chief doctrine is in these churches. This form I continue to teach, and I avoid some discussions." [1]

In the tenth Article he stated the Lutheran doctrine of the Lord's Supper in a generic form, not in the specific formulas of Luther, and the doctrine of Predestination he purposely omitted,[2] because of the inextricable mazes into which it leads. Though he composed the Confession and was ever recognised by his contemporaries as its author, yet he was for the time the common consciousness, the surrogate of his party. His object was not to state in particular what Luther held and taught, but what was held and taught in the churches of the subscribing princes and cities. This is the true idea in regard to a confession of faith.

But the Augsburg Confession comprehends by no means the whole of Melanchthon's labours from

---

[1] *C. R.*, 9 : 990.
[2] *C. R.*, 2 : 547.

April 15 to June 25, 1530.   His letters and learned
opinions of that period would make a fair-sized
volume.   They are written with that carefulness
which characterises all the productions of his pen,
and are of priceless value for the history of those
eventful days when the Evangelical Lutheran Church
was formally brought into existence.

CHAPTER XVII

NEGOTIATIONS FOR PEACE

Correspondence with Cardinal Campeggius—The Papal Confutation
—The Apology of the Confession—Publication of the Confession
and its Apology.

MELANCHTHON'S mental agony, caused by
the distractions of the Church, and his striving
for the restoration of harmony, did not cease with
the composition and delivery of the Augsburg Confession. He was apprehensive that greater evils
would come because of the severity of the Confession [1]; and thus that the very object for which the
princes had delivered the Confession, viz., the restoration of peace and concord,[2] would be defeated.
In this state of mind he wrote to Luther, June 27th,
and inquired " how much was to be conceded to the
adversaries." [3] But the latter, who, perhaps, alone
of his party believed that concord was impossible,
replied that " too much had been conceded in the

---

[1] *C. R.*, 2 : 140.
[2] *C. R.*, 2 : 125.
[3] *C. R.*, 2 : 146.

Confession,"[1] and exhorted his less heroic friend to greater firmness.

Notwithstanding the violence exhibited from time to time by representative Romanists, Melanchthon still clung to the delusion which he had expressed in the so-called Torgau Articles, and which he had carried with him to Augsburg, viz., that the dissension had arisen, not on account of *doctrine*, but alone on account of certain abuses which had been abolished by the Evangelicals. In the Epilogue to the doctrinal part of the Confession he had declared that there was nothing in the evangelical teaching " which differs from the Scriptures, or from the Catholic Church, or from the Roman Church, so far as it is known from writers." He also tells us that he would have made greater changes in the Confession, that is, would have made it milder, had he not been restrained by " the counsellors."[2] As before the reading of the Confession, so afterward, he thought that peace could be restored if the Romanists would only consent to the removal of certain vicious ceremonies and " human doctrines and statutes," such as the Mass, communion with only one element, the celibacy of priests, and monastic vows. He was encouraged in this thought by the deceptions practised on him by Cardinal Campeggius, the papal legate, who had invited him to an interview, had discussed with him the subjects at issue, and had conceded the use of both elements in the Eucharist and the marriage of the priests.[3]

---

[1] De W., 4: 52.
[2] C. R., 2: 140.
[3] C. R., 2: 174.

At the instance of the evangelical princes, Melanchthon addressed a letter to the Cardinal,[1] in which, after the usual complimentary allusions to the wisdom, moderation, and dignity of his " Right Reverend Lordship," he promises that the princes " will accept such conditions for the retention, confirmation, and establishment of peace, concord, and the authority of the ecclesiastical order, as his Right Reverend Lordship shall judge to be proper." He further says that the princes have no intention of abolishing the ecclesiastical order and the legitimate authority of the bishops.

Whether Melanchthon transcended his instructions in this letter, or not, cannot be determined; but it is certain that he was not the only one of his party who was alarmed by the threats and hostile attitude of the Papists, and was willing to make concessions.

In subsequent correspondence with the Cardinal through his secretary, Melanchthon reaffirms the agreement of the Confession with the Scriptures, with the Catholic Church, and with the Roman Church. His object in thus identifying the teaching of the Confession with the teaching of the Catholic and of the Roman Church seems to have been to force the Romanists to acknowledge the orthodoxy of the Lutheran teaching, since they, the Romanists, would not dare to repudiate the teaching of the Catholic Church. He nowhere identifies the

[1] *C. R.*, 2 : 171. There is strong reason to believe that the letter in *C. R.*, 2 : 169, is not genuine, therefore it is not quoted here. It is not essentially different from the one given below in full.

Lutheran teaching with the teaching of the papacy.

But Melanchthon little understood the character of Campeggius. The wily Italian had long been urging the Emperor to make war on the Lutherans and "to extirpate the poisonous plant by fire and sword."[1] And as little did he understand the mind of the Catholic theologians, who, on July 13, 1530, presented a *Confutation* of the Confession, so elaborate in form and so violent in manner, that the Emperor refused it, and returned it to the Committee with instructions to abridge it, and to eliminate all invectives.

While the Catholic theologians were further engaged in preparing their *Confutation*, Melanchthon wrote numerous letters to his friends, and several Opinions on theological subjects, among which is one *De Missa*, in which he refutes both the Zwinglian and the Romish hypothesis, and exhibits the Lutheran view that the "Lord's Supper is not a sacrifice, but a sacrament, by which grace is offered, by which we are moved to believe, and by which we comfort our alarmed consciences."[2]

Finally, August 3, 1530, the Papal *Confutation*,[3] chiefly the work of Eck, Fabri, Cochlæus, and Wimpina, was read publicly in the Diet. It is scholastic in form and weak in arguments. It actually strengthened the conviction of the Protestants that their cause was just. Melanchthon wrote to Veit

---

[1] Ranke, *Die Römischen Päpste im 16. u. 17. Jahrh.*, i., 111.

[2] *C. R.*, 2 : 212.

[3] Reprinted in Francke's *Libri Symbolici* and in Hase's *Libri Symbolici*.

Dietrich, Luther's friend and companion at Coburg, saying: "All good men in our party seem calmer and firmer in mind since hearing such absurdities. They know that among our adversaries there is no acquaintance with religion."[1]   And to Luther he wrote:

"All the good and wise men are more courageous, since they have heard that puerile *Confutation*.   Our rulers could easily obtain peace if they would court the Emperor and the more moderate princes.   But there is marvellous indifference, and, as I think, a quiet indignation that withholds them from such business."[2]

The Emperor declared that he would abide by the *Confutation*, and commanded the Protestants to do the same.   This widened the breach between the two parties.   Melanchthon now saw his cherished hope of peace about to be completely blasted. Again he had recourse to Campeggius, and wrote a letter to his secretary, which was designed evidently to reach the Cardinal himself.   As this letter exhibits the greatest length to which Melanchthon went in his striving for peace, it is here given in full, as follows:

"The advent of no one to this city has given me more pleasure than yours.   For I know that you are endowed with a certain remarkable sweetness of temper and with an amiability worthy of a learned and wise man.   Hence I have freely spoken with you both about my own private affairs, and of the public business; and on account of

[1] *C. R.*, 2 : 253.
[2] *C. R.*, 2 : 254.

your virtues I have been led to hope that you would be the promoter of peace in your deliberations.

" For this reason I have often shown that if a few things were kept in the background, these divisions could be healed. In my opinion it would contribute very much to the quiet of the Church and to the dignity of the Roman See, to make peace on the conditions which I have mentioned. For also our priests should in turn render obedience to the bishops. Thus the Church would unite again in one body, and the Roman See would have its own honour, so that, if anything wrong remains in the churches, it can gradually be corrected by the care of the bishops. It is also our earnest desire to be freed from these contentions, that we may give our whole attention to the diligent improvement of doctrine. And unless this be done, wise men can easily foresee what, amid so many sects, will come upon posterity. And in this matter it is easy to see how indifferent those are whom you now oppose to us. Yesterday the *Confutation* of our *Confession* was read. If it shall be published, condemning us, believe me it will not have great admiration among judicious men, and will irritate the minds of ours. Thus there is danger that by the renewal of this whole tragedy, greater commotion than ever will ensue. Hence I desire that these evils of the Church be not increased in virulence. Therefore I beg you to indicate to me in a few words, whether you have spoken with your Reverend Master about those conditions, and what hope he will hold out. If I can obtain anything favourable I will take care that the Roman See may not repent its kindness. The feelings and desires of many good men are united in this matter, who will do all they can to enlarge the authority of the bishops and to establish the peace of the Church.

" You see we cannot dissolve the existing marriages, nor have other priests.   Nor could the change in regard to both elements cease without contempt of the Sacrament.   It does not belong to the papal clemency to make war for such reasons, since there is nothing which is injurious to good men or to piety.   And if more new doctrines appear, it belongs to your prudence to take care that a much greater commotion do not occur in the Church.   I have written these things to you, a good and wise man, and I ask you to exhort yours to justice, and to indicate to me by this my friend, what hope your Reverend Master holds out.   As I am suffering with the gout I cannot come to you." [1]

The correspondence of Melanchthon with Campeggius has sometimes been pronounced *obsequious*, and so it seems to be when judged by our standards. But it is not more so than Luther's letter to Pope Leo, and the one to Henry VIII., and scarcely more so than is the Preface to the Augsburg Confession prepared by Chancellor Brück.   None of these writers, nor their writings, are to be judged by present conditions.

The seeming obsequiousness is in the times, and in the long superlatives of " the unblushing Latin," rather than in the men.   Campeggius was the representative of the greatest sovereign on earth.   It was but natural that Melanchthon should address him in the language which immemorial usage had allotted to one so eminent in station.   That the letters express too great confidence in the wisdom and moderation of the Cardinal, is to the discredit

<hr>

[1] *C. R.*, 2 : 248.

of Melanchthon only in so far as they show that
German frankness is no proper match for Italian
perfidy; and Melanchthon's willingness to restore
the rule of the Pope and bishops is subject to the
presupposition that they rule well, and promote
sound doctrine.   Besides, as the appointed leader
of the Protestant party, which professedly was striving for peace, Melanchthon felt his responsibility for
securing peace in the face of imminent war, at any
cost save that of the surrender of vital truth.   It
was not a truckling spirit nor personal fear that inspired the letter, but a sincere desire to avert impending ruin, and to preserve the freedom of the
Gospel in fundamentals.   This is shown by what
occurred the day after the reading of the Confession,
when in the midst of the assembled clergy this same
Cardinal Campeggius, " hurling thunderbolts like an
angry Jove," demanded of Melanchthon that he
should yield.   With a courage that has been compared to that shown by Luther at Worms, he answered: " We cannot yield, nor desert the truth.
We pray that for God's sake and Christ's our oppon-
nents will grant us that which we cannot surrender
with a good conscience." And when the Cardinal
cried out, " I cannot, I cannot, the keys do not
err," Melanchthon answered: " We will commit
our cause and ourselves to God.   If God be for us,
who can be against us ? We have forty thousand
wives and children of pastors whose souls we cannot
desert.   We will toil and fight, and die, if God so
will, rather than betray so many souls." [1]

---

[1] *C. R.*, 10 : 198.

Melanchthon was ever ready to hold out the hand of conciliation, but at no time was he willing to surrender the Gospel for the hierarchy.

Melanchthon did not hear the Papal *Confutation* read, nor would the Emperor furnish the Protestants with a copy. He simply demanded their submission. This they were not prepared to render. Neither the command of the Emperor, nor the rage of the bishops, nor the imminence of war could deter them from making a defence of their Confession. Melanchthon and some others were directed to prepare an Apology of the Confession, in which it should be explained why the Protestants could not accept the *Confutation*, and in which the arguments of their opponents should in turn be confuted. For this purpose they used notes taken by Camerarius at the reading of the *Confutation*, and perhaps availed themselves of some writings of the Romish theologians against the Confession. On September 22d, the Apology, thus prepared, was offered to the Emperor by Chancellor Brück, but was rejected. Later the Catholic majority published an edict in which they boasted that they had confuted the Confession out of the Scriptures.

On September 23d, Melanchthon set out with the Elector for home. At Coburg he tarried a few days with Luther, who praised God that his beloved Prince had been delivered from hell. Thence to Wittenberg the two friends, the heroic reformer and the faithful confessor of Christ, travelled together. But Melanchthon, having obtained a copy of the *Confutation*, laboured on his Apology as they journeyed. In the house of Spalatin at Altenburg he was writing on it while eating, until Luther snatched the pen out of his hand, saying, " Dear Philip, we can serve God not only by work, but also by rest." [1]

On October 4th, he was again in Wittenberg, after an absence of six months. What he had suffered in mind and body no pen could record, no voice could utter. His was the heroism of endurance, as Luther's was the heroism of daring. If Melanchthon sometimes bowed too low in the storm, it was that he might rise again with greater strength when the storm was over. And seldom has a man shown greater strength of conviction, or more transcendent skill as a theologian, than Melanchthon did in the elaboration of the Apology, which occupied his chief attention for several months. The work is as simple and edifying in form as it is profound and learned in contents. Some of the chapters were written over and over again for the sake of accuracy and thoroughness of treatment. He who would read the theology of Melanchthon at its best must read the Apology of the Augsburg Confession.

After his return to Wittenberg, in connection with his other labours, Melanchthon prepared the first edition of the Augsburg Confession. The Emperor had forbidden its publication without his permission. But very soon no less than seven unauthorised editions appeared—six in German and one in Latin. As these had been printed from relatively imperfect copies, they differed from each other and from the text presented in the Diet. Some seem to have

---

[1] Matthesius, fol. 143.

been purposely corrupted. From an authentic
Latin copy, and from his own German manuscript,
Melanchthon caused an edition to be printed, copies
of which reached Augsburg before the Diet adjourned.

Near the close of April, 1531, this edition was
published in quarto form with the Apology, under
the following Latin title ¹·

CONFESSIO FIDEI
exhibita inuictifs.   Imp. Carolo V
Caefari Aug. in Comicijs
Auguftae,
Anno
M. D. XXX.

Addita eft Apologia Confefsionis.

Beide, Deudſch
und Latiniſch.

Pſalm. 119.
Et loquebar de teftimonijs tuis in con-
fpectu Regum, & non confundebar.

WITEBERGÆ.

A copy with this title is found in the royal library
at Dresden.   Beneath the title Melanchthon wrote
with his own hand, *D. Doctori Martino.   Et Rogo ut
legat et emendet.*²

---

¹ *C. R.*, 26 : 235.
² *Ibid.*

CHAPTER XVIII

MELANCHTHON'S GROWING FAME

Schmalkald League—Peace of Nuremberg—Melanchthon's *Opinion*
Melanchthon Called to England, to Tübingen, and to France
—Negotiations with Henry VIII.

THE final decree of the Diet of Augsburg, published November 19, 1530, bore heavily against
the Protestants. They were given time for consideration until the fifteenth of the following April,
with the intimation that unless they yielded, forci-
ble measures would be applied. They now felt the
need of mutual defence. On the nineteenth of December the princes who had signed the Augsburg
Confession, and several cities which had accepted
the same testimony of faith, met at Schmalkald and
laid the foundation of the Schmalkald League, which
was ratified on the twenty-ninth of March, 1531, for
six years, and strengthened later by foreign alliances.
The object of this politico-ecclesiastical alliance was
the protection of Germany and the defence of the
Protestant cause against the sword of the Empire.
So powerful was this new combination that it

alarmed the Emperor, and led to the Peace of Nuremberg, July 23, 1532, which provided that the
affairs of religion should remain in the state in which
they then were until they could be settled by a
general council or a new diet.

The terms of this Peace were most favourable to
the Protestants. They enhanced the dignity and
moral influence of the leaguers, and secured them
new accessions of power. The Peace itself allowed
a time of quiet development for the principles of
the Reformation. Luther and Melanchthon saw
the cause for which they had long laboured and
prayed and endured hardship, at length triumph
through a large part of Germany; but while they
were rejoicing over the happy condition of affairs,
they were called to the death-bed of the Saxon
Elector, who departed this life, August 16, 1532.
He was buried in the Castle Church at Wittenberg,
Luther preaching a German sermon on the occasion,
and Melanchthon delivering an academic oration in
Latin. Because of the steadfastness of his faith,
and the firmness of his character, the Elector is
known in history as John the Constant. He was
succeeded by his son, John Frederick, whose zeal in
the Protestant cause was destined to pass through a
fiery experience. The new Elector was irritable in
temper and dogmatic in manner, but was wise
enough to consult his theologians on all important
ecclesiastical questions. When in June, 1533, the
papal nuncio came to Weimar, and proposed a
council on the condition that the Estates would
pledge themselves to submit to its decisions, he re-

JOHN THE CONSTANT, ELECTOR OF SAXONY.

ferred the matter to Luther and Melanchthon. As
these theologians opposed a council on such a condition, one was not called, though at a convention
held at Schmalkald, the Protestants had declared
themselves favourable to a council: " but it must be
a council in which Christ shall be Pontifex, who
prays the Father for the Church, saying, ' Sanctify
them by thy truth: thy word is truth.' "

As misunderstandings and estrangements still
existed and threatened the peace of the Church
and of the country, the Elector of Mayence and
Duke George of Saxony offered themselves as mediators. A conference was held in Leipzig, Melanchthon and Brück appearing in the name of the Saxon
Elector. The Catholic party would make no concessions on the main questions. They insisted
on Good Works as necessary to Justification, and
wanted Private Masses restored in the Protestant
churches. Soon the negotiations were broken off.

Melanchthon's letters during the summer of 1534
show much anxiety in regard to the peace and safety
of the Church. He expresses the conviction that
the commotions cannot be settled by human counsels. Only God can prevail. About the middle of
the summer he wrote a long *Opinion on the Settle-
ment of the Controversies in Religion.*[1] He concedes that for the sake of harmony some abuses
may be overlooked and condoned, but not those
which destroy the necessary articles of faith, or are
idolatrous, or drive men to open sin. He is willing
that the government of the Pope, and of the bishops,

---

[1] *C. R.*, 2: 740 *et seqq.*

shall remain for the sake of unity throughout the world, provided they do not abuse their authority by suppressing sound doctrine. He also favours common rites in the Church, but on the condition that such rites are to be regarded as indifferent things, which do not make for righteousness, and are not to be used to foster superstition. Confession may be retained, but an enumeration of sins must not be required. Justification is not bestowed on account of our contrition, or works, '' but alone through the mercy of God apprehended by faith, that is, trust in Christ.'' The old formulas for saying the Mass may be retained, but private masses are to be abolished. The doctrine of the Mass as a meritorious sacrifice is rejected. Communion in both kinds is in harmony with the institution of Christ and with the custom of the ancient Church. The Pope ought to remove the restrictions in regard to the Sacrament until the Church can be united, and the full use restored. The invocation of saints has neither example nor command in the Scripture, neither was it practised by the ancient Church. It is not necessary. The histories and examples of the saints may be retained, but there is to be no worship of the saints. Not all vows are of perpetual obligation.

'' Monks who are not fitted for the monastic life may renounce it. In the richer monasteries of Germany neither literature nor learning exists. Idle men who are of no possible use to the Church are simply fed. Hence such monasteries ought to be suppressed, and their revenues ought to be transferred to other uses of the

Church, and to the support of students in institutions of learning."

The Pope ought to abolish enforced clerical celibacy. It is purely a human institution.

The *Opinion* is learned, moderate, and conciliatory. It breathes throughout an earnest desire for harmony in the Church, but it does not surrender a single point of evangelical doctrine. The author expresses the hope that good and pious men will be able to agree in all points at issue.

The Reformation was now making steady progress throughout Germany, albeit it was sometimes assisted by the sword. In the year 1534, the Landgrave with an army, and aided by French gold, rescued Würtemberg from the Austrians, and restored it to Duke Ulrich, who had been banished in 1528. When Melanchthon learned of the Landgrave's success, he exclaimed · " I cannot help loving him. All good men must wish that he might be preserved for great things yet to come." King Ferdinand recognised Ulrich as an under-feudatory, and John Frederick recognised Ferdinand as King of the Romans. Melanchthon wrote, " I will do all in my power to allay the agitations about Religion." [1]

It was during this year (1534) that Melanchthon was invited to France, where " the Lutheran heresy" had begun to take root. Francis, the King, seemed inclined to the Reformation, but he did not desire to separate himself from Rome. His motives were political rather than religious. He was willing to

[1] See, for these facts, *C. R.*, 2 : 739.

ally himself with the German Protestants against
a common enemy, the Emperor. His scheme was
warmly espoused by William Bellay and his brother
John, the Bishop of Paris. Bellay was sent to
Strassburg to interview Bucer on the best means of
restoring harmony to the Church. Dr. Ulrich
Chilius was despatched to Wittenberg to lay the
King's request before Melanchthon. Inspired by
the hope of introducing the evangelical faith into
France, Melanchthon expressed a willingness to
follow the invitation. Both he and the Strassburg
theologians sent Opinions to Francis. At first these
Opinions were favourably received. But the in-
trigues of the Catholics and the violent conduct of
the reforming party soon excited the King's anger
against the Protestants, and brought on a bloody
persecution. Melanchthon expressed himself with
energy against the fanaticism of those who overthrew
the Gospel by their absurd methods.

A letter[1] of Melanchthon, written September 13,
1534, informs us that he had been called a second
time to England, and that he is impatiently awaiting
a third letter. He was also invited in September of
this year to return to his " fatherland," and to assist
in the reorganisation of the University of Tübingen.
He left the decision of the matter to his Elector,
who did not find it to his own interest to spare so
distinguished a teacher from Saxony. When Philip
now declined the call to Tübingen, the Elector was
so pleased that he enlarged his house, provided a
garden for him, and wrote him a friendly letter.

[1] *C. R.*, 2 : 785.

But the Swabians were not entirely satisfied. In October, they begged Melanchthon to attend a disputation between Ambrose Blaurer and the Catholic professors of the university. The Catholics especially desired his presence, because " he is not bitter and envious, but moderate, kind, and peaceable." [1]

The request of the Duke was seconded by " the University, by all the abbots, by prelates spiritual and temporal, yea, by the entire country." Melanchthon could not go, but he sent his friend Camerarius, who had become uncomfortable at Nuremberg, who acted an important part in reorganising the university. In September, 1536, Melanchthon went to Tübingen to visit Camerarius, and also visited the Duke at Nürtingen. He made many suggestions for the improvement of the university, and brought it about that John Brentz, who was pastor at Swabian Hall, should spend one year at Tübingen lecturing on theology. He returned home a little later with a present of a hundred gulden from the Duke, and with the consciousness that he had been of service to the university.

When new complications arose between Francis I., King of France, and the Emperor Charles V., the former sought an alliance with the Protestants of Germany; but as it was reported that he had formed a league with the Turks, his advances were treated with hesitation. He then solicited the services of Bucer and Melanchthon. To this end Barnabas Voreus, Lord de Lafosse, a confessed follower of Melanchthon, was sent to Germany with

[1] *C. R.*, 2 : 795.

15

letters of invitation and a safe-conduct. He also
carried with him a letter from Jacob Sturm, who
was then residing in Paris. This letter describes
the religious condition of France and the mind of
the King toward Melanchthon. It closes by saying:
" You are called not by me, but by many, nor is
your presence desired by those only who have suffered direct distress, nor by those only who fear
destruction; but you are called by the voice of God
and of Christ." [1]

This urgent call lay heavily on the heart of Melanchthon, but grave difficulties stood in the way of
its acceptance. At home loud complaints were
heard to the effect that his going to France would
look like a desertion of the Reformation. In Paris
was the Sorbonne, with which in former years he
had had sharp controversy, and, besides, he did not
fully trust the King. In May, 1535, he answered
Sturm's letter, and recites some of the obstacles
which beset him:

" You know how insolent the rulers are, and how they
hold the fascinated minds of the nobility. Yet I am
not much influenced by such things. What deters me is
the fear that nothing will be done which will promote
the glory of Christ and the peace of France and of the
Church. I have come to this conclusion: If the King
wishes to advance the glory of Christ and the peace of
the Church, let him be earnestly exhorted to call a Synod,
in which the restoration of the Church may be freely discussed. Other plans, it seems to me, are futile, yea,
pernicious." [2]

[1] *C. R.*, 2: 855.   [2] *C. R.*, 2: 874.

As Melanchthon's decision was delayed, the King himself wrote, June 23, 1535, beseeching him to come, either as a private individual, or in the name of his confederates, and assured him of his gracious pleasure. Cardinal Bellay and his brother William also wrote, expressing the deepest interest in Melanchthon's coming, and assured him of the favour of the King and of all good men.[1]

Melanchthon, who meanwhile had gone to Jena, on account of the plague that raged at Wittenberg, now greatly desired to go to France. To this end he sought permission from the Elector to visit France as a private person for three months. He was warmly supported in his request by a letter from Luther. The Elector, who thoroughly understood the King's political motives, refused the request with an emphasis that bordered on severity. Melanchthon was deeply wounded, not so much because the Elector refused to grant his request, as because he had expressed himself with so much harshness. He wrote the King, August 28, 1535, saying that though he was compelled to postpone his coming to France, his mind was still bent on the abatement of controversy.[2] Thus the matter ended. Neither Melanchthon nor Bucer went to France.

Early in 1531, Melanchthon had been requested to prepare an Opinion on the divorce of Henry VIII., King of England, from Catharine of Aragon. August 28th, in a lengthy argument, he declared

---

[1] C. R., 2: 879–886.
[2] C. R., 2: 913, 914.

the King's marriage valid, and without scriptural grounds for divorce. Nevertheless, if public policy requires an heir for the throne, " it would be safest for the King to contract a second marriage without abrogating the first, because polygamy is not for-bidden by the law, and is not without precedent." [1]

Some other German theologians counselled the divorce; but those of Wittenberg disapproved of it under any and all circumstances. Finally, when the divorce had been effected, and Henry had, in 1534, separated from Rome, and had sent his chaplain, Dr. Anthony Barnes, a second time, in March, 1535, to consult with the Wittenberg divines, Me-lanchthon was induced to write the King a letter. He counsels Henry to use his authority in moderat-ing others and in assisting to abolish abuses, and " to introduce a simple, specific form of doctrine." In giving this advice he followed the principle which had guided the Reformers in all their operations: the abolition of abuses and the maintenance of sound doctrine. Even when Henry's envoys pressed the suit of their royal master for the headship of the Schmalkald League, they were met by the demand that he should sign the Augsburg Confession. When Melanchthon at Barnes's suggestion dedicated to Henry the new edition of the *Loci*, with a Preface more diplomatic and flattering than our taste can approve, his object was not to secure a patron, " but to seek a censor whose good judgment in regard to doctrine he should consider unbiassed and fair." And when Melanchthon's colleagues, Luther, Jonas,

[1] *C. R.*, 2: 520.

Cruciger, and Bugenhagen, importuned the Elector to allow Melanchthon to go to England, the end aimed at was not so much alliance with Henry as it was the propagation of sound doctrine, since Doctor Antonius, *ille niger Anglicus*, as Luther calls him, had given the most positive assurance that doctrines were to be included in the negotiations.[1]

Also, this supreme regard for doctrine was still more conspicuously exhibited in " The Thirteen Articles of 1535," written by Melanchthon, December 25th, and signed by the Elector, the Landgrave of Hesse, and the English envoys. The first of these articles provides—

" That the Most Serene King shall promote the Gospel of Christ and the pure doctrine of faith in the manner in which the Princes and confederated Estates confessed it in the Diet of Augsburg, and have guarded it in the published Apology; unless perhaps with the common consent of the Most Serene King and the Princes themselves, some things should seem to need correction or change in accordance with the Word of God."[2]

As the Elector knew that Henry's motives were political rather than religious, he refused to spare Melanchthon from his university; and as further negotiations failed to induce the Wittenberg theologians to sanction Henry's divorce, Melanchthon soon relinquished all desire to go to England. June 9, 1536, he wrote to Camerarius: " I am now freed from anxiety about going to England. Since the

---

[1] Luther's *Briefe*, iv., 630, 632.
[2] *C. R.*, 2 : 1032.

occurrence of such tragedies in England, there has
been a great change of views. The late Queen, accused rather than convicted of adultery, has been
executed." [1]

Later the Elector wished to send an embassy of
statesmen and theologians, including Melanchthon,
to England, to secure Henry's subscription to the
Augsburg Confession, as a condition of his admission
to the Schmalkald League; but as this was opposed
by the other Estates, in September a letter, written
by Melanchthon, was sent in the name of the confederated Estates, inquiring for the King's view of
the articles agreed upon between his envoys and the
Wittenberg theologians, and announcing their intention to suspend their judgment in regard to a General
Council until " they should learn whether his Royal
Highness is disposed to defend the pure doctrine
of the Christian religion which we profess." [2] As
this letter was delayed in reaching the King, and as
meanwhile the attention of the Protestants was
attracted to other matters, the negotiations with
England were suspended.

---

[1] *C. R.*, 3 : 89.
[2] *C. R.*, 3 : 144.

SPES MEA IN DEO EST
IOHANNES FRIDERICVS DEI BENEFICIO SAXONIÆ DVX,
SACRI ROMANI IMPERII ARCHIMARSCHALCHVS ET
ELECTOR LANDGRAVIVS THVRINGIÆ, MARCHIO MISNIÆ,
ET BVRGGRAVIVS MAGDEBVRGI ETC:
VERBVM DOMINI MANET IN ÆTERNVM.
1543

THE ELECTOR JOHN FREDERICK OF SAXONY.

AFTER THE COPPER ENGRAVING BY G. PENCZ, 1543.

CHAPTER XIX

MELANCHTHON'S THEOLOGY

New Edition of the *Loci*—Exposition of Melanchthon's Theology: The Will, Good Works, the Number of Sacraments, Infant Baptism, the Lord's Supper—Luther's Approbation of the *Loci*.

DURING the four or five years that followed the Diet of Augsburg, Melanchthon was especially active with his pen. Among the most important of his writings of this period, besides the Apology, **are** two books on Rhetoric, *Cario's Chronicle*, a Preface to a work on astronomy, some editions and translations of Greek and Latin classics, a second edition of his *Commentary on Romans*, dedicated to the Archbishop of Mayence, and in 1535 a revised and enlarged edition of the *Loci*, with dedication, as already noticed, to the King of England, who sent him two hundred florins, with a letter subscribed, " Your friend, King Henry VIII."

Since this new edition of the *Loci* ranks as one of Melanchthon's most important writings, it deserves more than a passing notice. The author tells us in several letters, that he is revising the Confession and the *Loci* for the purpose of making the definitions more simple and luminous. To Camerarius he wrote, December 24, 1535: "In my *Loci* I seem to have second thoughts. You see I have tried to throw some light on obscure and intricate subjects."[1] During the ten years that intervened from 1525 to 1535, Melanchthon had opportunity to acquaint himself better with the Catholic system, to look more deeply into the teaching of the Fathers, to study the Scriptures more thoroughly, to profit by the criticisms of his opponents, and to learn better the practical needs of the Church. Hence this edition exhibits not only progress in theological science, but more calmness, greater accuracy in definitions, a larger reverence for the oldest teachers of the Church, and the quiet assurance that the Protestants are in possession of the true doctrine. Each individual *Locus*, or subject, is first stated systematically, often syllogistically, and is then followed by proofs from the Scriptures and from the Fathers, to show that the Protestants are in harmony with the true Catholic Church of Jesus Christ. The work also exhibits some important changes in theological views, and in methods of statement. We have space in which to mention only the following subjects:

1. *Free Will and Predestination.* The absolute determinism taught in the first edition by the declaration " that all things that occur, occur by necessity," is excluded. In the *Locus*, " Of the Cause of Sin and of Contingence," it is said:

---

[1] *C. R.*, 2: 861, 881.

" God is not the cause of sin.   Contingence must evidently be conceded, because sin, properly speaking, arises from the will of the devil and of man, and is committed without the approbation of God and without his forcing our wills.   Hence it is not by any means committed necessarily by absolute necessity."

The doctrine of necessity he calls " a dream of the Stoics," to which the pious must give neither their minds nor ears.   " The hardening of Pharaoh's heart is a Hebrew figure of speech which signifies permission, not an efficient will; as, Lead us not into temptation, means, permit us not to be led into temptation."   " There are three causes which concur in conversion: The Word, the Holy Spirit, and the Will, not indeed neutral, but resisting its own weakness."   He supports this proposition by quotations from Basil and Chrysostom, and says: " God precedes, calls, moves, assists us, but we should take care not to oppose.   For it is evident that sin arises from us, not from the will of God." Melanchthon had been led by the controversy on the Will between Erasmus and Luther, to see that the former had defended an important element of truth, namely, the essential freedom of the Will as over against the absolute predestinarianism of Lu ther.   From the time that he formally entered the theological faculty, in 1526, he had begun to move more independently in his sphere; and this is certainly to his credit; for though he had at the beginning learned his theology from Luther, he was under no obligation to dwell forever under Luther's shadow,

nor to abide by all the definitions and conclusions of
his master.   His highly ethical and practical nature,
and his biblical studies, had led him to esteem piety
and morality as the end of theological pursuits;
and he soon discovered that a doctrine which made
God the cause of sins, like the adultery of David
and the treachery of Judas, could not be favourable
to virtue.   In his *Commentary on Colossians* (1527),
he says: " Because Christ himself says, John viii.,
when he speaketh a lie, he speaketh it of himself, I will
not make God the author of sin, but the preserver
of nature, the restorer of life and motion, which life
and motion the devil and the wicked do not rightly
use."   This clearly implies that the devil and the
wicked have Free Will and are the cause of sin.   But
he plainly limits the freedom to choose in things
pertaining to nature, for he says that " the will cannot perform Christian or spiritual righteousness,"
but " has the power of performing natural and civil
righteousness, as, abstaining from theft, or from
murder, or from another man's wife." [1]   With this
agree the Visitation Articles of the same year.

In the Augsburg Confession, Article V., he had
presented the doctrine of divine sovereignty in the
clause, " Where and when it seems good to God."
In Article XVIII. he had asserted the essential
freedom of the Will in the declaration that " the
human will has a certain freedom for doing civil
righteousness and for choosing such things as belong
to reason."   In the *Commentary on Romans* (1532),
to the " scruple of particularity," he " opposes **the**

[1] Galle's *Charakteristik Melanchthons*, p. 274.

universal promises of the Gospel, which teach that God for Christ's sake, and out of grace, offers salvation to all." He further says that " we must judge of the will of God and of election, not from reason, nor from the law, but from the Gospel." He expressly places the cause of reprobation in unwillingness to believe the Gospel.[1] Thus Melanchthon was the first among the Reformers to depart from the Augustinian *particularity*, and to bring out the doctrine of the universality of the offer of salvation, and to direct the attention of men primarily to the redemption through Christ as a fact, and not primarily to the secret decree of God: " The Church does not depend on human counsel, nor on human virtues; but God in Christ has loved and chosen those who are to be saved," that is, those who believe the Gospel. Already, in 1531, he had reached essentially the same position, when he wrote to Brentz:

" You imagine that men are justified by faith, because by faith we accept the Holy Spirit and afterwards are justified by the fulfilling of the law, which is effected by the Holy Spirit. This supposition places righteousness in our work, in our purity or perfection, albeit such perfection ought to follow faith. But turn your eyes wholly from renovation and the law to the promise and to Christ, and know that we are justified on account of Christ, that is, that we are accepted before God and find peace of conscience not on account of that renovation. Such renovation is not sufficient. We are justified by faith alone, not because it is the root, as you

---

[1] *C. R.*, 15 : 680–686

write, but because it lays hold of Christ, on account of whom we are accepted." [1]

In this particular, viz., that justification precedes regeneration and prepares the way for it, the Lutheran Church has followed Melanchthon, as shown especially in the Form of Concord of 1580.

In the *Locus De Prædestinatione* he exhibits the doctrine of the universality of the offer of redemption with greater fulness. He says again: " Mercy is the cause of election "; and he declares that no one can seek the cause of election outside the Gospel without erring: " Hence let us not permit ourselves to be turned from the Gospel, but let us utterly reject other fancies." In writing of Free Will and Predestination, he insists that men must hear the Gospel, must apply the promise by faith, and each one must include himself in the universal promise by which the Holy Ghost operates. " God draws man, but he draws only him who is willing." In the *Commentary on Romans* he had said (p. 680): "It is not of him that willeth or runneth, but of God that showeth mercy; that is, mercy is the cause of election. It is not of us to will, or to run, and yet these things take place in the will, and in him that runneth and resisteth not."

This teaching of Melanchthon's has been called *Synergism*, and has been the subject of much dispute in the Lutheran Church. Some of the statements, taken in isolation from the full treatment of which they form a part, may be open to objection;

---

[1] *C. R.*, 2 : 501.

but, considered in their proper relations, the teaching is believed to be in accord with the plain import
of the Scriptures, and with the common Christian
experience. According to Melanchthon, God calls;
the Spirit works through the Word; the Will becomes active under the influence of grace and of
divine truth. Then it accepts or rejects the offer
of salvation. It has no self-moved activity in spiritual things. Of itself it can work no spiritual righteousness; it can contribute nothing to justification;
it cannot bring forth faith. Faith occurs when man
hears the Word of God, and when God moves and
inclines him to believe. Without the Word there
is no contact of the Spirit. Thus Free Will is simply
the power to resist the Will's own infirmity and to
accept the offer of grace when assisted by the higher
powers. Its subordination to the Spirit and to the
Word is always presupposed. Of the three concur-
ring causes, the Will is placed *third*, and becomes a
cause only when preceded and quickened into activity by the other two.

Thus Melanchthon is as far from Pelagianism on
the one hand as he is from Determinism on the
other. He preserves the golden mean. Over against
Luther's one-sided emphasis of the love of God, and
Calvin's doctrine of irresistible grace, Melanchthon
maintains and conserves the responsibility of man.
He thus imparts an ethical quality to the Lutheran
theology, such as otherwise it had not had. The
moral personality is insisted on, and is made responsible for the use of the means of grace, for the appropriation of salvation, and for righteous living.

It is the conclusion of the most competent judges that at this point even the Form of Concord adheres to Melanchthon's fundamental tendency; and " the later expounders of the Form of Concord, notwith standing their aspersions of Melanchthon, have simply adopted his conception of the way of salvation in order to save their own *ordo salutis* at its most critical point from the inconsistence and absurdity of pure accident." [1]   Moreover, some of the ablest modern Lutherans, Thomasius, Stahl, Harless, Hofmann, Kahnis, and Luthardt, have more or less followed the course taken by Melanchthon, and have developed the Lutheran doctrine of the Will and of Predestination away from the position taken by Luther in *De Servo Arbitrio*, and never renounced by him.   Indeed the proposition that God loves and elects man in Christ, and not by an absolute *beneplacitum*, has become classic in the Lutheran Church.

2. *Good Works*.   In these *Loci* Melanchthon sets out the doctrine of Justification with great clearness. He gives Justification its *forensic* sense, as meaning " to absolve, or to pronounce just."   Faith is described as " confidence in mercy promised for Christ's sake."   " It includes the knowledge of the history of Christ as the Son of God and a habit or action of the will which accepts the promise of Christ and reposes in Christ."

Thus every thought of the merit or of the righteousness of works is excluded.   Justification is named

---

[1] See Dorner, *Hist. Prot. Theol.*, i., 218 ; Herrlinger's *Melanchthon's Theologie*, 95.

a *gratuita acceptatio* for Christ's sake. But in Melanchthon's conception, faith in its essential quality is far from being an intellectual apprehension; much rather is it a moral quality which regenerates the heart and controls the will. In the Apology he had said that " faith is a new light in the heart, an energetic operation of the Holy Spirit by which we are regenerated." The justified person must therefore be looked upon as a regenerated person. Before Justification, faith accepts gifts of grace; after Justification, it works righteousness. In the *Loci* he says: " Our obedience, that is, the righteousness of a good conscience, or of works which God enjoins upon us, ought of necessity to follow reconciliation." He further says, " We are justified that we may live a new spiritual life." The relation of good works to Justification is that of effect to cause. Where they do not exist, faith is not a living apprehension of Christ. He continues: " Whom He justifies, the same also He glorifies. Hence eternal life is not given on account of the merit of good works, but freely on account of Christ. And yet good works are thus necessary to eternal life, because they ought necessarily to follow reconciliation."

The good works that are required are " spiritual affections, the fear of God, trust, worship, love, and the like." These are acceptable to God, " not because they satisfy the law, but because already the persons are acceptable." It is evident that there is neither Pelagianism, nor Antinomianism in such a doctrine of *Good Works*. In no sense does it substitute human righteousness for the righteousness of

Christ; neither does it abolish the law of the Ten Commandments, nor encourage an idle or dissolute life under false notions of Christian liberty.

In his *Commentary on the Gospel of John*, written for the use of Cruciger in his lectures, Melanchthon had said that in Justification good works are a *causa sine qua non*. This clause was injudiciously employed by Cruciger, and, at the instance of one Conrad Cordatus, it brought on controversy. But Melanchthon declared that it meant only that " new spirituality is necessary to eternal life," and he affirmed his full agreement with Luther. To Jonas he wrote that Christ is the cause of Justification, but that we must have contrition, and must comfort our consciences by the Word, in order that we may receive faith. It is evident that he wished to clear the doctrine of Justification from the false notion that a mere dead historical faith justifies. He meant to say that where there is no repentance and no Christian living, there is no Justification. The *sine qua non* is intended to signify the close and living connection between faith and sanctification. Good works are necessary to eternal life, or to salvation, as the fruit of faith. In after years, however, in order to avoid giving offence to an age which was justly suspicious of the very words *Good Works*, Melanchthon exchanged the formula, " Good works are necessary to eternal life," for " Good works are necessary "; and to this formula he adhered.

3. *The Number of Sacraments*. Melanchthon defines Sacraments as ceremonies or rites appointed in the Gospel, and having reference to the remission

of sins. Thus defined, he names Baptism, the
Lord's Supper, and Absolution, Sacraments. " For
these rites are appointed in the Gospel, and are employed to signify the promise that is peculiar to the
Gospel. We are baptised that we may believe that
our sins are forgiven. The Lord's Supper and Absolution admonish us to believe that our sins are
surely forgiven." In the Apology, Melanchthon
had declared that Absolution is a true Sacrament,
and there can scarcely be a doubt that he meant to
assign it the same dignity in the Augsburg Confession. Here he calls confession an ecclesiastical rite;
says it is not necessary, and that an enumeration of
sins rests upon no divine command. In the Lutheran
Church, Absolution is not reckoned among the Sacraments, nor put in a category with Baptism and the
Lord's Supper. This Church never has required an
enumeration of sins, and Private Confession has
fallen into desuetude.

4. *Infant Baptism.* Melanchthon puts the argument for Infant Baptism in the following syllogistic
form :

" It is certain that the Kingdom of God and the promise of salvation appertain to children. But there is no
salvation outside the Church where there is no Word and
no Sacrament. Therefore children must be united to
the Church, and the sign must be applied which testifies
that to them appertains the promise."

The major premise is established by numerous
passages from the New Testament and by the law of
16

circumcision. The minor is supported chiefly by the fact that the Church is the Kingdom of Christ, in which Christ operates through the Word and the Sacraments. There can be no Church without the Sacraments and the Word. He also quotes the Mosaic law, that the soul of every uncircumcised male shall be cut off from the people. The conclusion is that infants are to be baptised, and that by receiving the sign they become members of the Church, and God bestows upon them the promise. In opposition to the Anabaptist doctrine that infants cannot believe, he instances the fact that unbelief did not exclude them from the Mosaic covenant. He does not even intimate that infants can have faith. Nor has infant faith at any time been confessional in the Lutheran Church. The conclusion involved in Melanchthon's minor premise was fully accepted at Wittenberg, namely, that there is no salvation for the children of Jews and heathen,[1]—a harsh judgment which the Lutheran Church does not approve.

5. *The Lord's Supper*. On no other subject did Melanchthon bestow so much thought and investigation as on that of the Lord's Supper. As proof of this we reproduce a few quotations that have already appeared in this book. In 1537, he wrote, " For ten years neither day nor night has passed in which I have not reflected on this subject "[2]; and in 1529, he wrote to the Reutlingen pastors, " Not without the greatest struggles have I reached the conclusion that

[1] *C. R.*, 10 : 688.
[2] *C. R.*, 3 : 537.

Christ is truly present." [1] He also said, " I would rather die than affirm with the Zwinglians that the body of Christ can be in only one place." [2] At Augsburg he believed that he had expressed Luther's doctrine of the Lord's Supper in the tenth article of the Confession [3]; and he had already said that " Luther's doctrine is very old in the Church, and a good man will not rashly depart from the teaching of the ancients." [4] But when Œcolampadius, in his *Dialogue on the Teaching of the Ancients* (1530), showed that some of the passages from the Fathers relied on by Melanchthon were spurious, the faith of the latter in the correctness of some of his own representations was shaken. To Brentz he wrote, January 12, 1535.

" I am not willing to be the author or defender of a new dogma in the Church. I see that there are many passages of the ancients which certainly explain the mystery [sacrament] figuratively. There are also opposing passages, perhaps later, or spurious. We must be careful not to oppose the doctrine of the ancients." [5]

In this same letter he affirms " the true presence of Christ in the Supper," but he constantly refrains from defining the mode of the presence, and refers it to the *will* and to the *institution* of Christ. At Marburg, in 1529, he modified Luther's doctrine of oral manducation. In 1531 he forsook the theory of Ubiquity. He did not place either of them in the Confession, or in the Apology. A little later the

---

[1] *C. R.*, 1 : 1106.
[2] *C. R.*, 2 : 25.
[3] *C. R.*, 2 : 142.

[4] *C. R.*, 1 : 823, 830.
[5] *C. R.*, 2 : 824.

in pane (*in the bread*) was also given up.   Since 1538,
he seems to have surrendered the literal signification
of ἐστί (is) in the words of institution, but without
surrendering the doctrine of the real presence.   The
connection, whether physical or metaphysical, of
the body and blood of Christ with the material elements, and the presence of the body of Christ in the
bread, both so much emphasised by Luther in controversy, drop into the background with Melanchthon in view of the religious and ethical significance
of the Supper.   He regards the Eucharist more as a
pledge, a mystery, a communion with the entire
Christ, a salutary impartation of the God-man to
the believing human soul, a thanksgiving by which
we give thanks for the remission of sins.   " Whence
it occurs that Christ is in us not only by love, but
also by natural participation, that is, not only by
efficacy, but also by substance." [1]   Thus with Melanchthon, the religious significance of the Supper is
more important than the metaphysics of Dogma.
By joining the words of Paul (1 Cor. x. 16) with the
words of institution, Melanchthon sees in the Sacrament a fellowship with the body and blood of Christ;
and by associating the Sacrament directly with the
forgiveness of sins, he preserves the true Lutheran
type of doctrine, for with Luther, as with Melanchthon, the chief moment in the Sacrament is the assurance of the forgiveness of sins.   The Sacrament
is the application and appropriation of redemption.

All hangs on the words, " Given and shed for you
for the remission of sins."   Even the presence of

_____
[1] *C. R.*, 21 : 863.

the body and blood of Christ is entirely subordinate to these words. The heavenly gifts are but the sign and seals of the promise contained in these words. This position Melanchthon maintained with unyielding firmness, though in definitions, and in matters of form, he deviated from Luther. But the latter regarded the deviations of such small importance that he never called Melanchthon to account, nor uttered one word of disapprobation that has come down to us. Even when an Opinion of Melanchthon's " that under tyrants a person may use the sacrament with only one kind," had been treacherously divulged by Jacob Schenk, to whom it was given in confidence, and had excited some suspicion at the Electoral Court, and had led to inquiry, Luther simply said, " I will share my heart with Philip; I will pray for him." [1] Would to God that the same spirit of charity had always and everywhere prevailed in the Lutheran Church!

Moreover, Melanchthon always believed himself to be in harmony with Luther in the matter of the Supper; and well he might, since the latter, in 1525, had sanctioned the highly ideal and virtual presence of the body and blood, as it had been stated by Brentz and others in the Swabian Syngramma. [2]

Nowhere, perhaps, has the religious significance of the Supper been set forth more correctly in harmony with that which is *central* in the Lutheran doctrine than in the *Loci* of 1535.

---

[1] *C. R.*, 3 : 428.

[2] Köstlin's *Luther's Theologie*, ii., 147; English Trans., ii., 105.

" This cup is the New Testament, that is, the witness of the new promise. The sum of the Gospel or promise in these words is, This is my body which is given for you. Also: Which is shed for you for the remission of sins. Therefore the principal purpose of this ceremony is to testify that the things promised in the Gospel, remission of sins and Justification on account of Christ, are presented. As the chief thing we should consider that the sacrament is a sign of grace, that this Supper is a sign of the New Testament. But what is the New Testament ? Certainly it is the promise of the remission of sins and of reconciliation on account of Christ. Also this ceremony profits when we add faith, that is, believe that these promises belong to us, and that this sign is presented to our eyes and mind, to incite us to faith and to quicken the faith in us. For Christ testifies that his benefits belong to us when he gives us his body, and makes us his members, than which no closer union can be conceived. Likewise he testifies that he is active in us, because he is life. He gives blood to testify that he washes us. When we see these things done in that most Holy Supper, we ought to have faith."

In these views Melanchthon persisted to the end. As in 1527 he wrote, " The bread which we break is a communication of the body of Christ, not a communication of the spirit of Christ," [1] so in the last edition of his *Loci* in 1559 he wrote·

" This do in remembrance of me. It is not an empty spectacle, but Christ is truly present through the ministry giving his body and blood to him that eats. So also say the ancient writers. Cyril on John says: We must not

---

[1] *C. R.*, 26 : 19.

think that Christ is present in us by love only, but also by natural participation; that is, he is present not only in efficacy but also in substance." [1]

A few persons of narrow and partisan spirit tried to excite Luther against Melanchthon in view of the changes made in the *Loci*. But in this they utterly failed. Luther spoke kindly and sympathetically to Melanchthon about the criticisms. He knew too well how to distinguish between the form and the substance, not to perceive that Melanchthon had preserved and expressed the full truth of the Gospel. When the Elector read the German translation of the new *Loci*, he complained to Luther that the article on Justification was too meagre. There is no record of Luther's answer, but about this time he said to the students:

" Read Philip's *Loci* next to the Bible. In this most beautiful book the pure theology is stated in a quiet and orderly way. Augustine, Bernard, Bonaventura, Lyra, Gabriel Biel, Staupitz, and others have much that is good; but our Master Philip can explain the Scriptures and present their meaning in brief compass. By reason of affliction he has learned to pray, and he has disputed with the greatest and most learned opponents." [2]

This is high praise from a high authority, and ought to silence forever the clamours that have been raised against Melanchthon because he did not choose always to express his conceptions of divine truth in

[1] *C. R.*, 21 : 863.
[2] Matthesius, *Twelfth Sermon.*

the formulas of Luther.   If the great Luther could
magnify Melanchthon's work, there ought to be only
one opinion in regard to the small men who try to
belittle it; and as for the complaint of the Elector,
that was only a passing scruple.   He remained faithful to the estimate of Melanchthon which he had
formed when on the fifth of May, 1536, he added a
hundred florins to his and to Luther's salary, saying:

" In these times the merciful God has published his
holy Word through the work of the Reverend Doctor Martin Luther for the comfort and salvation of men; and in
connection with the other arts, particularly by the languages, through the special distinguished skill and diligence of the highly learned Philip Melanchthon, the true
Christian knowledge of the Holy Scriptures has been
advanced." [1]

And, what is more important, Luther placed what
may be called his testamentary seal on Melanchthon's *Loci*, and thus bequeathed it to posterity with
his blessing and benediction: In the Preface to the
first edition of his own works, he extols " Philip's
Loci Communes " above all other books of systematic divinity, and wishes that his own books might
be buried in oblivion in order to make place for
those that are better; and says finally:

" Philip Melanchthon was called hither by Prince
Frederick to teach Greek, but beyond doubt that I might
have a companion in the work of theology.   What God
has wrought through this organon, not only in letters,

---

[1] Seckendorf, iii., 142.

but in theology, his own works sufficiently testify, though Satan and his rabble rage.''

This was written in full view of the fact that in the edition of 1543 Melanchthon had still further changed the *Loci*, and had declared therein that '' Free will in man is the power by which he applies himself to grace.'' It would seem that the more Melanchthon revised the *Loci*, incorporating into it the acquisitions of study, and adapting it to new conditions, the better Luther liked it and the more loudly he praised it.[1]

---

[1] Volume 21 of *C. R.* contains the *Loci* in its different forms.

CHAPTER XX

THE WITTENBERG CONCORD

Melanchthon and Bucer at Cassel—Oberlanders Come to Wittenberg Articles of Union—Internal Feuds.

SOON after the Diet of Augsburg in 1530, the theologians of Upper Germany began to approach the Lutheran position on the doctrine of the Lord's Supper. The most active mediator of union was Martin Bucer of Strassburg. He prepared a formula in which he confessed that Christ is truly and essentially present in the Sacrament. Luther declared himself satisfied, " provided Bucer means it as the words sound." Melanchthon regarded it as a great thing that Bucer had confessed the true and substantial presence, and " seized the opportunity to unite the Church, and to harmonise distracting views." [1] As the Landgrave of Hesse had been and still was an ardent advocate of union, Melanchthon wrote him begging him to take the work of concord in hand, and promised to do all in

---

[1] *C. R.*, 2: 787.

his power to bring about Christian unity, " since in other articles there is no dissent." [1]

On the twenty-seventh of December, 1534, Bucer and Melanchthon, upon invitation of the Landgrave, met at Cassel to prepare a basis of agreement. The latter, that he might not appear wholly in his own name, requested an *Instruction* from Luther. This was given in language which brought out Luther's doctrine with a crassness that had not been before exhibited. He says: " *Our doctrine is, that in the bread or with the bread, the body of Christ is really eaten, so that all the motions and actions that are attributed to the bread, are attributed also to the body of Christ, so that the body is truly broken, eaten, and torn with the teeth.*" [2] He goes on to say that there is no middle ground, that it were better that each party should abide by its own opinion than that occasion should be given for new disputes. Writing of the *Instruction* to Jonas, December 16, 1534, he says, " I cannot recede from my position though the heavens should fall and bury me beneath their ruins." [3] Of course Melanchthon could not approve such a formula, and hence he afterwards declared that he went to Cassel " as the bearer of another's, not of his own view." [4]

There could be no approximation on the basis of Luther's *Instruction;* but the two conferees agreed on and signed the following statement:

---

[1] *C. R.*, 2 : 787.
[2] Seckendorf, iii., 8, xxviii.
[3] De W., 4 : 569.
[4] *C. R.*, 2 : 822.

" That the body of Christ is really and truly received, when we receive the Sacrament; and bread and wine are signs, *signa exhibitiva*, which being given and received the body of Christ is at the same time given and received; and we hold that the bread and body are together, not by a mixing of their substances, but as a sacrament, and are given with the sacrament.   As both parties hold that bread and wine remain, they hold that there is a sacramental conjunction." [1]

When Luther read the agreement he was delighted with it, and announced that union was virtually accomplished.[2]   That the other theologians might not have occasion for " protest or offence," Melanchthon acquainted them with the proposed formula, and solicited their opinions.   For the most part the opinions returned were favourable.   Everything now seemed propitious for union.   Melanchthon declared, " Could I purchase union by my death, gladly would I give my life," [3] and Luther wrote that he would do all in his power to strengthen and maintain concord.[4]   At Bucer's suggestion, it was soon arranged to hold a meeting of the Oberlanders and Wittenbergers at Eisenach, May 14, 1536.   But because of Luther's indisposition, the place of meeting was changed to Grimma, the time to May 21st.   The Oberlanders coming to Grimma and learning that Luther was still indisposed, decided to press on to Wittenberg.   Melanchthon and Cruciger went to

---

[1] *C. R.*, 2 : 808.
[2] De W., 4 : 588.
[3] *C. R.*, 2 : 837.
[4] De W., 4 : 612.

meet them, and gave them a formal invitation. Sunday, May 21st, at three o'clock P.M., they entered the university town on the Elbe. The next day the colloquy began. Luther insisted that Bucer and his associates should renounce their earlier teaching, and should confess the real presence of Christ in the Eucharist, independently of the faith of the recipient, and own that the body and blood are received by worthy and by unworthy communicants. When this was assented to by the Oberlanders, except that they made a distinction between reception by the *unworthy* and by the *wicked*, denying the latter, Luther expressed himself satisfied, and declared·

"We have now heard your answer and confession, viz., that you believe and teach, that in the Lord's Supper the true body and true blood of Christ are given and received, and not alone bread and wine: also, that this giving and receiving take place truly and not in imagination. Although you take offence in regard to the wicked, yet you confess with St. Paul that the unworthy receive the Lord's body, where the institution and word of the Lord are not perverted;—about this we will not contend. Hence, as you are thus minded, we are one, and we acknowledge and receive you as our dear brethren in the Lord." [1]

It was a great moment. Bucer and Capito shed tears, and the hand of brotherly recognition was given and received. Melanchthon, who of late had not been sanguine of good results, and during the

---

[1] Köstlin's *Martin Luther*, ii., 349.

colloquy had been active chiefly in averting passionate disputes, was now commissioned to draw up a form of concord. While he was employed at this the two parties discussed Baptism, Private Confession, and Absolution, and reached satisfactory conclusions. Bugenhagen, Menius, Myconius, Alber, Bucer, and Luther preached, and all went to the communion. The Oberlanders were especially pleased to see that the Wittenberg ministers officiated with perfect indifference either in civil or in priestly attire. They were offended by the presence of pictures and candles, and by the elevation of the elements; but were quieted when informed by Bugenhagen that some things were retained out of regard for the weak, and that he often officiated without candles, or clerical attire, or the elevation. He also told them that the elevation ought to be abolished. A few years later it was abolished, through the influence of Melanchthon.

On Friday morning Melanchthon laid the proposed Articles of Concord[1] before the Oberlanders. In the afternoon the parties met and discussed the matter of extending the concord to wider circles. Monday, the 29th, the articles on the Lord's Supper were subscribed by twenty-one persons. These articles deny transubstantiation, the local inclusion of the body of Christ in the bread, or the lasting union without the use, as when it is laid by in the pyx or displayed in processions. They affirm " that with the bread and wine the body and blood of Christ are truly and substantially present, presented,

---

[1] *C. R.*, 3 : 75. Translated in Jacobs' *Book of Concord*, ii., 254.

WITTENBERG IN 1546.

and received." They close by saying that "all profess that in all articles they want to hold and teach according to the Confession and Apology of the princes professing the Gospel."

The articles on the Lord's Supper are followed by an article on Infant Baptism, and one on Absolution. It is held that infants ought to be baptised, since to them pertains the promise of salvation, and "since it does not pertain to those who are outside the Church. God works new and holy movements in infants, without which they cannot be saved; though we must not imagine that infants understand." A desire is expressed that private absolution be retained for disciplinary ends, "so that the inexperienced may be instructed."

The *Wittenberg Concord*, as it is known in history, failed to effect a lasting union; but it remains as one of Melanchthon's most useful writings, and as a lasting monument of an honest effort on both sides to close the chasm between the forces of the Reformation, which, alas! yawns to this day. Luther begged that both sides might bury the past and roll a stone on it. But Melanchthon wrote that the difference was so great that what had just been done would only stir up reprehension.[1] In this he was not wholly mistaken. The Swiss were displeased with Bucer's concessions; the Nurembergers were dissatisfied that Bucer would not confess the presence of Christ even apart from the use of the Eucharist, and Amsdorf thought that a formal recantation should have been required of Bucer.

[1] *C. R.*, 3: 81.

With all his efforts to make peace, Melanchthon was not allowed to enjoy it.

In July of this year (1536) he sought and obtained permission from the Elector to visit his brother at Bretten, and Camerarius at Tübingen.   Evil tongues circulated the report that Philip had quarrelled with Luther and his other colleagues, and would not return to Wittenberg.   Others said that even should he return, all harmony was at an end, because of Melanchthon's erroneous teaching.[1] From Nuremberg Melanchthon wrote a letter to his colleagues in which he courts investigation, and declares that he had only sought to explain what they had taught. The letter is couched in lofty terms of righteous indignation, and closes by saying:

" Never have I meant to sever my teaching from yours, but if I am to be loaded with the suspicions and calumnies of certain men, and must be in dread of alienations, I would rather go to the ends of the earth.   I complain of these things to you rather than to others.   I am unwilling to be the cause of any dissidence between us. Heartily do I love and cherish each one.   Also I am devoted to the public welfare.   If my labours and a fair amount of diligence in every duty do not witness for this, then in vain do I cry out in this matter.   But I hope you thoroughly understand me.   I have never refused admonition and friendly conference.   Each one has his own gift.   I have taken nothing upon myself, nor have I ever wished to offer anything new.   I have read your writings and to the extent of my ability, I have wished to expound them in the most simple manner." [2]

[1] Camerarius, 163.

[2] C. R., 3: 180.

This manly speech had the desired effect. When Melanchthon returned to Wittenberg, November 5th, he found his colleagues wholly on his side, and indignant at the fomenters of discord. No further notice was taken of the matter at Wittenberg.

But scarcely had Melanchthon time to forget the strife with Cordatus about *Good Works* before he was brought under suspicion again. Jacob Schenk, a Freiberg preacher, inquired whether it were permissible under stringent circumstances to administer the communion with one element. Melanchthon answered that, to avoid offence, in the case of those not sufficiently instructed, it might be done. The answer did not please Schenk, and so he sent Melanchthon's letter to the Elector, who requested Luther and Bugenhagen to inquire into the matter. It was on this occasion that Luther said, " I will share my heart with Philip. I will pray for him." Melanchthon called Schenk the Freiberg sycophant.

Amsdorf, the passionate Magdeburg preacher, had long striven to excite Luther against Melanchthon; and now when, in 1537, Cardinal Sadolet, a mild and learned Catholic, wrote Melanchthon a letter praising his moderation, and when a little later a letter of Sadolet's complaining of Luther's violence was printed and circulated at Wittenberg, Luther grew suspicious, and others called Melanchthon a deserter. But when Luther learned that Melanchthon had not answered the Cardinal's letter, he became convinced that the Catholics were only courting Philip to win him over, and he exclaimed sarcastically: " If Philip would consent, they would readily

17

make him a Cardinal and let him keep his wife and children " He knew well that Melanchthon would never consent. It was about this time also that Melanchthon came into unfriendly relations with the learned but contentious Osiander of Nuremberg on the subjects of Private Absolution and Original Sin Osiander wished to retain Private Absolution to the exclusion of the General Absolution, and had also declared that Original Sin is a part of the soul. Melanchthon wished to retain both kinds of Absolution, and named Original Sin a corruption of all the powers of the soul. He communicated some propositions to Osiander on the subject of sin, but the latter only replied in an unfriendly and insulting manner. There was no open controversy, but Osiander became one of Melanchthon's most bitter enemies.

In the year 1537, Luther had a controversy with Agricola, who declared that Moses should be hanged, and that the Law should be relegated to the Court-House. Luther called him an *Antinomian*, and powerfully refuted him in several Disputations. Melanchthon at length restored peace between them; but Agricola remained hostile to the Wittenbergers, and especially to Melanchthon.

These controversies were so purely of a personal nature that they awoke no serious opposition to Luther or Melanchthon and utterly failed to alienate these two great men.[1]

---

[1] Amsdorf seems to have been the most active in creating in the mind of Luther suspicions of Melanchthon. Also γυναικοτυραννίς, as Cruciger writes, sometimes stood in the way of the most frank and confidential intercourse between the two Reformers.—*C. R.*, 3 : 398.

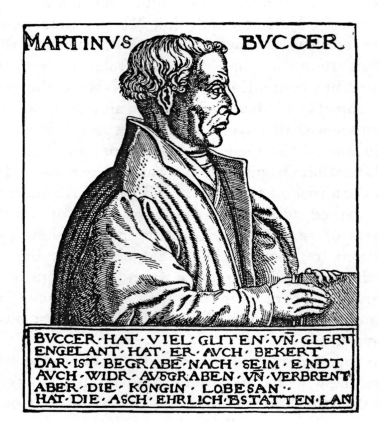

MARTINVS   BVCCER

BVCCER·HAT·VIEL·GVTEN·VN̄·GLERT
ENGELANT·HAT·ER·AVCH·BEKERT
DAR·IST·BEGRABE·NACH·SEIM·ENDT
AVCH·WIDR·AVSGRABEN·VN̄·VERBRENT
ABER·DIE·KŌNGIN·LOBESAN·
HAT·DIE·ASCH·EHRLICH·BSTATTEN·LAN

DR. MARTIN BUCER.

Indeed on the subject of Good Works, Luther so decidedly approximated to the position of Melanchthon, that the latter in sending a copy of Luther's discourse on the subject to Veit Dietrich, says: " Luther discourses eloquently on the subject which I defended, and on account of which I have been abused by ignorant men." [1]

[1] *C. R.*, 3 : 427.

CHAPTER XXI

MELANCHTHON'S WILL

Schmalkald Convention—Melanchthon's Subscription and Appendix to the Schmalkald Articles—Frankfort Convention—Calvin—Melanchthon Plans the Reorganisation of the Leipzig University —Melanchthon's Will.

JUNE 2, 1536, Pope Paul III. announced a council to be opened at Mantua, May 23d of the following year. The Protestant Estates now called a convention to be held at Schmalkald, February 7th, and the Elector instructed Luther and the rest of the theologians to revise the articles of faith and to report to him before January 25th. Instead of revising the Confession, Luther prepared new articles of faith, which, after having been approved and subscribed by his colleagues and some neighbouring theologians, were sent to the Elector, January 3d.[1] The series is divided into three parts. Part I. states briefly the doctrines of the Trinity and of the Person of Christ. Part II. discusses the Office and Work of Christ. Part III. contains the articles on which the Protestants were willing to treat with

---

[1] De W., 5 : 46.

learned and prudent men. These Articles, because
they were laid before the convention at **Schmalkald**
in February, 1537, are known as the **Schmalkald**
Articles. They are the most positive and antipapal
of all the Lutheran Confessions, and are in effect a
declaration of war against Rome. Melanchthon,
influenced by his love of peace, and by his prefer
ence for a Church government independent of the
State, subscribed with the following qualifications:

" I, Philip Melanchthon, regard the foregoing articles
as right and Christian. But of the Pope I hold that if
he will permit the Gospel, the government of the bishops
which he now has from others, may be *jure humano*
also conceded to him by us, for the sake of peace and
the common tranquillity of those Christians who are, or
may hereafter be under him."

At **Schmalkald** these articles were subscribed by
many other theologians, but not by the princes, inasmuch as they had decided to decline the Pope's
offer of a council, because the proposed council was
not to be held in Germany, " would not be a free
council," and " appealed the entire matter to the
arbitrament of the Pope." [1]

While the princes were deliberating on the political aspects of the situation, Melanchthon composed
an Appendix to the Articles, the object of which
was to set forth the position of the evangelical party
in regard to the Papacy.

This Appendix is a most learned refutation of the
claims of the Papacy touching the divine right of its

---

[1] *C. R.*, 2 : 1018–1022.

existence and of its supremacy over the bishops.
In this document Melanchthon considers the Papacy
as it was at that time, and not ideally and according
to its original intention, as he had conceived of it
in his qualified subscription to the Articles.   Hence
there is no contradiction between his actions.   Even
the Articles had conceded to the bishops the right
jure humano of governing the Church and of or-
daining preachers, on condition that " they would
faithfully discharge their office." The Appendix
is in every way in harmony with the Articles, and
with the sentiment that prevailed generally among
the Protestants on the subject of which it treats.
In learning, moderation, firmness, dialectic skill
and fidelity to evangelical principles, it is not surpassed by anything that ever came from its author.
Indeed he alone of all the theologians assembled at
Schmalkald had the necessary qualifications to compose such a tractate, and thus to render such a
signal service to the State and to the Church, by
exposing the unfounded assumptions of the hierarchy, and by vindicating the right of the churches
" to ordain for themselves pastors and other church
officers." The Appendix was signed by no less
than thirty-four ministers and theologians in the
Recess of the Convention.   For a time it had higher
authority than the Articles themselves, inasmuch as
it had in view the new relations in which the princes
and Estates had placed themselves by declining the
offer of a general council.

After that Melanchthon, at the instance of the
Estates, had composed several other treatises, and

with the other theologians had commended to the
princes a better administration of the Church property, he left Schmalkald, March 6th, and on the
14th was at home in Wittenberg.

The resolution of the princes at Schmalkald to
decline the papal offer of a council aggravated the
already greatly strained relations between themselves and the Catholic princes.   The latter, desiring
to strengthen the Papacy, met at Nuremberg, and
on June 10, 1538, formed the Holy League.   Two
leagues now stood in hostile attitude toward each
other; and though they both claimed to exist purely
for defence, yet so great was their mutual distrust,
that war appeared imminent.   Philip of Hesse actually counselled war; but the Electors, Joachim of
Brandenburg, and Louis of the Palatinate, offered
themselves as mediators, and proposed a council at
Frankfort, to which an imperial ambassador might
come.   The proposition was accepted, and February
1, 1539, Melanchthon set out with his Elector to
Frankfort.   The convention resulted in a truce,
April 19, 1539, the terms of which bound both sides
to keep the peace for fifteen months.

At Frankfort, Melanchthon wrote several important Opinions on subjects of current interest, and
addressed letters to influential princes and scholars.
The letter to Henry VIII. of England, dated March
26, 1539, was well calculated to produce a good
effect on the mind of that monarch.   After alluding
to Henry's "heroic virtues," he says:

"I commend to Your Majesty the public cause of the
Christian religion, for Your Majesty knows that the chief

duty of great princes is to promote and defend the heavenly doctrine. For this reason God associates them with himself in ruling. I am desirous, as I have often previously written, that agreement in the pure doctrine should be established in all those Churches which condemn the tyranny and wickedness of the Roman Bishop. Such agreement would show forth the glory of God, and would serve to attract other nations, and to prolong the peace of the churches." [1]

This letter adds another proof of the determination of the Reformers to make agreement in doctrine the first condition of their religious alliances.

At Frankfort Melanchthon made the personal acquaintance of Jacob Sturm and John Calvin. He here contracted a friendship with the latter which was broken only by death. Calvin has given a lively account of the Frankfort Convention, and of certain conversations held with Melanchthon. These conversations related principally to church union and to matters of discipline. Melanchthon is reported as assenting to certain articles prepared by Calvin, as having deplored the obstinacy and despotism of cert ain of his own party, and as having expressed the wish that the *Wittenberg Concord* might last until the Lord should lead both sides into the unity of His own truth. [2]

The Truce of Frankfort, which required the continued observance of the Peace of Nuremberg, was altogether favourable to the Protestants; and when in the same year, April 17, 1539, Duke George died,

[1] *C. R.*, 3 : 671.
[2] Bonnet's *Calvin's Letters*, i., 116 *et seqq.*

and was succeeded by his brother Henry, all ducal
Saxony was opened to the Gospel.

Soon Melanchthon and other Wittenbergers were
called to Leipzig to begin the work of reform. Melanchthon was commissioned especially to regulate
the affairs of the university and to bring them into
harmony with the proposed new order. He recommended, among other things, that, " because the
monks and sophists still utter their calumnies and
will not cease," they be forbidden to preach, to
dispute, and to lecture. He proposed Nicholas
Amsdorf, John Hess, of Breslau, or, in case he could
not come, Alexander Alesius, a Scotchman, and
Bernhard Zeigler, as professors of theology. Certain revenues from the cloisters were to be applied
to the university; stipends for theological students
were to be established; and the new professors were
to have a place and a vote in the counsels of the
university. His plans were adopted, and in a short
time, after some discussions between the new theological professors and the Dominicans, the university came under Protestant control. During the
summer, Melanchthon visited the churches in parts
of the Dukedom and assisted in the formal introduction of evangelical doctrine and worship. He found
many of the clergy ignorant and leading scandalous
lives. A little later in the same year he went to
Berlin to assist Joachim II. in introducing the Reformation into his dominions. Cochlæus attributes
the blame, as he calls it, of Joachim's conversion, to
Melanchthon. Be this as it may, we have a pleasing letter written by Melanchthon in the name of

the Elector to his father-in-law, Sigismund, King of
Poland, in which the last-named is informed that a
moderate reformation, free from fanaticism, is to be
introduced into Brandenburg.[1]

Melanchthon's letters of this year are of especial
interest. Not only do they contain an immense
amount of information touching current ecclesiastical affairs, but they show his deep interest in the
work of the Reformation, his ardent yearning for
harmony among the Evangelicals, and his fixed determination " to hold on to the true consensus of
the Catholic Church of Christ, as it is exhibited
in the apostolic Scriptures, in the old canons, and
by the writers of recognised authority."[2]

Such is the language he puts in the mouth of
Joachim, and, no doubt, it is at the same time a
faithful reflection of his own mind. His attitude
toward the venerable institutions of the Church was
conservative, but it was always subordinated to
sound doctrine.

Melanchthon had now reached the climacteric year
of forty-two. His health had greatly declined. He
writes that he " is worn out with labours, sorrows,
and insomnia." Believing that death was near at
hand he made his last Will and Testament,[3] which
he designed chiefly to be a confession of faith. As
this document exactly defines its author's theological position, and illustrates his method of study, and
shows the design with which from time to time he

---

[1] *C. R.*, 3 : 789 *et. seqq.*
[2] *C. R.*, 3 : 789 *et seqq.*
[3] *C. R.*, 3 : 825 *et seq.*

changed the *form* of his writings, we present it in full, as follows ·

" In the name of God the Father, of the Son, and of the Holy Spirit.

" It appears that the chief purpose for which at first wills were made, was that fathers might leave to their children a sure testimony of their views in regard to the religious faith which they wished to have transmitted to posterity, sealed, as it were, with the highest authority; also that they might obligate their children to retain and conserve the same views, as we see by the will of *Jacob* and of *David*. Therefore also Christ in this manner made his will. And because wills have contained explicit, sure, and unchangeable views of inspired doctrine, the magnitude of the matter has increased the authority of wills. Wherefore also as a memorial to my children, and to some friends, I have desired to begin my will by reciting my confession, and by enjoining upon my children, as becomes a father, the duty of abiding steadfastly in the same views.

" In the first place, I return thanks to God the Father of our Lord Jesus Christ who was crucified for us, the Creator of all things, because he has called me to repentance and to the knowledge of the Gospel; and I pray him for the sake of his Son, whom he wills to be a sacrifice for us, to pardon all my sins, to receive, justify, hear me, and to deliver me from eternal death. This I believe truly he will do. For thus he has commanded us to believe. And it is impiety to magnify our sins above the death of the Son of God. This latter I magnify above my sins. Moreover, I pray God for the sake of his Son our Redeemer, by the Holy Spirit to increase in me these beginnings of faith. I am indeed distressed by my sins, and by the scandals of others; but I magnify the death of the Son of God, that grace may abound over sin.

" In the second place, I declare that I truly embrace the Apostles' and the Nicene Creed; and in regard to fhe entire Christian doctrine, I hold as I have written in the *Loci Communes*, and in the last edition of the *Commentary on Romans*, in which, article by article, I have striven to say without ambiguity what I hold.

" In regard to the Lord's Supper I embrace the Form of Concord [the *Wittenberg Concord*] which was made here.   Therefore I united myself with our churches, and I declare that they profess the doctrine of the Catholic Church of Christ, and that they truly are churches of Christ.   I also enjoin upon my children to abide in our churches, and to flee the churches and society of the Papists.   For the Papists in many articles profess the most corrupt doctrine: they are absolutely ignorant of the doctrine of Justification by Faith, and of the Remission of Sins; they teach nothing about the difference between the law and the Gospel.   In regard to the worship of God they hold heathenish and Pharisaical notions.   To these errors they also add many others, besides manifest idolatry in their Masses and in the worship of dead men. Therefore I beseech my children on account of the command of God to obey me in this matter and not to join the Papists.

" And since I see that posterity is threatened with new commotions of doctrines and of the Church, and that there will probably be fanatical and trifling spirits who will overthrow the articles of the Son of God and of the Holy Spirit, I wish to warn mine to adhere to the views which I have professed with the Catholic Church of Christ in the *Loci*, where I condemn Samosatenus and

Servetus, and others who dissent from the received Creeds.

" It is also probable that new sophistries of a seductive nature will come after a while, when the old errors, somewhat changed in colour, will be re-established, and these conciliatory measures will corrupt the pure doctrine, as it is now taught. I also admonish mine not to approve these sophistical attempts to conciliate.

" The learned also are to be exhorted to watch, lest under the semblance of peace and public tranquillity they accept such doctrinal confession as was promulgated at the Syrmian Synod. This I can truly affirm, viz., that I have striven truly and properly to explain the doctrine of our Church, that the young may rightly understand our views and transmit them to posterity. If this form is profitable, as I think it is, I request *Caspar Cruciger* and others who have been my pupils, to conserve it in the schools.

" I know that certain persons have at times suspected that I have done some things to favour the adversaries. But I call God to witness that I have never wished to favour the adversaries; but I have sought accuracy in explanation in order that these things when freed from ambiguity might be better understood by the young. How difficult it was for me to attain to such order and method in explanation, many know, who know that in explaining, I often changed the form. It is evident that the Augustinian form is not sufficiently explicit. Hence I declare that with a pure motive I studied the method which is employed in the *Commentary on Romans*, and I desire to leave behind me distinct views, without ambiguity, because ambiguity afterwards produces dissensions. Nor has it been my purpose to present any new opinion, but clearly and properly to expound the Catholic doctrine, which is taught in our churches, which by the special blessing of God I declare to have been revealed in these recent times through *Doctor Martin Luther* in order that the Church which had almost perished might be cleansed and restored. Therefore so long as we can, let us preserve this light. And I pray God the Father of our Saviour Jesus Christ, the Creator of all things, to promote the studies of the pious, and to preserve the Church, and especially to bless our churches which on account of the Gospel are daily attacked.

"But I return thanks to Doctor *Martin Luther*, first because from him I learned the Gospel. Then because of the many kindnesses shown me by him, I wish him to be cherished by mine not otherwise than as a father. Because I have seen and discovered that he is endowed with an excellent and heroic quality of mind, with many great virtues, with piety, with eminent learning, I have always honoured and loved him, and have felt that he should be esteemed.

"I also return thanks to the Prince, *John Frederick*, Elector of Saxony, whose special kindness and liberality were extended to me. I pray God to keep him safe, to defend and direct him to his own and to the common safety of the Church and of many nations.

"Very grateful also was the kindness of Chancellor *Pontanus* [Brück], whom on account of the excellent character of his mind and his virtue, I have loved, and to whom I return thanks for all his kindnesses.

"I also return thanks to other good men, who have shown abiding constancy in our friendship, to my brother *George*, Joachim *Camerarius*, Chancellor *Francis* [Burkhard], Doctor *Jonas*, Doctor *Pommer*, *Cruciger*, Doctor *Augustin* [Schurf], Doctor *Milich*, Paul *Eber*, *Veit* [Dietrich]; and I pray God to preserve them.

" Nor do I suppose that these friendships are extinguished by my death; but I hold that after a little while we shall meet in eternal life, where we shall more perfectly enjoy our friendship and where our intercourse will be sweeter.

" I also entreat all persons graciously to pardon my errors, if in anything I have offended anyone. Certainly I have not wished to injure.

" I also return thanks to all my colleagues and fellow-teachers in the University, because in many ways both publicly and privately they have kindly assisted me."

This Will was written on or just before November 12, 1539, and was reaffirmed the following summer. It therefore stands in the closest chronological and doctrinal relation to the edition of the Augsburg Confession published in 1540, an account of which will be hereafter given. The *Loci* and the *Commentary on Romans*, to which it appeals, are the editions respectively of 1535 and 1532, the same which Luther so heartily endorsed and commended a few years later. It thus becomes a demonstration of the doctrinal harmony that existed between Luther and Melanchthon; and even if there were no other evidence, it fully justifies the affirmation of Nicholas Selneccer that Luther and Melanchthon did not differ in doctrine,—which affirmation, however, must not be pressed to the extreme of indicating absolute coincidence, but a coincidence which found its expression in common symbols, and in learned treatises, of which Melanchthon was the author.

CHAPTER XXII

MELANCHTHON AND PHILIP OF HESSE

Colloquy of Hagenau—Melanchthon's Sickness—The Landgrave's Bigamy—Confessio Variata—The Tenth Article of the Confession.

THE winter of 1539–40 wore away heavily for Melanchthon. His presentiment and "dream" of impending death came near being realised. When in May, 1540, attended by magisters and students he crossed the Elbe on his way to the Hagenau Colloquy, he exclaimed, "*Viximus in Synodis et jam moriemur in illis*," that is, " I have lived in conventions, in conventions I shall now die."

At Weimar he fell seriously ill, so that his life was despaired of. The Elector sent him the court physician and summoned Luther and Cruciger from Wittenberg. Solomon Glass has left us a graphic account of the scene in Melanchthon's chamber when Luther entered. He says:

" When Luther arrived he found Melanchthon apparently dying. His eyes were sunk, his senses gone, his speech stopped, his hearing closed, his face fallen in

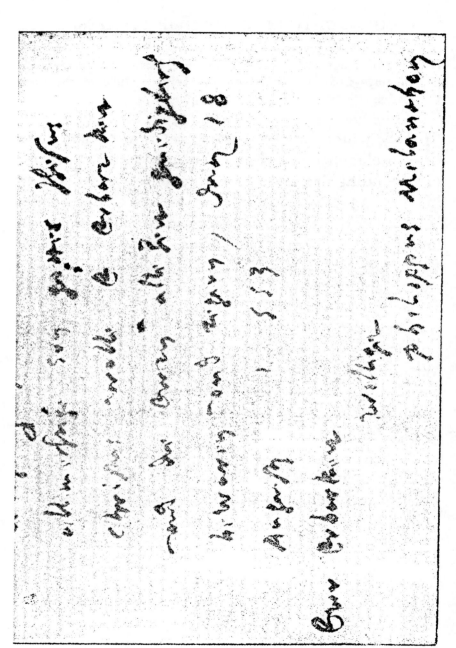

FACSIMILE OF CLOSING PORTION OF A LETTER FROM MELANCHTHON TO THE AUTHORITIES OF

and hollow, and, as Luther said, '*facies erat Hippo-cratica*" He knew nobody, ate and drank nothing. When Luther saw him thus disfigured, he was frightened above measure, and said to his companions, *God for-fend! how has the devil defaced this Organon!* He then turned forthwith to the window, and prayed fervently to God. *Then*, said Luther, *our Lord God could not but hear me ; for I threw my sack before His door, and wearied His ears with all His promises of hearing prayers, which I could repeat out of Holy Writ ; so that He could not but hear me, if I were ever to trust in His promises.* Here-upon he grasped Philip by the hand: *Be of good courage, Philip ; thou shalt not die. Although God has reason to slay, yet He willeth not the death of a sinner, but that he should be converted and live. He has pleasure in life, not in death. If God called and received the very greatest sinners that ever were on earth, Adam and Eve, again into favour, much less will he reject thee, my Philip, or let thee perish in sin and despair. Therefore give no place to the spirit of sorrow, and be not thine own murderer ; but trust in the Lord, who can slay and make alive again, can wound and bind up, can smite and heal again.* For Luther well knew the burden of his heart and conscience. Being thus taken hold of and addressed, Philip began to draw breath again, but could say nothing for a good while. Then he turned his face straight upon Luther, and be-gan to beg him for God's sake not to detain him any longer,—that he was now on a good journey,—that he should let him go,—that nothing better could befall him. *By no means, Philip*, said Luther; *thou must serve our Lord God yet longer.* Thus Philip by degrees became more cheerful, and let Luther order him something to eat; and Luther brought it himself to him; but Philip refused it. Then Luther forced him with these threats, saying: *Hark, Philip, thou must eat, or I excommunicate thee.* With these words he was overcome, so that he ate a very little: and thus by degrees he gained strength again."[1]

The immediate cause of Melanchthon's sickness was remorse over the part which he and Luther had taken in the bigamy of Philip of Hesse.[2] Influenced mainly by a desire to save the Landgrave from his besetting sin, they, without sanctioning bigamy as a principle, had given a *quasi* consent to his marriage with Margaretha von der Salle, but had enjoined strict secrecy. Their action cannot be approved. There was a better way, and that way should have been followed. As the matter has been much misrepresented, we reproduce the letter sent to the Landgrave by Luther and Melanchthon as their Opinion. It was written by Melanchthon:

" Since your princely Grace has through Master Bucer laid before us a certain longstanding trouble of your conscience, although it is difficult for us to answer in such haste, we would not let Bucer ride off without a letter. And first, we are heartily rejoiced and thank God that He has helped your Grace our of your dangerous sickness; and we pray that He will strengthen and preserve your Grace in soul and body to His praise. For, as your Grace sees, the poor miserable Church of Christ is small and forsaken, and verily needs pious lords and princes; as we doubt not God will preserve some, although every kind of temptation befall. With regard

---

[1] Seckendorf, iii., 314.
[2] *C. R.*, 3 : 1073.

to the question, of which Master Bucer spoke with us, first, this is our opinion. Your Grace knows and understands this yourself, that it is a very different thing to make a general law, and in a particular case to use a dispensation, out of weighty reasons, and yet according to divine permission; for against God no dispensation has force. Now we cannot advise that it be openly introduced, and thus made a law, that each be allowed to have more than one wife. But should anything of this get into print, your Grace may conceive that this would be understood and adopted as a general law, whence much scandal and trouble would ensue. Therefore this is by no means to be adopted; and we pray your Grace to consider how grievous it would be, if it were charged upon anyone that he had introduced this law in the German nation, whence endless trouble in all marriages might be feared. As to what may be said against this that what is right before God should be allowed altogether, this is true in a measure. If God has commanded it, or if it is a necessary thing, this is true; but if it is not commanded, nor necessary, other circumstances should be taken into account. Thus with regard to this question: God instituted marriage that it should be the union of two persons alone, and not of more, unless nature has been corrupted. This is the meaning of the saying, *They two shall be one flesh.* And this at first was so retained. But Lamech introduced the example of having more than one wife at once, which is recorded of him in Scripture as an innovation contrary to the first rule. Thenceforward it became customary among the unbelievers, till at length Abraham and his descendants took more than one wife. And it is true that afterward this was allowed in the Law of Moses, as the text says, Deut. xxi. 15, *If a man has two wives*, etc. For God gave way somewhat to

the weakness of nature.   But since it was according to
the first beginning and the creation that a man should
not have more than one wife, this law is praiseworthy,
and has thus been adopted in the Church: nor should
another law be made and set up against it.   For Christ
repeats this saying, Matt. xix. 5, *And they twain shall be
one flesh*, and reminds us how marriage was to be first
antecedently to man's infirmity.   That in certain cases
however a dispensation may be used,—as if a person
taken captive in a foreign land should marry there, and
on gaining his freedom should bring his wife with him,
—or if long continued sickness should supply a cause, as
has been held at times with regard to lepers,—if in such
cases a man takes another wife with the counsel of his
Pastor, not to introduce a law, but as a matter of necessity, such a man we could not condemn.   Since then it
is one thing to introduce a law, and another to use a dispensation, we humbly entreat your Grace to consider,
first, that care should in every way be taken that this
matter be not brought publicly before the world, as a law
which everybody may follow.   Next, since it is to be no
law, but merely a dispensation, let your Grace also consider the scandal, namely, that the enemies of the Gospel
would cry out, that we are like the Anabaptists, who take
several wives at once, and that the Evangelicals seek the
liberty of having as many wives as they please, according
to the practice in Turkey.   Again, what princes do, gets
abroad much further than what is done by private persons.   Again, if private persons hear of such an example
in their lords, they desire that the like should be allowed
to them; as we see how easily a practice spreads.
Again, your Grace has an unruly nobility, many of
whom, as in all countries, on account of the great
revenues which they derive from the Chapters, are vio-

lently opposed to the Gospel. Thus we know ourselves that very unfriendly speeches have been heard from divers young squires. Now how such squires and the country folks will behave toward your Grace in this matter, if a public proceeding be adopted, may easily be conceived. Again, your Grace, through God's grace, has a very illustrious name, even among foreign kings and potentates, and is feared on account thereof, which credit would be impaired hereby. Seeing then that so many scandals are combined, we humbly entreat your Grace to consider this matter well and diligently. This, however, is also true, that we by all means entreat and exhort your Grace to avoid fornication and adultery; and in truth we have long had great sorrow from hearing that your Grace is laden with such distress, which may be visited with punishments from God and other dangers; and we entreat your Grace not to esteem such matters out of wedlock a light sin, as the world tosses such things to the wind and despises them. But God has often fearfully punished unchastity: for it is recorded as a cause of the Deluge, that the rulers practiced adultery. Again, the punishment of David is a solemn example: and Paul often says, *God is not mocked: adulterers shall not enter into the Kingdom of God.* For faith must be followed by obedience, so that one must not act against one's conscience, nor against God's commandment. *If our conscience condemn us not, then have we confidence toward God:* and *if through the Spirit we mortify the deeds of the body, we shall live; but if we live after the flesh,* that is, against our conscience, *we shall die.* This we say, because it is to be considered that God will not trifle with such sins, as many people now grow bold to entertain such heathenish thoughts. And we have heard with pleasure that your Grace has seriously mourned on account thereof, and feels sorrow and repentance for them. These great and weighty questions press for your Grace's attention, pertaining to the whole world. Moreover, your Grace is of a slender and far from a strong constitution, and sleeps little; wherefore your Grace should reasonably spare your body, as many others are forced to do. And we read of the illustrious Prince Scanderbeg, who wrought many noble deeds against the two Turkish emperors, Amurath and Mahomet, and protected and preserved Greece as long as he lived. He, they say, specially exhorted his soldiers to chastity, and said that nothing takes away a brave man's spirit like unchastity. Again, even if your Grace had another wife, and did not seriously resist the evil practice and inclination, it would not avail your Grace. It behooves man in his outward walk to bridle his members, as Paul says: *Yield your members as instruments of righteousness.* Therefore let your Grace, in consideration of all these causes, the offence, the other cares and labours, and the weakness of body, weigh this matter well. Be also pleased to consider that God has given your Grace fair young princes and princesses with this consort; and be content with her, as many others must have patience under their marriage, to avoid offence. For that we should excite or urge your Grace to an offensive innovation, is far from our mind. For your country and others might reproach us on account thereof, which would be intolerable to us; because we are commanded in God's word to regulate marriage and all human matters according to their first divine institution, and, so far as possible, to keep them therein, and to avert whatever may offend anyone. Such, too, is now the way of the world, that people like to throw all the blame upon the preachers, if anything unpleasant fall out; and men's hearts, among high and low, are unsteady: and all sorts of things are to be feared. But if your Grace do not quit your unchaste life,—or that you write that this is not possible,—we would rather that your Grace stood in better case before God, and lived with a good conscience, for your Grace's happiness, and the good of your country and people. If, however, your Grace should at length resolve to take another wife, we think this should be kept secret, as was said above of the dispensation; namely, that your Grace, and the Lady, with some confidential persons, should know your Grace's mind and conscience through confession. From this no particular rumour or scandal would arise; for it is not unusual for princes to have concubines; and although all the people would not know what the circumstances were, the intelligent would be able to guess them, and would be better pleased with such a quiet way of life, than with adultery and other wild and licentious courses. Nor are we to heed everything that people say, provided our consciences stand right. Thus far, and this we deem right. For that which is permitted concerning marriage in the law of Moses, is not forbidden in the Gospel, which does not change the rule of outward life, but brings in eternal righteousness and eternal life, and kindles a true obedience to God, and would set our corrupt natures straight again. Thus your Grace has not only our testimony in case of necessity, but also our advice, which we beseech your Grace to weigh, as an illustrious, wise Christian Prince; and we pray that God may lead and direct your Grace to His praise and to your Grace's happiness." [1]

---

[1] *C. R.*, 3: 856. This *Opinion* was signed by Luther, Melanchthon, Bucer, Corvin, Fulda, Leming, Winter, Melander, and Raid. Translation from Hare's *Vindication of Luther.*

Luther, by the power of his faith, rose above his mistake, and denounced the Landgrave; but the more conscientious Melanchthon broke down under it.   He realised his error, and foresaw that the Landgrave's bigamy would bring reproach to the cause of Christ.   Perhaps the most inexplicable feature of the whole transaction is, that one so fearless as Luther, and one so frank as Melanchthon, should have enjoined secrecy in a matter which in itself they did not regard as wrong.

After his recovery from his sickness, Melanchthon wrote to Camerarius:

"I cannot describe the pain I suffered during my sickness, some returns of which I often feel.   I witnessed at that time the deep sympathy of Luther, but he restrained his anxieties that he might not increase mine, endeavouring to raise me from my desponding state of mind, not only by administering kind conversation, but salutary reproof.   If he had not come to me I should certainly have died."

Melanchthon was excused from going to Hagenau. At the convention no important conclusions were reached.   On the twenty-eighth of July, 1540, a new diet was appointed to meet at Worms in October.   Meanwhile, or perhaps earlier, Melanchthon published a new Latin edition of the Augsburg Confession.   Already in the year 1535 he had written to several of his friends that he was engaged in revising the Apology (Confession) and the *Loci*. His object was to make some of the discussions more luminous.   To Myconius in particular he wrote:

NICHOLAS AMSDORF.

" I am revising the Apology [Confession], and am making it almost wholly new, *ut habeat minus Sophistices*," that is, " that it may have less sophistry." [1]   It is thus plain from his letters that Melanchthon was revising the Confession and the *Loci* at the same time; and that he did not conceal his work from his Wittenberg colleagues is evident from a letter written by him to them all, November 1, 1536, in which he speaks of having revised the Apology (Confession) in order " to express some things more explicitly "   He continues: " I do not shun your opinion nor that of *Amsdorf*.   I have nothing in view except to explain most accurately what you teach, because I know that some persons have mistaken notions about such great subjects." [2] Bindseil examined all of Melanchthon's letters from May 1, 1535, to the end of the year 1540, and as he nowhere found in them any allusion to the preparation and publication of an edition of the Confession during these years, he concluded that the revised edition was completed and printed in 1535, and wonders that no copy bearing that date is known to exist.   Peucer, Melanchthon's son-in-law, contends that this new edition was prepared in 1538.   Selneccer gives the same date of preparation.   But as no copies of the *Variata* of that, or of an earlier, date have been found, we cannot now go back of the edition which bears the title:

---

[1] *C. R.*, 2: 861, 871.
[2] *C. R.*, 3: 180.

CONFESSIO
FIDEI EXHIBITA
INVICTISS. IMP. CAROLO
V. Caesari Aug. in Comicijs
AVGVSTÆ.
ANNO. M. D. XXX.
Addita est Apologia Confessi-
onis diligenter recognita.
PSALMO. CXIX.
*Et loquebar de testimonijs tuis in
conspectu Regum, et non con-
fundebar.*
VITEBERGAE. 1540.

This is the *Confessio Variata*, or the *Altered Confession*, of history, which for a time was more widely
used both publicly and privately than any and all
other Latin editions of the Confession.

This revised edition can no more be regarded as a
private writing by Melanchthon than the first edition of 1530–31 can be so regarded, since that edition
was not authorised by the Elector, nor by the theologians, and " was changed, especially in the German
text, in many places,"[1] whereas the evidence is in-
disputable that the edition of 1540 was prepared by
the command, and with the advice and assistance
of Luther, for the purpose of having it presented at
the diets. Not only do we have the testimony of
Peucer, Melanchthon's son-in-law, to this fact, but
that also of the theologians and superintendents at
the Altenburg Colloquy in 1569; and David Chy-

---

[1] Oehler, *Symbolik*, p. 133.

træus, Nicholas Selneccer, and Martin Chemnitz, all of whom assisted in the preparation of the Formula of Concord of 1577–80, testify that the *Variata* was presented at the Diets of Worms and Regensburg, and at the subsequent diets, and was constantly appealed to by the Lutherans as their Confession which was delivered to the Emperor in 1530. These are facts which have never been called in question. Moreover, it was approved by Westphal, an arch anti-Calvinist, by the rigidly Lutheran *Weimar Confutation Book*, and was expressly named and subscribed by nearly all the princes assembled at Naumburg in 1561, as a fuller and ampler explanation of the original Augsburg Confession. It was highly praised also by John Brentz, a strict Lutheran. It is thus absolutely conclusive that Melanchthon's contemporaries applauded and sanctioned his efforts to improve the Augsburg Confession; and no one found fault with it during the author's lifetime.[1]

The first to call invidious attention to the *Variata* was John Eck, the bitter foe of the Reformation. At the Diet of Worms, in January, 1541, he took exceptions to the alterations in the text. Melanchthon at once replied: " The meaning is the same, though in the later edition here and there some things have been softened or rendered plainer."[2] This put an end to the complaint, and the edition continued to be employed in the Diet by the Evan-

---

[1] See Weber's *Kritische Geschichte der Augs. Conf.*, ii., 300–310. Also Köllner's *Symbolik*, i., 253, 254.

[2] *C. R.*, 4 : 34, 37.

gelicals, notwithstanding the fact that the Saxon
Elector had charged his delegates to abide by the
Augsburg Confession.

At the Weimar Disputation between Strigel and
Flacius, August 5, 1560, the former refuted the
latter out of the *Variata*. In the afternoon Flacius
returned to the debate with the supplementary answer that Balthaser Winter, the deceased Superintendent of Jena, had said that he had heard the
deceased George Rorer say that Luther did not like
it that Melanchthon had changed the Confession.
Strigel, referring to Eck's procedure at Worms,
replied that that was a papistical subterfuge, and
the debate passed on to the discussion of the next
proposition.[1] That is, against the written testimony of the most eminent and upright men of
the age, we have only this reputed hearsay of a
hearsay of a dead man, an after-thought conjured
up to cover the mortification of defeat—an anti-
Philippistic fabrication, which is now regarded by
historians as worse than apocryphal. Hence he
who charges Melanchthon with intentional corruption of the Confession not only involves *him* in
falsehood, but makes Luther, Brentz, Chytræus,
Selneccer, Chemnitz, and others either partakers of
his sin, or the dupes of his deception.

Melanchthon's letters show that during the period
of revision he was most solicitous about improving
the Fourth Article, Justification by Faith. He
says: " We ought to thank the adversaries because
they compel us to revise this article, which amid

---

[1] Salig, *Hist. Augs. Conf.*, iii., 604.

other less important disputes has almost ceased to be heard."[1]   In the *Variata* the Fourth Article is greatly expanded, and is guarded against the possibility of being misunderstood.   It is against the Tenth Article chiefly that objection has been raised. In the *Unchanged Confession* the Tenth Article reads as follows: "*De Cœna Domini docent, quod corpus et sanguis Christi vere adsint et distribuantur vescentibus in Cœna Domini, et improbant secus docentes.*"   That is · "Of the Lord's Supper they teach that the body and blood of Christ are truly present and are communicated to those that eat in the Supper; and they disapprove those that teach otherwise."

In the *Variata* the Tenth Article reads thus: "*De Cœna Domini docent quod cum pane et vino vere exhibeantur corpus et sanguis Christi vescentibus in Cœna Domini.*"   That is: "Of the Lord's Supper they teach that with the bread and wine the body and blood of Christ are truly presented to those that eat in the Supper."

There can be no doubt that Melanchthon intended to place the Lutheran doctrine, generically stated, in the Tenth Article of the *Invariata*.   He wrote to Veit Dietrich, June 26, 1530: "The Landgrave has subscribed the Confession with us, though the article of the Lord's Supper is in accordance with Luther's doctrine."   But more than once it has been conceded that the Tenth Article of the *Invariata* does not exhibit the Lutheran doctrine of the Lord's Supper in a form sufficiently explicit.   Erhard Schnepf says

---

[1] *C. R.*, 2 : 484, 504.

that when the Confession was adopted at Augsburg,
many persons regarded the adverb *vere* (truly) as
ambigious.[1]   That the article is capable of a Roman
Catholic interpretation is shown by the fact that
both officially and privately it has been so interpreted by Romanists.   The instances are too
numerous and too well known to need specification.[2]
These things being so, it can be readily understood
what the theologians of Electoral Saxony meant
when they said : " Because of the adversaries of the
pure doctrine of the Gospel, and their cavils, a
clearer and plainer statement had to be made in
order that opportunity for cavilling might be removed," [3] — which corresponds in substance with
Melanchthon's reply to Eck, viz., that certain
things had been softened or rendered more explicit.
Schmidt says that Melanchthon's aim was

" to find the most distinct forms in order to prevent any
misunderstanding.   In the Apology he had treated
Christian doctrine in the usual manner in order to make
approach and agreement with the Catholics the easier.
But now approach seemed scarcely possible.   By the
Schmalkald articles against the papacy the Protestants
had openly broken with the Roman Catholic Church.
Besides, the enemy had abused the Confession of 1530
by explaining its mild language in *their own* sense, and
in order to demand new concessions from the Protestants.

---

[1] *Confes. de Eucharistia.*
[2] See the first Catholic *Confutation*, also that of August 3d ;
Cœlestin's *Hist. Augs. Con.*, ii., p. 235 ; *Ibid.*, iii., p. 43 ; Alois
Knöpfer's *Ch. Hist.*
[3] *Altenburg Colloquy*, p. 314.

Hence a more definite wording of the Confession had become necessary." [1]

All the known facts go to justify this conception. Besides, there was no longer any need of the damnatory clause, since the Oberlanders had accepted the Confession and Apology.

The interests of peace, the union of the evangelical forces against a common foe, and the keeping of faith with the Oberlanders, required at that time, according to Melanchthon's own words, " that the discords should be healed rather than exasperated." [2] It was only when Melanchthon could no longer answer for himself, when the bitter animosity of the Jena school had broken out in fierce accusations against Wittenberg, that Melanchthon was charged with having changed the Tenth Article in favour of the Calvinistic doctrine of the Supper. It was a pure calumny, manufactured in the interest of partisan zeal. The evidence is conclusive that Melanchthon never departed from the Lutheran view of the Lord's Supper, nor ever hesitated to reaffirm his adherence to the Augsburg Confession of 1530, as in the Repetition of the Augsburg Confession in 1551, in the Preface to the Mecklenburg *Kirchenordnung*, in the *Examen Ordinandorum*, and at Worms in 1557, when he expressly rejected the Zwinglian doctrine.

The formula by which in the *Variata* he expresses the Lutheran doctrine " that with the bread and wine the body and blood of Christ are truly pre-

---

[1] *Philipp Melanchthon*, p. 375.
[2] *Letters*, iii., p. 230.

sented to those that eat in the Lord's Supper,"
makes a difference in words, not in the original intention, and brings the Tenth Article into harmony
with the *Wittenberg Concord*, which had been officially endorsed by the princes in 1537. The words
are those chosen by Melanchthon under the counsel
and with the approval of Luther, and endorsed both
privately and officially by the men of their generation as the words best suited to express the Lutheran
doctrine without ambiguity, and to free it from the
fact as well as from the possibility of a Roman
Catholic interpretation. Nor would it be possible
to interpret these words in a Calvinistic sense without substituting *credentibus*, " those that believe,"
for *vescentibus*, " those that eat." And this is the
conclusion to which candid and orthodox Lutherans
have at length come.

CHAPTER XXIII

MELANCHTHON AT REGENSBURG

The Diet of Worms—The Regensburg Diet—The Regensburg Book—The Partial Agreement—Melanchthon's Aphorisms—His Steadfastness and Independence—His Report on the Regensburg Book—Publication of his Works.

THE Diet of Worms was opened January 14, 1541. The Protestants presented the Augsburg Confession, that is, the *Variata*, as the basis of the Colloquy. Eck and Melanchthon were chosen as the speakers. Eck who had examined the German original at Mayence, complained that the copy of the Confession laid before the Diet did not agree with that which had been presented to the Emperor at Augsburg. Melanchthon answered that " the meaning was the same, though in the later copies milder and plainer words were used." Eck made no further complaint, and at once took up the articles. The Colloquy was now begun. As never before did Melanchthon's skill in debate manifest itself. He commanded the admiration of all. He showed marvellous acquaintance with the Scriptures and with the fathers, and spoke in the most beautiful Latin. Francis Burkhard wrote to Chancellor Brück: " Doctor Eck has found his man; it looks to me like the meeting of David and Goliath. I do not doubt that the truth will come off victorious."[1] Others said: " Master Philip's speech is as the song of the nightingale; Eck's like the croaking of the raven."[2] Melanchthon's eloquence was surpassed only by his modesty. When Eck sought to entrap him by some sophism, he paused to consider the matter, and then said, " I will give you an answer to-morrow." " Oh," replied Eck, " there is no honour in that, if you cannot answer me immediately." Then fell the memorable words: " My good Doctor, I am not seeking my own glory in this cause, but truth. I say then, God willing, you shall have an answer to-morrow."[3]

The discussion centred chiefly round the doctrine of Original Sin, but no agreement was reached. January 18th, the Colloquy was brought to a close, or rather transferred to Regensburg, where the Imperial Diet was to be held the next Spring. Melanchthon wrote to Camerarius: " My anxiety has been greatly increased by this debate. It is not arms and violence that I fear, but deceitful speeches and sophistries. In these colloquies we cannot sufficiently guard ourselves against treachery."[4] In

---

[1] C. R., 4: 23.

[2] C. R., 25.

[3] Adami Vitæ, p. 329. See Melanchthon's report of the Diet in C. R., 4: 34 et seqq.

[4] C. R., 4: 88.

several letters he gives accounts of the Colloquy, and speaks hopefully of Granvella, the Imperial Chancellor, who had presided; but he has no good words for Eck.   Melanchthon returned home at once after the proroguing of the Diet, and took up his work in the university.   He was thoroughly disgusted with colloquies, and begged to be excused from going to Regensburg.   But his wish was not gratified, as the Elector needed his ablest theologians at the Diet. March 14, 1541, he left Wittenberg, and on the 16th he joined the other delegates at Altenburg.   On the Bavarian frontier the carriage in which he rode was overturned, and he was violently thrown to the ground.   His wrist was so badly sprained that for a time he could not write.   The injury followed him through life.

The Diet was opened April 5th.   Frederick, Count Palatine, and Granvella presided.   The Emperor selected Julius von Pflug, John Gropper, and John Eck from the Catholics, and Philip Melanchthon, Martin Bucer, and John Pistorius from the Protestants, to discuss the articles of religion. When the debate was about to begin, April 27th, the Emperor presented the colloquists, through Granvella, with a book, with the request to examine it, and to correct whatever they found in it contrary to the Scriptures, but to suffer all that was Christian to remain.   This book, of uncertain authorship, known as the *Regensburg Book*, was half Catholic and half Protestant, and contained doctrines to which neither party could consent without giving up its principles.   Eck said it *Melanchthonised* too

much, but Melanchthon totally disclaimed it.
Various articles were discussed, and agreement was
attained on Justification, the Freedom of Man,
Original Sin, Baptism, Good Works, and Episco-
pacy, but not on any other articles.[1] During the
discussion of the Eucharist, Melanchthon uttered
two aphorisms, that have come to be regarded as
axiomatic in the Lutheran doctrine of the Lord's
Supper: " Nothing has the nature of a sacrament
apart from the divinely appointed use." " Christ is
not present for the sake of the bread, but for the
sake of man." Eck was so confounded by Melanchthon's speech that in default of argument he
first raved, then got drunk, and falling sick never
returned to the Diet.[2] Granvella was so impressed
by the speech that he said, " This is a grave matter,
and is worthy of the attention of a council."[3]
When Melanchthon's aphorisms were reported to
Luther, he exclaimed: " Brave Philip, you have
snatched from the papacy what I should not have
dared to attempt," and he wrote to the Elector that
Melanchthon and the other delegates had stood
bravely by " the dear confession."[4]

Melanchthon's steadfastness was also greatly
praised by his colleagues, who reported that he declared that he would rather die than yield anything
in the Conference against his conscience, for it would
be death to him to go contrary to his conscience.[5]
The independence also which Melanchthon exhibited

---

[1] Seckendorf, iii., 35.   [4] De W., 5 : 357.
[2] C. R., 9 : 626.   [5] C. R., 4 : 225.
[3] Ibid.

at Regensburg is worthy of all praise.   It had been insinuated that he was simply the mouthpiece of Luther.   In a noble and manly letter to the Emperor he declares that he has no instructions from Luther, and only general directions from the Elector to adhere to sound doctrine.

" I know," he says, " that the doctrines of our churches are the doctrines of the Church Catholic. This, I think, is confessed by many wise men, though they think that in removing abuses we are harsher than is necessary.   They wish to retain a kind of saint-worship, private masses, and the like.   Hence they want us to take a backward step, and to approve the beginnings of abuses.   Since I cannot do this, I ask again to be dismissed." [1]

When Melanchthon's steadfastness was reported to the Elector, he wrote to his commissioners · " We have heard with great satisfaction that Master Philip has conducted himself with firmness and decision. May the Almighty God graciously sustain him in his course." [2]

On June 24th, Melanchthon presented a report on the Regensburg Book.   It contains a masterly discussion of all the articles in dispute, and closes with as brave words as ever came from any man's pen:

" For the reasons given I conclude upon the Word of God and with a good conscience that I cannot and will not receive this book, and I pray God the Father of our

[1] C. R., 4 : 318.
[2] C. R., 4 : 346.

Lord Jesus Christ that he will grant us all good counsel and help, and will protect and govern his Church, which he has redeemed by his Son and still wonderfully preserves. And that everyone may know what I believe, I will here declare that I hold the doctrine of our churches as it is comprehended in our Confession and Apology, and by God's grace I intend to abide in it. And I thank God that he has enlightened his Church; nor do I wish to give occasion for obscuring the pure doctrine again. No one can truthfully charge that I have pleasure in useless strife. For it is manifest from my writings that with the greatest diligence I have sought and maintained mildness and moderation. I also pray God for peace and Christian unity; and I am ready for a further declaration." [1]

At length, on July 29th, the Recess of the Diet was announced. The unreduced differences were to be referred to a council, or to a diet of the Empire; the Protestants were to refrain from writing against the articles agreed upon; the Bishops should intro duce a Christian reformation; the Nuremberg Peace should be maintained.

The Regensburg Diet marks a climax in the reformatory movement. Neither before nor afterward was the Emperor, or the Curia through its legates, so conciliatory; but the Papalists would not recede from what the Protestants regarded as fundamental errors. Hence there could be no agreement. At Rome, Germany was regarded as lost, and the gravest apprehensions were entertained concerning the Netherlands and France. The fact is, the Reform-

[1] *C. R.*, 4 : 413-431.

ation had gained such a distinct dogmatic consciousness that it could not recede from its position, and
it had acquired so much political strength that it
could not be suppressed by the sword. If the
Schmalkald League had helped to give the movement political strength, Melanchthon more than any
other man had helped to give it dogmatic consciousness and confessional dignity.

On the thirtieth of July, 1541, Melanchthon left
Regensburg for home by the way of Leipzig, where
he had sought a place for his friend Camerarius,
whom he commended to Duke Henry as " peaceable, quiet, and conscientious, and so learned in
philosophy and eloquence as to be surpassed by few
at home or abroad." [1]   Henry called Camerarius, August 14th, and, dying soon thereafter, was succeeded
by his son Maurice.   August 7th, we find Melanchthon in Wittenberg, and October 26th he addressed
a letter to Camerarius, now at Leipzig.   During the
autumn and winter he was as usual very active with
his pen.   In December, an edition of his works
was published at Basel.   January 20, 1542, he was
present when Luther consecrated Nicholas von
Amsdorf as Bishop of Naumburg.   In March Luther wrote: " Master Philip is well and hearty.   He
is doing more than all the rest.   He is the Atlas
who sustains heaven and earth." [2]   Some idea of
his labours may be gained when it is learned that
his letters alone during the year 1542 extend from
page 749 to page 942 in the *Corpus Reformatorum.*

[1] *C. R.*, 4 : 638.
[2] De W., 5 : 452.

CHAPTER XXIV

THE COLOGNE REFORMATION

Melanchthon Invited to Bonn—Hermann's *Consultation*—Controversy—Strained Relations between Melanchthon and Luther.

THE incoming year (1543) imposed new duties.
The Reformation had extended its influence
to the region of the Lower Rhine. In December,
1542, Archbishop Hermann of Cologne had invited
Bucer to Bonn to preach the Gospel. In January,
1543, he invited Melanchthon to come to him to
assist in instituting reform in religion, and requested
the Elector of Saxony to allow him to come. As
the request was in support of " a godly and christian
work," and was favoured by Luther and Camerarius,
the Elector gave his consent to Melanchthon's
going, and sent him a hundred gulden and an escort.
May 4th, attended by Justus Jonas, Jr., and Jerome
Schreiber he entered Bonn. He found the religious
ignorance greater than he had supposed it was. To
Luther he wrote:

" I think there is scarcely a place in Germany where
there is so much barbarism, even heathenish superstition

as in these parts.   Heretofore the people ran to the images.   Now I observe that the preaching of Bucer and Pistorius is largely attended, and I note that they both preach purely and correctly.   There are also others in the neighbouring towns who teach correctly, and rightly administer the sacraments." [1]

Two plans of reformation had been submitted: One by John Gropper, the archiepiscopal chancellor, who wrote " only painted articles," as Melanchthon called them ; and one by Bucer, who had taken the Brandenburg-Nuremberg Church Order as his guide. Melanchthon spent three days in revising some of Bucer's articles on doctrine, and wrote several new articles, but left those on the sacraments as Bucer had written them, because they were in harmony with the teaching in all Lutheran churches.[2] The result of his and Bucer's labours are embodied in the book known as Hermann's *Consultation*, which Lutherans have unhesitatingly claimed as a genuine Lutheran Church Order, which, translated into English and published in 1547, exerted an important influence on *The Book of Common Prayer*.

The *Consultation* was rejected by the Chapter and clergy of Cologne.   Gropper wrote a book against it, called *Antididagma*.   It was also lampooned by a Carmelite monk, named Billich, whom Melanchthon describes as " a fatted priest of Bacchus and Venus."   The Chapter and clergy, having gained the upper hand at Cologne, preferred charges

---

[1] *C. R.*, 5 : 112.
[2] De W., 5: 670.

against the Archbishop before the Emperor and the Pope. April 16, 1546, the aged Hermann was deposed.

While at Bonn Melanchthon was very uncomfortable in his surroundings, but very busy with his pen. Besides his contributions to the *Consultation*, he wrote a *Response* to Billich's satire. He first refutes the slanders that the Protestants have forsaken the doctrine of the Church Catholic; that they oppose the civil government; and that they are influenced in their movements by considerations of worldly gain. He then paints in striking colours the superstitions of the Roman Church, the corruptions of monasticism, and the evils of celibacy. Of doctrine he says: " We mutilate no church dogma, but only attack recent errors which have crept in contrary to the Gospel and the judgments of the purer church." The *Response* was published with a characteristic Preface by Luther. It covers twenty-two folio pages, and has been pronounced one of the noblest defences of Protestantism ever penned.[1]

Some idea of the double discomfort of Melanchthon's situation at Bonn may be learned from the following letters. To Peter Martyr he wrote, July 14th: " I have attended many conventions, yea, battles; but I have never happened among more rabid and impudent sycophants."[2] And to Paul Eber:

" I am living here the life of a sailor. My lodgings

---

[1] Witt. Ed., i., 95 *et seqq.*
[2] *C. R.*, 5 : 143.

are by the Rhine just where the boats land, whence comes the foul stench of the bilge-water. In the house everything, the table, the bed, the fireplace, are crowded together just as in a boat. The wine is wretched; the cooking is Westphalian. The cleanliness is far from that of France, or of the Upper Rhine. It is also expected that the imperial army will pass through these parts." [1]

July 28th, Melanchthon " tore " himself from this scene of controversy and discomfort and turned his face homeward. At Frankfort, he adjusted a controversy over some ceremonies connected with the sacraments, and proceeded thence to Weimar, whither he had been summoned by the Court. August 15th, amid an ovation of students and professors, who had gone forth to meet him, he entered Wittenberg.

Hermann's *Consultation* was soon published, and became the innocent cause of much sorrow to Melanchthon. The article on the Lord's Supper is Lutheran, but it is not stated in rigid Lutheran formulas. The subject is treated practically, rather than doctrinally. The Archbishop sent a copy of the *Consultation* to the Elector of Saxony, who sent it to Amsdorf for examination. Amsdorf, who was more Lutheran than Luther, and had long been hostile to Melanchthon, severely criticised the articles on the Will and Sacrament, and sent his criticisms to Luther, who had not yet read the *Consultation*. The latter was pleased with the criticisms, and con-

---

[1] *C. R.*, 5 : 142.

demned the *Consultation* because " it says not a
word against the fanatics," and does not mention
" the oral reception of the true body and blood." [1]
Luther was at the time violently excited against the
Swiss on account of their views of the Sacrament.
He calls Bucer *Klappermaul* (babbler), and in private
conversations, in public lectures and sermons, he
spoke against the Sacramentarians with all the
vehemence of former years. Gossips, busy-bodies,
and strife-makers were doing their despicable work.
The report went out that Luther was going to make
an attack on his old friend.

Melanchthon was now plunged into the deepest
grief, and began to talk of going into exile. August
28th (1544), he addressed Bucer as follows:

" I wrote you by Milich that our Pericles is about to
thunder most vehemently on the Lord's Supper, and that
he has written a book, not yet published, in which you
and I are beaten black and blue. Amsdorf, whom he
recently visited and consulted on the matter, is applaud-
ing the assault. To-morrow, as I learn, he will summon
Cruciger and me. I pray God to grant the Church and
us a salutary result. Perhaps it is God's will that the
subject be agitated again, that it may be further explained. I am calm and will not hesitate to withdraw
from this penitentiary should he attack me." [2]

Finally, in October, 1544, Luther published his
book under the title, *A Short Confession on the
Holy Sacrament against the Fanatics*. Zwingli and

[1] De W., 5 : 708.
[2] *C. R.*, 5 : 474.

Œcolampadius, both long since dead, are branded
as heretics and murderers of souls.   The Reformed
generally are named " eingeteufelte, durchteufelte,
ueberteufelte lästerliche Herzen und Lügenmäuler."
That is· " Blasphemers and liars, possessed and
permeated through and through by the devil."   But
neither Melanchthon, nor Bucer, nor Calvin, is
named or alluded to.   Malicious persons had striven
to excite Luther against Melanchthon; but in this
they signally failed; for even after he had decided
to write this new Confession, he had declared, " I
have absolutely no suspicion in regard to Philip " [1];
and a month after the publication of this Confession
he wrote to the Venetians: " If you should hear
that Philip or Luther has yielded to the insane
error of the Sacramentarians, for God's sake do not
believe it " [2]; as in the previous year he had spoken
of Bucer as orthodox, and by letter had commended
Melanchthon's *Loci* and his commentaries on Romans
and Daniel to the Venetians; though in his ardent
hostility to the Swiss, he not only affirmed in this
letter the oral reception of the body and blood, but
actually so far forgot himself as to write: *De trans-
substantiatione rejicimus inutilem et sophisticam dis-
putationem, nihil morati, si quis eam alibi credat, vel
non.*   That is: " We reject the useless and sophistical dispute about transubstantiation, but we do not
care whether anyone elsewhere believes it, or not," [3]
—which gave Melanchthon great distress, as he fore-

[1] De W., 5 : 645.
[2] De W., 5 : 697.
[3] De W., 5 : 568.

saw the controversies that would arise from Luther's " concession of transubstantiation, which is the source of idolatry." [1]

During this same crucial period the Elector also expressed his entire confidence in Melanchthon, and actually forbade Luther to attack him, since he was faithful and true, and could not be spared from the university [2] Yet this precaution was unnecessary, for there is not a word to be found in Luther's private correspondence, nor elsewhere from his pen, nor a recorded syllable from his lips, to show that he at any time meant to attack Melanchthon, or that during this period he had become seriously alienated from him, or that he was displeased with his doctrinal position; though his attitude towards his colleagues during the summer of 1544 was one of suspicion and unfriendliness.   He had quarrelled violently with the law faculty over the validity of secret betrothals, and at home he " was inflamed by the domestic firebrand," Frau Luther, " who could not endure those theologians who had married wives from the common people," and who, besides lording it over her husband at home, was just then meddling with public affairs.[3]   Under these circumstances Luther had " become quite morose and very irritable " His imperious temper had gotten the better of his reason, and had made him misanthropic, and so despondent that in disgust he left Wittenberg with the intention of never returning.   No one

---

[1] C. R., 5 : 208.

[2] C. R., 5 : 746.

[3] C. R., 5 : 314 and note 4.

could tell where his thunderbolts would strike; yet
it was perhaps a weakness in Melanchthon that he
did not go to Luther during this period of tension,
as he did afterward, and explain his position.   But
when Luther had actually gone from Wittenberg, it
was Melanchthon who declared that he would not
live there without him, and actually went to Merseburg and brought him back.[1]

When Melanchthon saw he had not been attacked
by Luther, and when Luther himself had become
calmer, the old friendly relation was restored.   Melanchthon sat again at Luther's table, and the two
took journeys together, and joined their labours in
promoting the cause which was dear alike to each.
As a basis for new negotiations with the Catholics,
Melanchthon prepared a formal statement of doctrines and ceremonies to be laid before the approaching conference at Worms.   The work is known as
The Wittenberg Reformation.[2]   It is essentially a
confession of faith in expressed harmony with the
Augsburg Confession, and was signed by the entire
Wittenberg theological faculty, thus showing that
the faculty was united in doctrine and in ceremonies.
The Elector thought it too mild, but his Chancellor,
Brück, praised it for its mildness, and because it
" bore no traces of Luther's turbulent spirit."   He
particularly notes its harmony with the Augsburg
Confession, and thinks it will effectually silence the
cry of the Catholics that the Protestants are seeking
their own glory.   He is pleased also with the fact

---

[1] Matthes, *Philipp Melanchthon*, p. 246.
[2] *C. R.* 5 : 577 *et seqq.*

that the other theologians have united with Melanchthon in this document.[1]

A part of *The Wittenberg Reformation* was laid before the Diet at Worms, and a part was withheld; but no part of it became the basis of negotiations. The Emperor simply requested the Protestants to submit to the Council. This they refused to do, and demanded the continuance of peace. To gain time to prepare for more violent measures, the Emperor adjourned the Diet, August 4, 1545, and announced another to meet at Regensburg, January 6, 1546, which was to be preceded by a colloquy on religion.

As the Protestants suspected that war was now resolved upon, they assembled at Frankfort, in December, to renew and strengthen the Schmalkald League. They reached no important conclusions, except to resolve to attend the Colloquy, and to oppose the Council which was opened at Trent, December 13, 1545. Melanchthon was commissioned to set forth "the reasons why the estates of the Augsburg Confession will not attend the Council of Trent." After presenting a list of grievances against the papacy, and severely taxing its errors, he says:

"We have allowed no new opinions to be propounded in our churches. On the contrary, we profess the old, true, only pure doctrine of the Church of God; and that it may be known what that is, we point to our Confession delivered at Augsburg, which contains a summary in harmony with the Apostolic, the Nicene, and the Athanasian Creeds."

[1] *C. R.*, 5 : 660.

This *Recusation*, as it is called, ranks as one of Melanchthon's most incisive writings. In its very positive and aggressive tone it reminds one of the *Schmalkald Articles* written by Luther. It shows that in dealing directly with the Roman Catholic errors, its author had no concessions to make. Luther himself, who died before the document was completed, could not have desired anything more decisive. It closes by saying:

" We have no pleasure in strife, neither do we mistake our perils and distresses; but we cannot allow the light of the Gospel and the necessary doctrine of God's Church to be extinguished, nor can we pollute our souls, and all future generations, by fellowship with cruelty." [1]

Melanchthon had been ordered to hold himself in readiness to attend the Regensburg Colloquy as chief disputant on the side of the Protestants. Early in January he returned with Luther from a visit to Mansfeld, broken down in health. Luther now importuned Brück orally, and the Elector by letter, January 9, 1546, not to send Melanchthon to Regensburg,

" because he is really sick, and ought to be in bed rather than at the Colloquy. Philip ought not to be sacrificed in such a vain and unnecessary work, for the opposite party are wicked faithless people. Philip is a true man. He fears and shuns no one, but he is weak and sick. It cost not a little effort to fetch him from Mansfeld, for he did n't want to eat or drink. Should he be taken from

---

[1] Bindseil's *Supplementa* to Melanchthon's Works, p. 239 *et seqq.*

the University half the students will leave in consquence of his absence. Doctors Zoch and Major should be sent. For though the latter is timid in such matters, on account of inexperience, yet he is more learned than the Emperor's Ass " [1]

The letters of Brück and Luther to the Elector furnish the most indubitable proof of the confidence which both reposed in Melanchthon, and show the interest they took in his comfort. There is no intimation that the great lover of peace would betray the evangelical cause, or surrender a point of doctrine. When Melanchthon was informed that Luther had counselled against his going to Regensburg, and had learned the reasons, he expressed himself entirely satisfied; though he said he would rather go to Regensburg than to engage again in the wretched transactions which had previously called him and Luther to Mansfeld. However, as the Elector ordered him to Torgau to speak for himself, he went thither and was formally excused. While at Torgau he wrote an *Opinion* on the Colloquy. He advised that the Article of Justification should be considered first. If the opposite party would not allow this Article, the Colloquy should be brought to an end with the protest: " Since the opposite party will not listen to this plain article it is useless to proceed." [2]

The Protestants followed Melanchthon's advice. When it became apparent that no conclusion could

---

[1] *C. R.*, 6 : 10 ; and De W., 5 : 774.
[2] *C. R.*, 6 : 15.

be reached, the Emperor demanded that the colloquists should not divulge the transactions. He
also cast obstacles in the way of peace, and tried
to throw the blame on the Protestants. Now it
was that Melanchthon cried out that the Emperor
might enjoin silence on his Spaniards, but not on
German freemen. He wrote an *Opinion*, and advised
the delegates to protest. This they did, March 20,
1546, and returned home, '' promising to come again
whenever the Emperor should command it.''

CHAPTER XXV

THE INCREASE OF SORROWS

Luther and Melanchthon's Last Correspondence—Luther's Death—
Melanchthon's Funeral Oration over Luther—His Letter about
Luther—Alliance against the Protestants.

THE year 1546 was one of the darkest and saddest
of Melanchthon's life. In October and December of the previous year he and Luther had
together gone to Mansfeld to settle the shameful
disputes between the counts. Their success had
been only partial, and the counts desired that they
should continue the good offices of mediation.
Melanchthon was excused from going because of ill
health. Luther made ready to go, and, January
20th, invited Melanchthon to sup with him. This
was the last time that Melanchthon sat at Luther's
table Three days later Luther started for Mansfeld, not to return alive. The letters which passed
between the two during the next three or four weeks
furnish an abiding proof of the admiration and love
which each had for the other. Melanchthon's letter
of February 18th, the day on which Luther died,
is addressed, "To the Reverend Doctor Martin

Luther, distinguished for his learning, virtue, and wisdom, Doctor of theology, Restorer of the pure doctrine of the Gospel, my most dear Father." This was written in answer to Luther's letter of February 14th, addressed, " To Philip Melanchthon, most worthy Brother in Christ." Earlier, Luther had addressed him as " the faithful servant of God, and most dear Brother." February 19th, letters reached Wittenberg announcing Luther's death. Melanchthon at once wrote to Jonas, who had gone with Luther:

" This morning we received your very sad letters, one to the illustrious Prince Elector, and the other to the Reverend Pastor of our Church, in which with great sorrow you write of the death of the Reverend Doctor *Martin Luther*, our most dear Father and Preceptor. He was the chariot and the charioteer of Israel, raised up by God to restore and purify the ministry of the Gospel. For we must confess that by him doctrine was revealed which is beyond the range of the human mind. Bereft of such a teacher and leader we are deeply pained, not only on account of the University, but also on account of the Church throughout the world, which he directed by his counsels, teaching, authority, and by the aid of the Holy Spirit." [1]

In announcing Luther's death to the students, he exclaimed : " Ah! the Charioteer and the Chariot of Israel is gone; he who guided the Church in these last days of the world." [2] To others he wrote that " Luther was endowed with many heroic virtues,

[1] *C. R.*, 6 : 57.
[2] *C. R.*, 6 : 59.

and was divinely called to restore the Gospel." The
funeral oration[1] which he pronounced in the Castle
Church, February 22d, is one of the loftiest tributes
ever paid by a great man to a greater. Luther is
placed in the line of " unbroken succession " with
Moses, Joshua, David, Elijah, Elisha, Jeremiah,
Daniel, Zacharias; with Polycarp, Irenæus, Basil,
Augustin, Bernard, Tauler, and others.

His services to the Church in the restoration of
sound doctrine and in the purification of worship are
briefly recounted, his splendid virtues are fitly
praised, and his fervent piety is duly extolled.

The Oration is chaste, eloquent, and discriminat-
ing. It shows Melanchthon's profound admiration
for Luther's character and achievements, and his
sincere sorrow for his death.

If it be lacking in pathetic tenderness, this is not
because Melanchthon's love for Luther had been
chilled by former misunderstandings, but because
the events of the last twenty years, and his acquired
style of composition, had imparted dignity rather
than pathos to his eloquence. But the Oration will
ever remain as a monument of its author's magnanimity, and a testimony to the services of Luther,
from one who understood both him and his achievements better than any other man, and who viewed
both the man and his achievements with an eye free
from envy and prejudice. Nor are the lofty terms
of praise contained in this Oration inconsistent with
a judgment of Melanchthon's expressed in a letter
to Christopher von Carlowitz, April 28, 1548:

[1] Given in full in an English translation in the Appendix.

" Formerly I bore an almost unseemly servitude, since Luther often gave way to his temperament, in which there was not a little contentiousness, and did not sufficiently consider either his own dignity or the public welfare." [1]   In Melanchthon's own words we have an explanation which truthfully describes Luther's nature.   To Dietrich von Maltz he wrote:

" I will make no elaborate apology to a man who is wise and candid.   I only ask that over against the one word φιλονεικία [love of contention] of that letter, be placed my many other laudatory speeches concerning Luther, written in many passages after his death, as in the funeral oration and in the preface to the second volume of his works.   Then why is that one word extracted from that letter, when many other severe things were there said against the adversaries, and that, too, in a letter written to a man of whose thoughts and purpose you are not ignorant ?   In a word, I affirm that I value the truth above my life.   What more do our Aristarchuses, who judge so harshly of that letter, require of me ?   Perhaps they do not consider what φιλονεικία means ?   It is not a crime, but πάθος, a ' temperament,' belonging to heroic natures, such as writers attribute to Pericles, Lysander, and Agesilaus.   There were heroic impulses in Luther.   It is no wonder that we whose natures are more sluggish are sometimes amazed at that vehemence, especially since there are some things belonging to many of the controversies, about which I prefer to speak to you privately, rather than to excite complaint and dissension." [2]

[1] *C. R.*, 6 : 880.
[2] *Unschuld. Nachr.* (1707), p. 85.

In the funeral oration Melanchthon had said:

"Some by no means evil-minded persons, however, express a suspicion that Luther manifested too much asperity. I will not affirm the reverse, but only quote the language of Erasmus: God has sent in this latter age a violent physician on account of the magnitude of the existing disorders; fulfilling by such a dispensation the divine message to Jeremiah: 'Behold I have put my words in thy mouth. See I have this day set thee over the nations, and over the Kingdom to root out and to pull down, to build and to plant.'"

Only blind admirers of Luther can fail to see that in all these passages Melanchthon has given a true description of Luther's nature. That Luther was polemical, passionate, vehement, and impatient of contradiction, is too well known to require proof. One has only to read his controversies with Henry VIII., Erasmus, Duke George, Duke Henry of Brunswick, and Cardinal Albert, to find exhibitions of violence and of coarse abuse which no friend of Luther's would undertake to defend or to justify. To acknowledge these things frankly does not detract from Luther's greatness, nor cast reproach on his moral character, nor discredit the justness of his contentions. It were far better for Luther's friends to exhibit these shadows of his "heroic virtues" in love, than to leave them to be exposed by his enemies in malice. True friendship is not blind to the faults of a friend. There is probably no word in any language which better describes Luther's nature than φιλονεικία; and that Luther's φιλονεικία gave

Melanchthon many hours of sadness, Melanchthon's letters abundantly show.

But Melanchthon's severest trials began with the death of Luther. Hitherto he had looked to the greater Reformer for guidance and solace. Now by force of circumstances he had himself become the theological head of the Reformation. He was born to teach, to write, to dispute, to negotiate, not to control the passions of men and to direct them in a time of excitement. By his powerful personality Luther had kept the refractory elements at bay, and had held his followers well in line; but no sooner was he gone than disputes and parties arose in the Lutheran Church, which live to disturb its peace to the present day. That Melanchthon did not settle these, and could not control them, was his misfortune, not his fault. It is morally certain that Luther himself could not have controlled the discordant elements of German Protestantism ten years longer, had he lived; for Protestantism had introduced and sanctioned independence of thought, and the Germans are by nature impatient of constraint. Moreover, Luther had already lost control over many theologians of the younger generation.

But before the breaking out of the theological war in which Melanchthon spent the last dozen years of his life, he was called on to experience the horrors of civil war. Inasmuch as the Emperor had concluded peace with the French, and had obtained a truce with the Turks, he resolved to restore Germany to the Holy Roman See. This could be done

only by force of arms. To this end he began to
make preparations for war. When asked the reason
for these warlike preparations he replied that, as he
" was unable to restore peace to Germany by mild
measures, he was obliged to proceed against the dis-
obedient by the power of the Empire." To make
the work of subjugation easier and success sure, he
entered into an alliance with the Pope. The pretext
for the Pope's action is found in the fact that the
Protestants had refused to submit to the Council of
Trent. The text of this alliance, as given by Sleidan,
is as follows:

" *Whereas for many years* Germany *hath persisted in
great errors such as threatened extraordinary danger ; for
the averting of which a council hath been called, that commenced at* Trent *in* December *last, and whereas Protestants reject and disown the same, therefore the Pope and
Emperor for the glory of God and the public good, but
especially the Welfare of* Germany, *have entered into league
together upon certain Articles and Conditions : And in the
first place, that the Emperor shall provide an Army, and
all things necessary for War, and be in readiness by the
Month of* June *next ensuing, and by Force and Arms compel those who refuse the Council, and maintain these Errors,
to embrace the ancient Religion and submit to the Holy See :
But that in the meantime, he shall use his endeavours, and
try all means, to accomplish that, if he can, without a War :
That he shall make no Peace nor Capitulation with them
upon Terms prejudicial to the Church and Religion. That
the Pope, besides the hundred thousand Ducats which he has
already advanced, shall deposit as much more in the Bank
of* Venice, *to be employed by his Lieutenants, in the War*

*only and for no other use : but if no War happen, he shall
receive his money again : that, moreover, he shall in this
War, maintain at his own charges, for the space of six
months, twelve thousand* Italian *Foot, and five hundred
Horse, who shall be commanded by a General and other
inferior Officers commissioned by him : But if the War be
ended before six months expire, he is no longer obliged to
keep his Force in pay. That the Emperor, by virtue of a
grant from the Pope, may for this Year raise one half of
the Church Revenues all over* Spain : *That he may also sell
as much of the Abbey-Lands of* Spain *as do amount to five
hundred thousand Ducats ; but all of this only for the use
of the present War, and upon condition also that he mort-
gage to them as much of his own Lands ; and because this
is a new thing, and without a precedent, he shall at the discretion of the Pope, give all the security he can : That if
anyone endeavour to hinder this their design, they shall join
their Forces, and assist one another against him ; and to
this both shall be obliged, so long as the War continues, and
six Months after it is ended. That all may enter into this
League, and share both in the Profits and Charges of the
War : That the College of Cardinals shall also ratify this
League ; and that what is said of June, is to be understood
of the Month of June this present year.* And both Parties
signed this League." [1]

---

[1] Bohun's Sleidan, p. 381.

CHAPTER XXVI

THE SCHMALKALD WAR

Melanchthon's Opinion concerning the Threatened War—Defeat of
the Protestant Forces—Capture of the Elector—The University
Closed—Melanchthon an Exile—Return to Wittenberg.

THE Protestants of Upper Germany, Würtemberg, Hesse, and Saxony, alarmed at the warlike preparations on the Danube, began to assemble
their forces. Already, in April (1546), Melanchthon
had written an *Opinion*, at the command of the Saxon
Elector, " Concerning War against the Emperor."
The *Opinion*, which was signed by all the Wittenberg theologians, is remarkable for its firmness and
wise circumspection. After declaring that the doc
trine which God had made known to the churches
could not be rooted out, he proceeds ·

" As regards myself it were easier for me to suffer and
die than to encourage a vague suspicion; but if it be
true that the Emperor intends to fall upon these states
on account of religion, then undoubtedly it is the duty of
these states by the help of God to protect themselves and
their subjects, as St. Paul says: ' The magistrate beareth

not the sword in vain, for he is the minister of God to punish those who do evil, as murderers.' Such resistance is as when a man repels a band of murderers, be he commanded by the Emperor or by others. This is a public tyranny, a *notorious violence*. As to how the Spaniards, Italians, and Burgundians will act in these lands, we know by what they have done in Julichs. Hence every father should offer his body and life to repel this huge tyranny." [1]

To Amsdorf he wrote, June 25th:

" It is certain that the Emperor Charles is preparing a great war against the Elector of Saxony and the Landgrave. Large armies are now assembling in the neighbourhood of Guelders, and Italian forces, supported by the Pope, are expected. Charles does not deny that he is going to make war on the Elector of Saxony. At Regensburg he summoned the representatives of the Estates and bade them not to assist the Elector. But the Estates replied nobly and resolutely, that they would not desert a neighbouring prince in danger. Such is the beginning of the war. But as God protected the house of the widow of Sarepta, so I pray that he will defend our princes, who are just in government, and in many ways serve the churches and promote the study of doctrine." [2]

A little later he published an edition of Luther's *Warning to his Beloved Germans,* with a Preface which sounded the tocsin of war, and which shows that this man who had spent so many years in nego-

---

[1] *C. R.*, 6: 123.
[2] *C. R.*, 6: 181.

tiations for peace, and had borne reproaches on account of his efforts to spare his native land the shedding of blood, could exhibit the highest courage, and could counsel war as a final means of repelling religious tyranny.   The Protestants marshalled their forces, twenty-seven thousand strong, on the Danube, before Charles had time to gather his army. Had they made an attack at once they could easily have ended the war in September, and could have forced Charles to terms.   But they hesitated and delayed and then retreated, leaving the Emperor master of the Danube.   They now proposed terms of peace, but the Emperor ordered them to surrender at discretion.   Learning that Maurice, Duke of Saxony, had united with the Emperor, and had already invaded the Electoral dominions, the Elector and the Landgrave hastened home.   Charles soon conquered the confederated cities of Upper Germany, humbled Würtemberg, and deprived the Archbishop of Cologne of his Electoral dignity. The next spring he advanced against the Elector of Saxony, fought and won the battle of Mühlberg, April 24th, and took the Elector prisoner.   He afterward deprived him of his Electoral dignity, and bestowed the same upon Maurice, thus transferring the Electorate from the Ernestine to the Albertine line, with which it remains to this day.

Melanchthon had not been hopeful of the results of the war.   But what distressed him most was the dissolution of the university, and the dispersion of the professors and students.   He took up his abode at Zerbst, though he was offered asylum with the

Elector of Brandenburg, and at Brunswick, and at Nuremberg. In view of the possible re-establish ment of the university he preferred to remain in the vicinity of Wittenberg. When he learned of the defeat and capture of the Elector he wrote to Cruciger in a way that reveals the magnitude of his distress:

" DEAREST CASPAR: Not if I were able to weep as many tears as the Elbe rolls deep waters before our walls, could I weep out my sorrow on· account of the defeat and imprisonment of our Prince, who truly loved the Church and Justice. Many important considerations increase my distress. I deeply commiserate the prisoner. I foresee a change of doctrine and a new confusion of the churches. A great ornament is destroyed in the dispersion of our University, and we are torn asunder. Then, too, if it were possible to consider the matter, I would rather die in your society and at your altars than wander in exile, in which I am daily growing weaker. The Eternal God and Father of our Lord Jesus Christ keep our pastor, you, and our other colleagues." [1]

When he heard that Spanish and Italian soldiers had invested Wittenberg, and were committing murders and many nameless crimes, he removed with his family from Zerbst to Magdeburg, thence to Brunswick, and thence to Nordhausen. His letters during this period of exile exhibit the deepest concern for his friends, the Church, and the university. He says: " There is fixed in my heart and in my very soul the greatest love for our little nest on the Elbe and for our friends who are there

[1] C. R., 6: 532.

and in the neighbourhood, so that I cannot separate from them without the greatest pain." [1]   In a few days he learned it was quite safe for him to return to Wittenberg.   Then he wrote: " I have decided to return for a short time to Wittenberg, or at least to Dessau, to consult with the friends in regard to the common exile."   He was now contemplating a visit to his native land, and was considering a call to the University of Tübingen.   He had no expect-ation at this time of being called back to Wittenberg to take up the work which had been interrupted by the war.   He also continued to express the deepest sympathy for his fallen Prince.   In a letter of condolence and comfort he declared his willing-ness to serve under him in the humblest school-work in poverty rather than elsewhere in riches.   He also promised that he would not depart from the Elect-or's dominions without his Grace's knowledge. But he did not know at that time, June 9th, that the sons of John Frederick, to whom a portion of their father's dominions, including Weimar, Jena, Eisenach, and Gotha, had been left, intended to open a university at Jena.   His heart was still at Wittenberg.   June 16th he wrote to a friend:

" Though I do not approve all the confusion there, yet if I can gather together the scattered remnants of the University, I would not go elsewhere.   For I love that University as my native land, as in it I lived in the most intimate relations with learned and honourable col-leagues, and with a fair amount of zeal taught the things

[1] *C. R.*, 6: 560.

CHARLES V. IN 1547.

FROM THE PAINTING BY TITIAN IN THE PINACOTHEK AT MUNICH.

most necessary. The son of our captive Prince has only requested that I should not leave these parts without first informing him of my intention. If a place should be given me even in a humble school in his dominions, I would not hesitate to serve him; for I am not thinking of a brilliant position, but of my grave." [1]

When asked by the young dukes to name the place where he wished to reside, he wrote that he would come to Weimar to learn further their inten, tions, and to give his " simple and humble opinion." On the seventh of July he went to Weimar, but with the determination not willingly to separate himself from his colleagues, and not to choose a position in which he could not again unite with them in labour; for in all his letters of these months he declares that he will act only in conjunction with his colleagues. July 10th, in a written *Opinion*, which only recently has been recovered, he sets forth the difficulties of founding a new university: It will cost a great deal of money; " the princes are poor and in debt "; it will probably increase the hostility toward John Frederick and his family. In this *Opinion* he openly insists on Wittenberg as the place for the university, since studies have already flourished there, and Wittenberg is favourably situated in the Saxon lands for the university.[2] But, as the Court persisted, he sketched a plan and named the professors. As not all of these were acceptable, and as Melanchthon was required to give a categorical answer as to

[1] *C. R.*, 6 : 578.
[2] Bindseil's *Supplementa*, p. 541.

whether he would come to Jena or not, he at once broke off all negotiations, and.on the 14th returned to Nordhausen, without knowing how it would go with him at Wittenberg, since he had not yet been invited thither by the new Elector.

The facts in the case show conclusively that the plan of founding a new university at Jena did not arise from opposition to the theology and tendency of Melanchthon. Exactly the opposite was the case. At the beginning, the Weimar Court wished especially to foster and to cultivate that theology, and above everything it sought to have Melanch thon as its chief teacher. Even the school that was opened at Jena, March 19, 1548, was opened under Melanchthon's auspices. The two teachers, Stigel and Strigel, were pupils and friends of Melanchthon. The Inaugural of Strigel treated a favourite thought of Melanchthon's, and wholly in his spirit, viz., that even in times of trouble, learned studies must be fostered. Only subsequent events, together with the rivalries of princes and the jealousies of theologians like Amsdorf and Flacius, brought on the sharp antagonism to Wittenberg, which, in 1558, erected the Jena gymnasium into a university, and made it the stronghold of opposition to Melanchthon and to Wittenberg.[1]

The one thing which influenced Melanchthon most was the deep conviction that for the sake of the Church the university ought to remain at Wittenberg. He saw that the downfall of the university would be a greater victory for the Catholics

---

[1] Hartfelder, p. 537.

than even the capture of John Frederick had been.
He wrote to Nicholas Medler: " The churches are
not to be deserted because the government changes.
The schools are bound up with the churches.   For
whence are we to have ministers of the Gospel, if·
the schools should be destroyed ? " [1]   He could
have gone to Tübingen, or to Frankfort-on-the-
Oder, and who would have blamed him ?   But the
love of the Church, and devotion to his colleagues,
constrained him.   To Prince George of Anhalt he
wrote :

" Were this purely a private matter, I could very easily
decide.   I would return to my native land which received me at my birth.   Now my native land is with the
company of most learned and virtuous men with whom
I have lived so many years, and by whose labours learning has been widely spread over these countries.   May
God for the sake of his holy sanctuary confirm what he
hath wrought." [2]

A day or two later he wrote to Augustin Schurf :

" Though from the very beginning of my exile I was
invited to my native land, yet I was unwilling hastily to
leave these parts.   Nor do I doubt that I have acted
wisely.   Either the longing for my colleagues, or other
good reasons, detained me; for I have come to the conclusion that if at Wittenberg, or elsewhere, I can live
among my old colleagues, most learned and honourable
men, I will choose no other home, no other friends.

[1] C. R., 6 : 812.
[2] C. R., 6 : 598.

I shall judge my native land to be where they are. But I doubt whether the victorious Duke wants to have two universities." [1]

In order to reach a conclusion in regard to his future, and his " migration," he left Nordhausen, July 16th, for Zerbst, to consult with Dr. Schurf, Paul Eber, and others. At Merseburg, on the 18th, he learned that the Wittenberg theologians had been summoned to Leipzig by the new Elector, and that a messenger had been sent to Weimar for him. He now proceeded to Leipzig, where Maurice promised the theologians " that he would not allow any papal abuses to be introduced; nor would he tolerate anything contrary to the Word of God, but as a Christian Elector he would protect the Word of God and its ministers to the best of his ability." [2]

The theologians were treated with the greatest kindness by Maurice, who lodged them at his own expense, and bestowed upon them suitable presents. Melanchthon was offered a professorship at Leipzig, but this was declined in favour of the " little nest on the Elbe," whither on the 25th he travelled with the other theologians. He also declined calls to Denmark and to Königsberg, though at Wittenberg he lived for a time at his own expense. His delight was " to gather up the planks of the shipwrecked University." In almost the same words in two letters written August 10th, he tells us why he re-

[1] *C. R.*, 6 . 599.
[2] *C. R.*, 6 : 605.

DUKE MORITZ OF SAXONY.

FROM A PAINTING BY CRANACH THE YOUNGER.

turned to Wittenberg: " Had I declined to come I certainly would have impeded the restoration of the University." [1]

There can be no question as to the motives which influenced Melanchthon's choice. They were devotion to his colleagues, and a desire to re-establish the university in the interests of the Church. He had made no unconditional promise to the sons of John Frederick. He was not a courtier, and hence he was under no obligation to follow the fortunes of a fallen court. As a citizen it was his duty to obey the powers that be, and to try to repair the ruins of war. Wittenberg was the original seat of the Reformation. It were far wiser to restore it than to found a rival university which was sure to be conducted with partisan zeal. Fault was never found with his colleagues for returning to their old places; but that he, the most celebrated teacher in Germany, should take service under the apostate Maurice, was construed by the Weimar Court as an act of unfaithfulness and of ingratitude toward his former lord; to which was subsequently added the charge of intending to change the Lutheran doctrine. But as Melanchthon's promise did not involve the founding of a new university, and as the conditions imposed involved a desertion of his old colleagues, he compromised neither his veracity, nor his honour, nor his fidelity, by returning to Wittenberg. As to the charge of wishing to betray the Lutheran faith, that is absolutely refuted by the *Confessio Saxonica*, composed in 1551, and by his repeated affirmations

[1] *C. R.*, 6: 628, 629.

of adherence to the Augsburg Confession and its Apology.

When he was informed of the slanders circulated by the Weimar Court and its adherents, he wrote to Caspar Aquila, August 29th:

" When there was hope of restoring our University, and my colleagues urgently entreated me to return, the name of the University, association with my colleagues, the sad and desolate condition of this Church to which hitherto so many nations looked, influenced me to come hither. It seemed a singular blessing of God that our little town was not utterly destroyed, and I thought it would be another blessing of God if our University could be restored. To the many who wickedly blame me for my return I make no reply, except to pray that surcease may be granted to my sorrow. *A melancholy mind always errs*, says Ennius. Perhaps in my great distress I was too eager for the companionship of my old friends, with whom I had so long been associated in the most honourable toil. It may be that the condition of the times did not justify me in hoping for so much in regard to the reparation of the University, the success of which is not yet assured. Certainly I sought neither pleasure nor gain. I am living here like a stranger at my own expense, sorrowing and praying, and passing no day without shedding tears. If the restoration succeeds, I hope the churches in these parts will be blessed. If it do not succeed, then I must go into exile again. It is not strange that we have sought for an end to this distraction. Those who magnify my error into a rejection of doctrine, do me injustice. Oh that they would also consider their own errors! " [1]

---

[1] *C. R.*, 6 : 649.

Melanchthon now gave himself up to the university, "which had been so serviceable in promoting liberal studies and Christian doctrine." In a short time he secured ample means for it, and wrote, "If there were peace in the country, I think there would be plenty of students." To the accusations that he meant to change the doctrine, and had forgotten the Elector, he replied:

"When those of whom you wrote, say that the preachers of this place have deserted the truth, they do great injury to the Church, which is already sufficiently distressed. By God's grace the voice of the Gospel now resounds as unanimously in the city of Wittenberg as it did before the war. And almost every week ministers of the Gospel are publicly ordained, and sent into the neighbouring districts. It was but this week that six pious and learned men were sent forth, all of whom declare even as formerly that they will preach the pure Gospel to their hearers. And they are likewise examined as in former times. The facts of the case prove that we have not changed our minds in regard to doctrine. We also offer up public and private prayers for the imprisoned Prince. We do not hear anyone speak evil of our Prince; and the authorities of the city would not permit anything of the kind. Therefore I beseech you, do not believe those who slander us, or the Church here; I hope that God himself will confute them and deliver us from their envenomed tongues. I myself honour the imprisoned Prince with devout reverence, and daily commend him to God with tears and supplications, and I pray God to deliver and guide him. As this is true I am amazed at the levity of the slanderer who accuses me of the cruelty of preventing prayer for the Prince. But I will beseech God to protect his Church everywhere and also to deliver us from such slanders in this our great distress." [1]

In numerous other letters during the closing months of this year (1547), he most earnestly protests that he has made no change in doctrine, and that he is opposing the Lutheran Confession to the decrees of the Council of Trent. But from this time on, the Weimar princes and their theological adherents began to entertain the most irreconcilable grudge against Melanchthon. They also bitterly hated Maurice, and looked with envy on Wittenberg, which, by the reputation of Melanchthon and under the protection of Maurice, was again becoming the head and centre of German Protestantism. Melanchthon was training the ministers of the Church, and these were extending the fame of their teacher and of the university. He was everywhere recognised as the most eminent theologian of the Church, and his advice was sought on all kinds of vexed ecclesiastical questions. This was more than the Weimar princes could bear. They soon announced themselves as the exclusive defenders of the doctrines of the Lutheran Church, which from that time on embraced two hostile camps. The contests between the theologians of ducal Saxony and those of the Electorate are memorable.

[1] *C. R.*, 6: 651.

CHAPTER XXVII

THE INTERIMS

The Augsburg *Interim*—Letter to Carlowitz—Several Formulas—
The Leipzig *Interim*.

AS the Schmalkald War had completely shattered
the Schmalkald League, so Protestantism
seemed on the verge of ruin. At the Diet of Augsburg, September, 1547, a form of doctrine was proposed which was to be binding in the churches until
a satisfactory decision of the Council should be
reached. The book is known as the *Augsburg Interim*. Not more than two or three of its twenty-six
articles contain the pure evangelical doctrine. Its
acceptance would have been the preliminary to the
acceptance of the decrees of Trent. Maurice hesitated and sought the advice of his theologians.
These strongly counselled against the *Interim*.
Melanchthon especially rejected some of the articles
of Trent because they were contrary to divine truth.
He would not burden his conscience with them.
He also declared that he would not burden his conscience with the *Interim*. To Camerarius he wrote:

329

" So long as I live I will act as I have hitherto done, and I shall speak the same things wherever I shall be. I shall continue the same worship of God and shall speak with my accustomed moderation and without violence." [1]

The period was a critical one. Protestantism had not before been in such peril. It was uncertain how Maurice would act, or what the political exigencies would require of him. For twenty years Melanchthon had laboured and prayed for the peace of the Church. In his negotiations both with the Reformed and with the Catholics, he had laid stress on the *essentials* of the Gospel, and not on things *indifferent*. To the same principle he still adhered with heroic firmness, even in the face of the Emperor's hate and of the Elector's less than half-hearted support. Fault was found with him by some of the Protestants because he did not make greater concessions to the Catholics. Christopher von Carlowitz, one of Maurice's counsellors, a hearty hater of Luther, acting in the pay of Charles, more intent on his master's political interests than on the cause of religion, exhorted Melanchthon " to advance the plans which had been proposed for the promotion of the union of the churches," and *demanded* that he should approve the *Interim*. On the twenty-eighth of April, 1548, Melanchthon replied as follows:

" In regard to the exhortation, I assure you I desire that the illustrious Prince shall decide in accordance with his own judgment, and with that of his council, as

---

[1] *C. R.*, 6 : 878.

shall seem most salutary for himself and the state. When he shall have decided, if there be anything which I cannot approve, I will not act seditiously, but I will either keep silent, or I will leave, or I will bear whatever befalls. Formerly I bore an almost unseemly servitude, since Luther often gave way to his temperament, in which there was not a little contentiousness, and did not sufficiently consider his own dignity and the public welfare. And I know that always we must modestly overlook some defects in government, just as we must bear the evils of storms. But you say I am not only required to be silent, but also to give my approval [of the *Interim*]. Now I doubt not that you as a wise man understand the natures and dispositions of men. By nature I am not controversial, and I as greatly love peace among men as anyone. Neither have I started the controversies which distract the state. But I have fallen into them when they had been started, and I have taken part in them with a sincere desire to ascertain the truth."

He then proceeds to say that he does not object to some ceremonies contained in the *Interim*. Again:

" Gladly will I promote the harmony of these churches; but I am by no means willing either that they shall be disturbed by a change of doctrine, or that worthy men shall be driven away. When I think of a new distraction of the churches, I am deeply grieved."

He closed by alluding to the dilatoriness of the chiefs of the Schmalkald League during the campaign on the Danube in 1546.[1]

Carlowitz, instead of holding this letter in con-

[1] *C. R.*, 6: 879.

fidence, as Melanchthon plainly intended that he should do, showed it to friend and foe. The Catholics made copies of it, one of which was sent to the Pope, and another was read to the Emperor, who exclaimed, " Now you have him, hold on to him." Some of Melanchthon's Protestant enemies published it with the most slanderous perversions and spiteful comments.[1] In a word, it became a campaign document in the hands of two contending parties. The Catholics rejoiced over it as an evidence of division in the ranks of the Protestants, and some of the Protestants blamed it for its concessions, its characterisation of Luther, and its allusion to the heads of the Schmalkald League. But to Protestants and Catholics alike it can be said that the letter adheres to essentials in doctrine, and concedes only things indifferent. Its characterisation of Luther is only too true, and all historians agree that the irresolution of John Frederick and others is responsible for the outcome of the Schmalkald War.

To have written such a letter at that time may be regarded as unwise and impolitic, and we may with Ranke wish that it never had been written. In itself it shows the transparent honesty of Melanchthon. It contains no taint of treachery, nor of hypocrisy, nor of ingratitude, and no intimation of a surrender of fundamental truth. The evil lay in the evil that was made out of it, and in the deceitful purpose of the man who obtained it, and then divulged it. Carlowitz, as the letter shows, wrote of

[1] See *Concilia Witebergensia*, p. 325.

CONTEMPORARY CARICATURE ON THE INTERIM.

the necessity of preventing war, of conciliating the Emperor, of saving the Protestant cause from utter ruin. All this could be done by a little concession on the part of Melanchthon! He should therefore sign the *Interim* and secure these great ends! His answer in substance is: I do not have Luther's heroic nature. I will make concessions in *adiaphora*, but not in doctrine. If I cannot bear the Elector's decrees, I will go into exile. He did not expect his moderation to please those in power, but he was resolved, by the help of God, to bear whatever might befall him, because he preferred truth to life. We have only to know all the circumstances of those terrible times, and to put ourselves in Melanchthon's place, in order to judge righteously as well as charitably of the matter. The letter is a polite but firm way of saying, *I will not accept the Interim;* and to this Melanchthon adhered; for not only did he write criticism after criticism on the *Interim*, but when called to Leipzig, June 9th, to consult about it, he said, " If approbation be demanded, it is not doubtful what answer should be given "; and added, " This sophistical book will be the cause of new wars and of greater alienation in the churches." [1] All this he did and said notwithstanding the fact that the Emperor had twice demanded that he be delivered up, or driven into exile. To the Prince of Anhalt he wrote that he would suffer banishment and death rather than approve a change in doctrine. Indeed Melanchthon's course in relation to the *Interim*, in the face of a deceitful

[1] *C. R.*, 6: 922.

Court, of an apostate Elector, and of an all-victorious
Emperor, is marked by prudent but firm opposition.
Nothing could induce him to betray the doctrine
which he and others had long taught at Wittenberg.
His conduct was that of a martyr. His faith in
God, to whom he committed " these perils," is sublime. It is impossible to read his letters at this
period without feeling the deepest sympathy for him
and the many other good men who " were being
crucified with anxieties for the Church and for
peace." When, a little later, the civil counsellors
presented a strongly Catholicising statement known
as the *Celle Interim*, Melanchthon called it " a
botch," and declared that " the consciences of the
politicians are more concerned for other things than
for the maintenance of pure and uncorrupt doctrine." [1] This *Celle Interim* was subscribed at
Jüterbok, December 17th, by Maurice of Saxony
and Joachim of Brandenburg as the norm of teaching for their churches. The theologians were not
consulted.

When the Saxon theologians were told that they
were to abide by the *Celle Interim*, Bugenhagen exclaimed, " Then we thank God, for we know that
at Celle we adopted nothing unchristian, but rejected
what was unchristian." [2] And Melanchthon, while
at Jüterbok, presented a long refutation of " the
idolatrous blasphemies of the private masses and
the canon [of the mass]." [3]

---

[1] *C. R.*, 7 : 232.
[2] Voigt, *Briefwechsel*, p. 96.
[3] *C. R.*, 7 : 235.

It was thus evident that Melanchthon was disputing every inch of ground demanded by the two electors and their courtiers. These latter declared that unless concessions were made, the same persecutions would come upon Saxony that had come upon South Germany, where four hundred pastors with their families had been driven into exile, and where all the churches had been given to the Catholics. At the same time, Agricola, his old enemy, now court-theologian of the Elector of Brandenburg, was complaining to Maurice that by his much writing to the theologians and preachers, Melanchthon would create an alliance against the *Interim*. The Emperor was still demanding that he be driven into exile. Never did a man occupy a more difficult and responsible position. The drawn sword hung over the Church and the people; and it looked as though everything would be lost unless concessions should be made in *adiaphora*, that is, in the external usages of the Church.

It was under these circumstances that Melanchthon went from Jüterbok to Leipzig to attend a diet which had been called by Maurice for December 21, 1548. The other theologians present were Gresser of Dresden, Pfeffinger and Camerarius of Leipzig, and George of Anhalt. In his *Declaration* to the Diet, Maurice distinctly says that the chief article, Justification, shall still be purely taught in his dominion.[1] This was the fundamental thing. It was thought that if this could be saved the churches might yet be saved. To the *Celle Interim*, the *work*

[1] *C. R.*, 7 : 254. See Vogt's *Bugenhagen*, p. 431.

of the civil counsellors, was prefixed an article on
Justification, and one on Good Works, composed
by Melanchthon at Pegau, in July.   The article on
Justification maintains without equivocation the
central Lutheran principle, that " God does not
justify man by the merit of his own works which
man does, but out of mercy, freely, without our
merit, that the glory may not be ours, but Christ's,
through whose merit alone we are redeemed from
sin and justified." [1]   The document thus composed
was laid before the Diet.   It was due to Melanchthon that the fundamental principle was saved.   To
the other portion of the document he submitted,
but not until further resistance seemed to be futile.
He did not give the document his unqualified approval.   He simply regarded " the transactions at
Leipzig as tolerable," in view of " the various perils
that threatened the churches and the State."   He
" wanted some things considered differently and
done differently." [2]

The document retained as *adiaphora* various
Catholic ceremonies, as Extreme Unction, Fasts,
Corpus Christi, and most of the usages of the Mass.
Perhaps the most dangerous feature was that it
yielded ordination exclusively to the bishops; but
this was done with the expressed understanding
that the bishops exercise their office well, and " use
the same for edification and not for destruction "—
a restriction which balanced the concession, and for
which there was abundant precedent, as at Schmal-

---

[1] *C. R.*, 7 : 51.
[2] *C. R.*, 7 : 275, 292.

JOACHIM CAMERARIUS.

FROM A CONTEMPORARY COPPER-PLATE.

kald in 1540, when it was conceded by Luther and others, that *Ordination, Visitation,* and *Jurisdiction* might remain in the hands of the bishops [1]; and also in *The Wittenberg Reformation,* where Ordination is conceded to the bishops on condition that they hold the true doctrine and ordain proper persons.[2]

Yet it will not be denied that this document, which soon began to be known as the *Leipzig Interim,* conceded too many Catholic uses, and thus opened the door to Catholic abuses. The consideration which finally prevailed with the theologians in making such large concessions, is found in a letter of George of Anhalt to Francis Burkhard, written by Melanchthon:

" They hope to avoid perils, if we retain some rites in themselves not vicious. We are also accused of unjust obstinacy if in such things we are unwilling to promote the public tranquillity. In this matter they err who think that perils can be avoided; yet we do not violently contend about such things, because there are other greater controversies, about which there are most bitter disputes. That we may retain things essential, we are not rigid in regard to things non-essential, especially since those rites have to a great extent remained in the churches of these parts. We know that much is said against these concessions; but the desolation of the churches, such as is occurring in Swabia, would be a greater scandal. If by such moderation it can be brought about that neither doctrine nor worship be changed, fault cannot be justly found with us." [3]

---

[1] *C. R.,* 3 : 943.

[2] *C. R.,* 5 : 585.

[3] *C. R.,* 7 : 252.

CHAPTER XXVIII

THE ADIAPHORISTIC CONTROVERSY

The Reaction—Flacius Illyricus—The Adiaphoristic Controversy—
Melanchthon Defamed—His Letter of Defence.

THE *Leipzig Interim* was published (1548) " out
of obedience to the imperial command, and
from the love of peace "; but it soon brought on
the Adiaphoristic controversy in the Lutheran
Church. Complaints and inquiries reached Melanchthon from Berlin, Frankfort, Hamburg, and
other places. He replied in substance that the
churches should bear the yoke of *adiaphora*, but
should stand fast in the pure doctrine, since Christian liberty does not consist in rejecting external
uses, but in the free confession of the truth; and
not *adiaphora*, but faith, prayer, and a pious life
constitute the worship of God.[1] From what he
wrote again and again it is evident that it was Melanchthon's " supreme determination to preserve
purity of doctrine and the true worship of God in
the churches committed to our faith." [2] This he

[1] *C. R.*, 7 : 322.
[2] *C. R.*, 7 : 370.

thought could at that time be done best by submitting to certain things of long standing in the Church, which were neither enjoined nor forbidden in the Divine Word. But this was a mistake in judgment, induced partly by his reverence for antiquity, partly by his love of good order, partly by his yielding temper, or the lack of the heroic element in his nature. The times were sadly out of joint; and it is not at all improbable that had no concessions been made, the same distress would have come upon Saxony that had already befallen Swabia. The *Interim* and the reaction which it brought gave the politic and ambitious Maurice time to test the sense of his people, and to get ready for that second act of perfidy which saved Germany to Protestantism.

The ablest and most violent opponent of the *Interim* was Matthias Flacius, born in Illyria, March 3, 1520. He had studied at Venice, Basel, Tübingen, and Wittenberg, and was now living at Magdeburg. He was a very learned, but bitter, violent, and calumnious man. From Magdeburg, which was called " the chancery of God," Flacius, Amsdorf, Wigand, and Gallus, the self-styled " exiles of Christ," poured forth a flood of vituperation against the *Interim*, and against Melanchthon, as though he was its author. To apprise the reader of the contents of one of his pamphlets, Flacius placed the following advertisement on the title-page:

" From this pamphlet you will learn the innocence of the author and the origin and progress of the Adiaphora, and all the causes of those delusions, and that, too, from the mouths of the authors themselves. You will learn that the occasion was in part the desire of the wicked to betray and to crucify Christ, and to set the Roman Barabbas free; in part it was the false faith, the fear and carnal wisdom of weak Christians. The matter is the union of Christ and Belial, of light and darkness, of the sheep and the wolves, the service of two masters who are mortal foes, Christ and Belial. The form is the false paint and deceitful colouring of order, discipline, and uniformity. The end is the restoration of the papacy, the setting up of Antichrist in the temple of Christ, the confirmation of the wicked, that they may triumph over the Church and Christ, the distress of the pious, weakness, the leading into doubt, unnumbered offences." [1]

It is freely conceded here that Flacius rendered at this time an important service to Protestantism. He had the correct idea of *adiaphora*, viz., that, as things neither enjoined nor forbidden by the Divine Word, they may be received in the exercise of Christian liberty, but are not to be imposed by authority. He also had the correct idea of the relation of the State to the Church, viz., that the former should not dictate the faith and the form of worship of the latter. Early in the Reformation the Wittenberg theologians had urged the rulers, as "necessity bishops," to reform the Church. This principle worked well enough for them when it was applied on their side; but now that two influential electors of Protestant lands were in league with the papacy, it returned to vex them and their followers,

---

[1] Preger, i., 85.

and it vexes German Protestantism to this day. Here the courtiers, as the representatives of the Saxon Elector, simply took the matter in their own hands, and overwhelmed the theologians by vociferous intimidations, inserted into the *Interim* their own propositions, and then interpreted the silence of the theologians as approval. The consolation left to the latter was that they had saved the evangelical principle in its essence; that they had preserved the Church from destruction; and that every *adiaphoron* allowed might be reconciled with evangelical truth. Melanchthon's letters give the full proof that he did not approve the *Interim ;* that he regarded it as " a servitude imposed upon the churches by the rulers," which had to be borne, lest greater evils come. Moreover, he had no confidence in the *Interim*, and predicted " that in two years it would die out, and would bring greater trouble and confusion." [1]

At Wittenberg men were ordained almost every week " by the customary rite," and sent into the churches to preach the pure Gospel; and Bugenhagen protested publicly from the pulpit that the Wittenberg theologians were not responsible for the *Interim*, and he called upon professors and citizens to make this known by letter. [2]

Melanchthon called the *Interim* " the work of the courtiers," and constantly insisted, also, that as a matter of fact no change had taken place in doctrine

---

[1] See Ranke, v., 64, 65, vi., 509 ; *C. R.*, 7 : 342, 350, 351, 356.

[2] Voigt, *Briefwechsel*, p. 96.

and in ceremonies. He wrote that he could easily bear the reproaches heaped on himself personally, if only the seeds of further dissensions should not be sown.

Flacius continued his calumnies. He even obtained, either by theft or through breach of confidence, Melanchthon's private letters, and published them with the most scurrilous and defamatory comments. Finally Melanchthon could stand it no longer, and in October, 1549, he wrote a letter which ought forever to silence all criticisms in regard to his motives, and all suspicions in regard to his fidelity to the Lutheran faith, both during and after the unfortunate interimistic contest and controversy. The letter, which is calm, dignified, and pious, is as follows:

" *To the Candid Reader :*

" As it ought to be the principal care of all men rightly to know and to worship God, so, since God reveals himself in the Church and wishes his Word to be heard there, and all persons to become members of that society and to gather under the banner of our Lord Jesus Christ, as is said in Isaiah, *He shall be an ensign to the people*—so it is necessary to consider carefully, and, in view of the diversity of the human race, to inquire wisely what and where the true Church is, that wherever we are, we may unite with it in faith, worship, and confession. The Church is scattered throughout the world; but from the profane and impious part of the human race it is distinguished by infallible signs, so that we may know truly that the Church is the society, wherever it is, which preaches the pure Gospel, and retains the proper use of the sacraments, and does not persistently defend idolatry. Since those who have learned the prophetic and apostolic doctrine, and know that it is not a fable, can judge of these things with mind, eyes, and ears, surely the Church can be recognised.

"Amid the wreck of empires and the dispersion of men, pious souls have this comfort, that wherever they hear the pure word of sound doctrine, and witness the proper use of the sacraments, and see that idolatry, and errors which oppose the Word of God, are rejected, they know of a truth and do not doubt that there is the house of God, that there God is in the ministry of the Gospel, that there the worshipper is heard, that there God is rightly worshipped, and that there the Son of God gathers an eternal inheritance, as he has said: 'Where two or three are gathered together in my name, there am I in the midst of them.'

"In periods of public dissensions there is need of this consolation, and I present it here because our churches which have this sure and steadfast consolation, are now greatly disturbed by the clamours of certain persons. Let each one see and hear for himself. The same doctrine in all respects is taught that appears in our books. There is the same use of the sacraments, that there was before the war. Errors and idolatry are discarded, as our books show.

"But *Flacius Illyricus* exclaims that *the doctrine is changed, and that certain ceremonies formerly abolished have been restored.* I will first reply concerning doctrine. The voice of all the teachers in our churches and schools openly refutes this calumny. And to avoid a prolix statement, I refer to the whole body of doctrine written in the *Loci Communes*, which is in many hands. In that book I did not aim to set up any new doctrine, but faithfully to embrace the common doctrine of those churches which adopted the Confession presented to the Emperor Anno M.D.XXX., which I consider the invariable doctrine of the Church Catholic, and which I wish to have understood as having been written honestly and without sophistry and calumnious intentions.

" I am conscious of having compiled that epitome not from a desire of differing from others, nor from a love of novelty, nor from contentiousness, nor from any wicked desire whatever. The circumstances made it necessary. When, in the first inspection of our churches, we encountered the discordant clamours of the ignorant in regard to many things, I brought together a summary of the doctrine which had been taught by Luther in different volumes of interpretations and discourses, and I studied a mode of expression suited to accuracy, perspicuity, and harmony in those who were being taught; and I have always submitted my writings to the judgment of our Church and of Luther himself. In regard to many questions I was careful to consult Luther, whose books are widely circulated, and I sought to know his opinions. I am satisfied that this doctrine is the invariable consensus of the Church Catholic of our Lord Jesus Christ, and I pray God to keep me in the profession of this doctrine for the good of the eternal Church. I mention these things that no one may accuse me of hindering the faith of others by my own doubts.

" In the next place it is requisite to offer a few words of reply to the charge respecting *Ceremonies*. I certainly could have wished, especially in the present afflictive circumstances, that the churches should not have been disturbed by any change; but if such be the case it does not originate with me. But I confess that I have persuaded the people of Franconia and others not to abandon their churches on account of any service with which they could comply without impiety. For though Flacius cries out vehemently that the churches had better be deserted, and the princes alarmed by the fear of sedition, I should not choose to be the author of such wretched advice. It is plain that we must endure much greater burdens in the cause of literature and religion than mere dress—as the hatred of the great, the insolent contempt of the populace, the malevolence of hypocritical friends, the dissensions of the priesthood, poverty, persecution, and other evils which accompany even a quiet government: but these turbulent times produce many greater miseries.

" But as we must not desert our posts on this account, we must sustain lighter servitude if it can be done with a good conscience. The distressing situation of the present times, in which there are such divisions in sentiment and opinion, seems to me to require that these oppressed churches should be comforted and strengthened by all the aids that piety can afford, and that we should take care that the most important doctrines should be faithfully explained and transmitted to posterity, and that the universities be supported as the depositories of general literature.

" The representation of Flacius respecting somebody's (who I know not) having reported that I have declared we ought not to withdraw from the churches, although the ancient abuses should be reinstated, is absolutely without foundation.

" Now mark this crafty man: In order to excite suspicion and inflame hatred, he produces many sentences dropped in familiar discourse, which he calumniously misinterprets, and also attributes to others sayings of his own invention, that he might appear not only to have witnesses, but agents at his command. Nor have I ever thought or said what he falsely imputes to me, that we ought to remain in those churches in which old errors are restored, such as Mass services, invocation of saints, and other impious services which we have condemned in our publications. I do openly declare that such idolatrous rites should neither be practised nor tolerated. And that students may be the better instructed in every particular, I have explained the occasions and origin of the controversy with great care and labour.

"Here, if I were inclined to indulge my grief, I might justly complain of Flacius, who circulates such falsehoods to my detriment, and might detail the origin of those distresses which overwhelm the whole Church, explaining those circumstances which tend to strengthen the boldness and confirm the power of our adversaries against the truth. But I am unwilling to open these wounds, and I beseech these advocates of liberty to allow me and others at least to endure our afflictions in peace, and not excite more cruel dissensions.

"He boasts that he will continue to be the advocate of the pristine state of things. If by this expression he refers to particular empires and governments, and confines the Church only to its own walls, his idea is very incorrect; for the Church is scattered abroad in various kingdoms, publishing the uncorrupted word of the Gospel, and serving God by tears and groans of genuine worship. But as he states that he was once so familiarly acquainted with me, he could testify my pains and sorrows and zealous care. We lament the disturbed state of public affairs and of kingdoms, and yet we do not ask for garrisons and ramparts of defence; but in our churches we publish the Gospel truth, serving God in the knowledge and faith of his Son, and aiming, to the best of our feeble efforts, to promote the literary pursuits of our youth and the preservation of discipline.

" If this advocate of the primitive state of things can restore this golden age to our churches, let him triumph as much as he will.

" Why he should particularly attack me who have never offended him, as Marius did Antonius, I know not, for he is aware that I have been always opposed to the corruptions of religion, and have censured the prevailing errors. Now he says I have encouraged them, because it has been my advice not to quit the churches on account of a surplice or anything of that kind. If dissensions arise on these subjects, the commandments respecting charity should not be forgotten, especially as he knows our great afflictions, and that we neither seek dominion or wealth. We should not imitate the example of worldly disputants whose impetuosity is often such as to exemplify the proverb: ' Unless a serpent eat a serpent, a dragon will never be born.'

" He now not only threatens to write against me, but to do something worse. I could wish that we rather co-operate to illustrate essential truth, for there are sources enough of contention; so that we should proclaim a truce, and form an alliance, a mode of proceeding more conducive to our personal advantage and that of the whole Church: lest it should happen as Paul says, ' Take heed that you do not devour one another.' I shall frame my answers with a view to utility, and hope, that both by my writing and by the opinion of the pious, I am sufficiently defended against calumny. Many good and learned men in different places are greatly grieved that the churches are so unjustly censured. But I recommend Flacius and others to consider what will be the consequence, if mutual animosities revive the quarrels of thirty years. How deplorable would this be!

" Wherever he reports his idle stories and things professedly spoken in familiar conversations, he shows what kind of regard he has for the confidence of friendship and the rights of social intercourse.

" We naturally unbosom ourselves with more freedom among our friends, and often I have myself, in maintaining a discussion, strongly opposed an opinion which I really embraced, not in jest, but for the purpose of obtaining information from the views of others.

" Many are acquainted with my natural turn of mind, and know that I am prone rather to indulge in jocoseness, even in the midst of afflictions, than to anything like sternness. To catch and circulate my words on these occasions as he has done is mean and unkind, to say no more. But if, as in some parts of his letter he threatens me with the sword, any evil should occur, and destruction should befall this miserable head, I will commend myself to Jesus Christ the Son of God, our Lord, who was crucified for us and raised again, who is the searcher of hearts and knows that I have inquired after truth with a careful simplicity of mind, not wishing either to gain factions and influence, or to indulge an unbridled curiosity. Nor has it been without great and diligent attention to the whole of Christian antiquity, that I have endeavoured to unravel a variety of intricate questions and to direct the studies of youth to important learning.

" But I will not speak of myself. In all civil dissensions I am aware that calamities are to be expected. The minds of men become inflamed, and I perceive Flacius prepared with his firebrands; but to God I commit my life and his own true Church here and in other places, respecting which I feel far more solicitous than of my own life. This, however, is my consolation, that God has promised his perpetual presence in the Church, and his Son declares, ' Lo! I am with you alway, even to the end of the world.' He will preserve the people that maintain the doctrines of the Gospel and that truly call upon his name; and I pray with the utmost fervour and importunity of soul that he will preserve his Church in these regions.

" This brief reply to the clamours of Flacius I have written, not so much on my own account as for the sake of our churches in general, among whom many pious minds are deeply wounded by his writings. Let them be consoled by this assurance, that fundamental principles are faithfully retained in our churches, namely, the un-corrupted ministry of the Gospel, all the articles of faith, and the use of Christian sacraments without alter-ation. The Son of God, it is most certain, is present with such a ministry, and, as I have already said, hears the supplications of such an assembly. Adieu, candid reader.

" October, 1549." [1]

There are no traces of a weak and vacillating spirit in this letter. There is in it decision enough to have put its author under the ban of the Empire, and to have brought upon him the displeasure of the Elector, for it is an unequivocal avowal of every principle of the Reformation, as it is an unanswer-able refutation of the slanders heaped upon him by his calumniator. Yet this letter did not silence the calumniator. He went on with his slanders and

---

[1] *C. R.*, 7 : 478.

mendacity.   In September of the next year (1550),
Melanchthon in two letters charges downright lying
upon Flacius.   To his friend John Matthesius he
wrote:

" REVEREND AND DEAREST BROTHER :

" I know that as a wise man you carefully look into
the hearts and dispositions of men.   Hence I hope you
have considered also my motive, and that you are not
influenced by the sycophantic writings of Illyricus, who
invents *manifesta mendacia*.   Never have I said, never
have I written, never have I thought, what he says I
have said, viz., that the proposition, '*We are justified by
faith alone*,' is an absurd trifling about words.   On the
contrary, I have spoken and written much more in regard
to the meaning of the *exclusive particles*, than many
others.   Not without effort have I corrected the opinion
of others who did not properly explain the particle *sola*.
But I will reply to those virulent calumnies.   I pray God
to foster and extend the churches in these parts.   We
are labouring faithfully in the promulgation of the doctrine of the Gospel, and of the useful arts.   To-day I am
writing propositions to be discussed by Prutenus, who is
to become a doctor of theology." [1]

He wrote to George of Anhalt that he " could
more easily bear exile and death than this venom of
vipers." [2]   That Flacius was actuated chiefly by
personal malice towards Melanchthon is evidenced
by the fact that he had but little to say against
Agricola and the Elector of Brandenburg, who from
the beginning abetted and promoted the *Interim*, as

---

[1] *C. R.*, 7: 658.

[2] *C. R.*, 7: 658.

MATTHIAS FLACIUS.

AFTER A CONTEMPORARY ENGRAVING.

its chief patrons. But the Saxon theologians, and especially Melanchthon, must be crucified, because, forsooth, they acted too leniently towards that which Agricola *originally helped to call into being.* A still sadder part is that later detractors of Melanchthon have drawn their representations mostly from the calumnies and *manifesta mendacia* of Flacius, rather than from the facts in the case and from the disavowals of the conscientious and truth-loving Melanchthon, whose Opinions, letters, and conduct during the entire interimistic period demonstrate the absurdity of charging him with tergiversation, or with the desertion of a single Lutheran doctrine.

This interimistic and adiaphoristic controversy forms a sad chapter in Lutheran history, but it cannot be further discussed in these pages.

CHAPTER XXIX

THE COUNCIL OF TRENT

Various Writings—The Saxon Confession—Council of Trent—The Treaty of Passau—Examen Ordinandorum—More Controversies.

THE letters of Melanchthon for the year 1550 cover nearly two hundred pages in the *Corpus Reformatorum*. They are addressed to kings, princes, theologians, town councils, and personal friends, and show the intense interest which the writer had in all the affairs of the Church. Many of the letters discuss questions of doctrine. But the most significant productions of his pen belonging to this year are Prefaces to the third and fourth volumes of Luther's German works. He urges the reading of Luther's books, and the transmission of them to posterity, thus again giving a sufficient reply to the charge of wishing to corrupt the Lutheran doctrine. He also published this year his *Exposition* of the Nicene Creed, for the purpose of showing the agreement of the Lutheran theology with the teaching of the ancient Church. In an *Opinion* addressed to the Elector he opposes the continuation

of the Council of Trent: Because the Estates of the
Augsburg Confession had not been formally invited;
some things had been decreed against them in their
absence; the Council had been called by the Pope,
who could not be allowed to act as a judge. The
Emperor should call a free council in Germany, in
which the Protestants might not only be heard, but
could take part in the proceedings.[1]

When finally the Emperor promised the Protest
ants a safe-conduct to Trent and a hearing in the
Council, the Elector summoned Melanchthon, Bugenhagen, and Camerarius to Dresden in January,
1551, to hear their views in regard to the matter.
Melanchthon then presented an *Opinion*, in which he
says that everything which had been done by the
Council should be gone over again; that the Protestants should agree on articles of faith which they
wished to defend, and " that they should defend no
articles except those which are now publicly taught
in the churches of Misnia ; and what those articles
are, can be learned from the Catechism of these
churches, or from the Augsburg Confession, and
from the first Brandenburg Liturgy."[2]

It was decided that Melanchthon should not go
to Trent; but he was commissioned to prepare a
new confession of faith. That he might work in
greater quiet he retired to Dessau, where from the
sixth to the tenth of May, 1551, he wrote *The Repetition of the Augsburg Confession*, or *The Confession of
the Doctrine of the Saxon Churches*, commonly known

[1] *C. R.*, 7 : 637.
[2] *C. R.*, 7 : 736.

23

and referred to as *Confessio Saxonica*.[1] It is a
luminous and somewhat elaborate restatement of
all the chief doctrines of Christianity according to
the Lutheran conception. It not only reaffirms the
Articles of the Augsburg Confession, but it defends
them out of the Scriptures and the teaching of the
early Church, and refutes the opposite doctrines and
some articles already promulgated by the Council of
Trent. The document is thus both positive-didactic
and polemical.

The intention was to lay this Confession before
the Council of Trent in the name of the Lutheran
theologians. That it might bear a representative
character, the professors at Leipzig and the superintendents of the Saxon churches met at Wittenberg,
and, July 10th, subscribed it " as the common doctrine taught in the churches and universities." The
Margrave John of Brandenburg, George Frederick of
Ansbach, the Counts of Mansfeld, and Duke Philip
of Pomerania, sent their theologians to Wittenberg,
who also signed it as the Confession composed " by
their dear preceptor, Master Philip."

This must have been a proud moment for Melanchthon. In the face of the *Interim* and of
the Flacian calumnies, the best representatives of
Protestantism thus testified that he had given a
clear and unequivocal expression of their common
faith.

It was decided not to publish the Confession until
after it had been presented at Trent. But it was
not taken thither, and in March, 1552, it appeared

---

[1] *C. R.*, 27: 327 *et seqq.*

in print at Basel without the knowledge of the author.

The Council of Trent, which had been indefinitely prorogued September 17, 1549, reassembled May 1, 1551, and adjourned to September. Public sessions were held October 11th and November 25th. December 13th Melanchthon received orders to make ready to go to Trent. On the fifteenth of December he went to Dresden to receive instructions; but he received only the general direction to repair to Nuremberg and there to wait further orders. He reached Nuremberg, January 22, 1552, and was lodged in the St. Ægidius Cloister, where he delivered more than thirty public lectures. He received much attention from the most distinguished citizens, and employed a portion of his time in writing. Among other things he here wrote the Preface to Volume III. of Luther's *Commentary on Genesis*, in which he severely criticises " the Tridentine Areopagites " and " their heathenish and Pharisaical conceits."[1] Having received no instructions up to March 10th, he left Nuremberg and returned home. The Electoral delegates who had gone to Trent, failing to get a public hearing, left there on the fourteenth of March, and on the twenty-eighth of April the Council adjourned *sine die*.

The affairs of the Protestants now took an unexpected turn. The opposition encountered by the *Interim* showed Maurice how deeply Protestantism was rooted in Saxon soil. Suddenly raising the siege of Magdeburg, which he had been commanded

---

[1] *C. R.,* 7: 918.

to subdue, and concluding an alliance with France, he turned his arms against the Emperor, cut off his retreat to the Netherlands, and forced the treaty of Passau, August 2, 1552, which liberated John Frederick and the Landgrave, and gave the Protestants full amnesty, a general peace, and equal rights until the meeting of a national and general council to be arranged for at the next diet.

Oppression now ceased; the exiled ministers returned home; the hated *Interim* came to an end. Maurice, who by one act of treachery had brought Protestantism into peril, now by another act of treachery saved it from ruin. The next year he died from a wound received in the battle of Sievershausen, fought against his former friend and comrade in the Schmalkald War, Albert, Margrave of Brandenburg.

When the liberated John Frederick returned to his Thuringian home, Melanchthon, in the name of the Wittenberg theologians, sent him a letter of congratulation, and dedicated to him the fourth volume of Luther's Latin works, in which dedication he compares the Elector to Daniel in the den of lions and to the three Hebrew youths in the fiery furnace. The ex-Elector returned his thanks to the theologians for their sympathy, but impliedly accused them of having departed from Luther's doctrine. And yet it was exactly during the period of the ex-Elector's captivity that Melanchthon by the composition of a new creed had shown himself to be the continuator of Luther's doctrine; while during the summer of this year (1552) he had been engaged in revising the

Mecklenburg Liturgy, and in composing a list of articles known as the *Examen Ordinandorum* [1]—two books which have ever since been ranked among the classics of the Lutheran Church. Both were used far beyond the bounds of Mecklenburg, the one in the conduct of worship, and the other in the examination of candidates for the ministry.

Scarcely was Melanchthon, the man of peace, free from one controversy until he was precipitated into another. Andrew Osiander, the talented and learned, but contentious, conceited, and ambitious Reformer of Nuremberg, was driven into exile by the *Interim*. He made his way to Duke Albert of Prussia and was soon appointed *Professor Primarius* of theology in the new University of Königsberg. In his *Inaugural* he declared that we are justified not by the imputation of Christ's righteousness, but by union with Christ, in that Christ dwells in us. He also declared that Christ is our mediator only according to his divine nature; not at all according to his human nature. This new exposition of the central doctrine of Lutheranism brought him into collision with his colleagues. Osiander appealed to Melanchthon, who at first regarded the controversy as merely a war of words, and so counselled the Königsbergers to stop their disputing. Very soon Osiander turned against Melanchthon, and declared that both he and all his followers were nothing but ministers of Satan, and that Melanchthon knew nothing about Christian doctrine. He also condemned Melanchthon's books, and asserted that a

---

[1] *C. R.*, 23 : 21 *et seqq.*

more dangerous man than he had not appeared in the Church since the days of the Apostles.

In 1551, Duke Albert sent a copy of Osiander's writings to each of the States of the Augsburg Confession. By order of the Saxon Elector, Melanchthon wrote the *Opinion* of the Wittenberg faculty. He asserts that " we must look upon Jesus Christ, God and man, as our Mediator, must cast ourselves on his wounds, and must find sure consolation in the fact that we have forgiveness of sins, and are heard, on account of this Mediator; " and further: " That faith rests on the Lord Jesus, God and man, and on his merits and intercessions." [1]

Osiander now attacked Melanchthon in the coarsest manner, accusing him of corrupting the Lutheran doctrine and of having introduced the custom of binding candidates for the doctor's degree to the Augsburg Confession. He also wrote, " I will open a vein in him, and will spill his blood all over Germany." He then published two scandalous books, entitled respectively, *The Bleeding of Philip*, and *The Refutation of the Weak and Worthless Answer of Philip Melanchthon.*

As Melanchthon did not wish the people to be further offended by this unseemly dispute, early in January, 1553, he made reply in the form of an academic oration in Latin. The principal point of interest in this oration is the statement that the binding of candidates to the Confession had been introduced about twenty years before by Luther, Jonas, and Bugenhagen, as a safeguard against the

---

[1] *C. R.*, 7 : 898.

fanaticism of the Anabaptists, Servetus, Campanius, Schwenckfeld, and others.[1] October 17, 1553, Osiander died, but the controversy continued to rage for several years, when finally the Königsbergers renounced the teaching of Osiander, and pledged themselves to the Augsburg Confession and to Melanchthon's *Loci*, whereupon they were denounced by the Flacian party as Philippists.

One extreme usually begets another. In opposition to Osiander, Francis Stancar, an ex-Italian priest, who had joined the Reformation, announced the proposition that reconciliation is effected alone through the suffering which Christ bore in his human nature; that is, Christ is a Saviour only by his human nature. This view of the work of Christ was first opposed by Andrew Musculus. Then Melanchthon was called in as peacemaker; but very soon he was attacked by Stancar and accused of three hundred errors. In June, 1553, Melanchthon wrote a *Reply to the Contentions of Stancar*. He states the teaching of the Church to be " that God was born of a virgin, suffered, died, rose again. The divine nature did not suffer, die, rise again, because the person is considered in the concrete."[2] It may be said that the *Reply* to Stancar, and the *Oration* against Osiander, give the best scientific treatment of the Lutheran doctrine of the Person of Christ and of Justification by Faith to be found among the writings of the Reformers. They still have standard value.

[1] *C. R.*, 12 : 5.
[2] *C. R.*, 23 : 87 *et seqq.*

In these years a controversy was carried on between George Major, superintendent of Mansfeld, and the Flacian party, on Good Works. Major maintained that good works are necessary to salvation, not by the *necessity of merit* but by the *necessity of conjunction*, that is, they must exist in conjunction with faith, otherwise faith is dead. Amsdorf defended the proposition that good works are injurious to salvation. At first Melanchthon held himself aloof from the dispute, and advised Major to give up his formula, as it was capable of being misunderstood. But he went on defending it, and so the controversy continued to rage. At length Melanchthon wrote a short *Opinion* on the subject, in which he asserts that " Good Works are necessary, not as extorted by force, but because appointed by an immutable divine order, by which the creature is subject to the Creator." [1]

[1] *C. R.*, 8 : 194.

STATUE OF MELANCHTHON
IN THE CASTLE CHURCH IN WITTENBERG.

CHAPTER XXX

CONTROVERSIES ON THE LORD'S SUPPER

Naumburg Convention—Augsburg Religious Peace—Controversies on the Lord's Supper—Attempts at Reconciliation.

MAURICE, who died July 11, 1553, was succeeded by his brother Augustus. The new Elector at once confirmed the grants made to the university by Maurice, and sought in every way to promote peace in the churches. To this end it was thought wise to hold a convention at Naumburg. The twofold purpose of the convention was to formulate articles of faith to be presented at the next imperial diet, and to oppose a common declaration to the errors of Osiander and Schwenckfeld. Melanchthon, accompanied by John Forster and Camerarius, reached Naumburg, May 20, 1554. The next day witnessed the arrival of delegates from Hesse and Strassburg; and on the 23d Pacæus and Salmut came from Leipzig. On the 24th a *Declaration* written by Melanchthon was presented and signed by ten representatives. The *Declaration* reaffirms the Augsburg Confession; rejects the errors of Schwenckfeld and Osiander; lays down the principle

that " unity in the true doctrine is absolutely necessary "; holds that in church government four things
are highly necessary, viz., Proper Studies, Ordination, Consistories with rigid discipline, and Visitation ; and refuses to commit Ordination to the
bishops, because they persecute sound doctrine.[1]
But the Flacians were not satisfied, and still kept
up their opposition to Wittenberg and to everybody
outside of their own circle.

February 5, 1555, the long-deferred diet was
opened at Augsburg. After much strife and contention the Augsburg Religious Peace was concluded, September 25th. According to its general
principles the nobles had free choice between the
Catholic religion and the Augsburg Confession, and
the religion of the subjects was to depend upon that
of their rulers. Practically this made Protestantism
the religion of Germany, but it did not by any
means extinguish its internal strifes. Discord ran
riot. The spirit of controversy filled the air. The
Christian charity that suffereth long and is kind was
unknown, at least it was not exemplified. On the
one side there was the Melanchthonian school, represented by Wittenberg and Leipzig, which sought
to apply the doctrine and the principles of the Reformation in an irenical and conciliatory manner.
On the other side were the Weimarians, both Court
and theologians, and their theological adherents of
several Lower Saxon cities, who sought to make the
gulf between themselves and their religious opponents, both Catholics and Reformed, as wide as possi-

---

[1] *C. R.*, 8 : 282-291.

ble. This latter party took "holy father Luther," as they called the great Reformer, as their shibboleth and began to imitate his decision, and to apply his methods in a wholly one-sided manner.

Controversy would naturally follow the lines of former years. Hence it soon gathered round the Lord's Supper. The Melanchthonian formulas, which not only had not been condemned, but on the contrary had been approved by Luther, that nothing has the nature of a Sacrament apart from the divinely appointed use, and that Christ is present not on account of the bread, but on account of the recipients; that with the bread and wine, the body and blood of Christ are given—this view, which is found in the *Examen Ordinandorum* and in the exposition of the Nicene Creed, and which is perfectly consistent with the teaching of the Augsburg Confession, the Apology, and the Schmalkald Articles, had been universally accepted as the Lutheran doctrine of the Supper. In 1552, Joachim Westphal, a Hamburg pastor, attacked Calvin and Peter Martyr, and made allusion to Melanchthon and his scholars. Calvin and Bullinger answered Westphal. The controversy was continued for some time with an equal amount of bitterness and violence on each side. Westphal and his followers carried their doctrine to the most absurd extremes. They were not content with the adverbs *vere* and *substantialiter*, by which the presence of Christ in the Supper had been described in the Confessions; they added *corporealiter*, *dentaliter*, *gutturaliter*, and *stomachaliter ;* they said that Christ's body descends like other food into the stomach, and that after the consecration Christ abides in the elements; that his body is everywhere present, even in wood and stone. They seriously asked what would become of a mouse, should it eat of the consecrated host. They carefully swept up the crumbs that fell from the consecrated host and burned the ground on which a few drops of wine happened to have been spilled, on the supposition that these were particles of the veritable body and blood of Christ. Some demanded the adoration of the host, and Dr. Morlin said: " Thou must not say mum! mum! but thou must say what this is which the priest has in his hand."[1]

Melanchthon refused to endorse " such remnants of the papacy," and named such a monstrous perversion of the Lutheran doctrine $\alpha\rho\tauo\lambda\alpha\tau\rho\acute{\epsilon}\iota\alpha$, that is, bread-worship. Nicholas Gallus (1554) and West phal (1557) wrote each a book to show that Melanchthon was on their side, and that at least during the lifetime of Luther he had not endorsed the sacramentarians. Calvin urged Melanchthon to make war on the bread-worshippers, and was impatient when Melanchthon delayed answering his letters, and remained silent. He even attributed Melanchthon's silence to weakness.[2] The situation was a painful one. The great Wittenberg Master simply did not permit himself to be drawn into a controversy which he had not started. It would not have been possible for him to defend the Romish absurdities and superstitions of the Flacian party in

---

[1] C. R., 9: 962 ; Salig., iii., 455, 456, 528.
[2] Bonnet's *Calvin's Letters*, iii., 61, 157.

his own Church, and nothing short of a full endorsement of their position as *Lutheran* would have satisfied them. Personally he was friendly with Calvin, and doubtless had the conviction that the Calvinistic doctrine of the spiritual enjoyment of the body and blood of Christ sacrificed no essential element of religious truth. But there is not a single line in all of Melanchthon's writings to show that he ever endorsed the particular Calvinistic formulas of a *glorified* body, and of a communion in Heaven to which the believer's soul is lifted by faith. On the contrary his formulas show that he maintained that the communion takes place on earth in connection with eating and drinking. Moreover, he ever associates the Supper with the forgiveness of sins, as its essential factor; while with Calvin the Supper is regarded more as a food for the soul of the believer.

Under such circumstances Melanchthon might well write that it was not difficult, but dangerous, to say what ought to be said. To Calvin he wrote, " Certain persons are renewing the contest about bread-worship, moved principally by hatred towards me, that they may have a plausible excuse for crushing me." [1] It is to the praise of his wisdom that he maintained a dignified silence, though at one time he had resolved, under a certain contingency, to reply, since he " feared neither exile nor death." [2] In his correspondence he again and again declared that he continued to teach in accordance with his numerous writings, with the *Wittenberg Concord*,

---

[1] *C. R.*, 8 : 362.
[2] *C. R.*, 8 : 482.

with Luther's Catechism, and the *Examen Ordin-andorum*. Anything new from his pen would only have added fuel to the fire. Yet his silence did not satisfy the Flacians. They evermore accused him of *Calvinising*, on the ground that not to endorse their semi-Romanism, and not to confute Calvin, was to *Calvinise*.

In the year 1556, an effort was made to effect a reconciliation between Melanchthon and Flacius. The terms proposed were those of Flacius's own composition, and involved the humiliation of Melanchthon. When the terms were rejected, Flacius broke out in a most violent publication, in which he demanded a public recantation by Melanchthon and his friends as a condition of peace. When finally others interceded for peace and proposed terms that were artfully meant to make Melanchthon " cut his own throat," the latter replied that he had always sought the peace of the Church; that he had introduced no new doctrines, and had taught the doctrines received in the Church. " If this form of doctrine does not please *Flacius*, let him publish another body of doctrine. If the churches shall prefer it, I will make no opposition." [1]

Melanchthon also wrote a letter to Flacius in which he denies that the Leipzig *Interim* was " a conspiracy of the theologians," as had been charged. He also says:

" Then we were censured with all kinds of reproaches by the courtiers. Now we are censured by you. At length the Prince said with his own voice, that he did not seek to have the doctrine, nor anything necessary,

---

[1] *C. R.*, 9: 103–105.

changed, but to retain external rites in the ordering of the festivals, lections, and in attire. Subsequently the counsellors named these *Adiaphora ;* for in the beginning the word was imposed upon us. I knew that even the slightest changes would be offensive to the people. Yet when the doctrine was to be retained intact, I preferred that ours should submit to this bondage, rather than forsake the ministry of the Gospel, and I gave the same advice to the Franconians. This I did. The doctrine of the Confession I never changed. In regard to these moderate rites I contended less because they have been retained in very many churches of these parts. Then you began your opposition. I ceased; I did not contend. Ajax in Homer in his fight with Hector was satisfied when Hector fell and acknowledged him as victor. You make no end of criminations. What foe strikes those who have surrendered and grounded their arms? Conquer! I yield. I will not contend about these rites. I greatly desire that the Church should have peace. I confess that in this matter I made a mistake, and I ask pardon from God because I did not flee those insidious counsels. But I shall refute the false charges made by you and Gallus." [1]

In April, 1557, Flacius was called to Jena as professor of theology. The new university became the centre of rigid Lutheranism, and exerted a strong influence over the Duchy of Saxony, in Magdeburg, and in parts of Northern Germany. But the larger part of the evangelical churches of the country, viz., those of the Electorate, Pomerania, Hesse, and Southern Germany, acknowledged the services of Melanchthon and blamed the violence of the Flacians.

[1] *C. R.*, 8 : 839.

CHAPTER XXXI

CLOSING YEARS AND DEATH

Frankfort Recess—The Flacian Party—Melanchthon Attends the Colloquy of Worms—The Weimar *Confutation Book*—The Bavarian Articles—The Heidelberg Scandal—Last Sickness—Death and Burial.

THE Lutherans were now divided into two hostile camps. The princes, assembled at Frankfort in March, 1558, sought to put an end to the controversies by the publication of a fair and candid declaration, known as the *Frankfort Recess*,[1] which is based partly on an Opinion by Melanchthon and partly on an essay by John Brentz. The *Recess* states that man is justified by faith alone in Christ; that new obedience is necessary in the justified, that is, necessary according to divine appointment; that Christ is truly and essentially present in the Supper with the bread and wine, and is given to Christians to eat and drink.

The *Recess* was decidedly rejected by the Weimar dukes, who caused the Weimar *Confutation Book* to be published in 1559 as a refutation of all the heresies

---

[1] *C. R.*, 9 : 489.

of the times, and as the assertion of the most rigid Lutheranism. The object of the book was to establish pure Lutheranism in the land. Hence the ministers of Thuringia were required to sign this book; but it did not preserve harmony even in the ducal dominions. The spirit of antagonism had so possessed the authors of the book, Flacius and others, that they soon quarrelled with John Frederick the Second, and were driven from Jena.

That the Flacian party did good service in hastening the rejection of the *Interim*, has been already conceded in these pages; but " the profane scurrility " and " the most diabolical calumnies of the Flacians," as Melanchthon characterises their conduct, is worthy of unqualified reprehension. In their mad presumption, and in their insane zeal for pure Lutheranism, they transcended all just limits, and became the most dangerous errorists. Indeed the Lutheran Church has uniformly rejected the errors of Osiander, Flacius, Amsdorf, and Stancar; but she has never placed herself on record against a single doctrinal proposition of Philip Melanchthon, when such proposition was presented in the full Melanchthonian form and sense. In the Confession and its Apology, both of which he wrote, in his *Loci*, and in the many admirable definitions and expositions scattered through his voluminous writings, and in his spirit, which still lives, Philip Melanchthon is an abiding power for good in the Lutheran Church. Even the authors of the Form of Concord, Andreæ, Chemnitz, and Selneccer, retained the full Melanchthonian doctrine of the Will in the earlier drafts of

that famous book, and sacrificed it at last only at
the behest of a few intractable zealots; but still retained its fundamental tendency, as already shown,
in opposition to the absolute predestinarianism of
Luther and the Flacians, and in its affirmation of
the universality of divine grace.[1]

In the spring of 1557, Melanchthon was invited to
assist in reorganising the University of Heidelberg,
but his Prince refused to spare him from Wittenberg.
It was the purpose also of his Elector to take him
to Denmark to attend a synod in which the Lord's
Supper was to be discussed. In administering the
communion a pastor had been so unfortunate as to
spill some wine. This accident furnished the occasion for the calling of a synod. But Melanchthon
shrank from the proposed journey to the North,
giving as his reason that at his birth an astrologer
had told his father he should suffer shipwreck in the
Baltic. It is altogether probable that Melanchthon
dreaded a conference with the excited theologians
far more than he feared the stormy rage of the sea.
For some reason the Elector changed his mind,
and ordered Melanchthon to attend a colloquy at
Worms; but even with the prospect presented by
this journey Melanchthon was not pleased. To
Camerarius he wrote:

"I am now engaged in preparing for a trip to the
Rhine. I dread the dire sophistry and rage of the hypo-
crites more than Ulysses dreaded Scylla and Charybdis.
I would rather stay at home and say prayers with my

---

[1] Gieseler's *Ch. Hist.*, iv., 486, Translation.

little granddaughters than elsewhere to listen to the riddles of the Sphinx.'' [1]

On the fifteenth of August, 1557, Melanchthon set out for Worms, accompanied by Peucer. Paul Eber and Cracovius had gone on ahead. At Frankfort he heard that the Flacians were demanding the condemnation of all errors and errorists among the Protestants as a condition preliminary to the holding of a colloquy with the Catholics. He wrote to friends that the virulence of his enemies was giving him great trouble. August 28th he reached Worms, and was received with the highest reverence by nearly all of the theologians.

The Flacians spared no pains to excite the whole body of theologians against him, and when they failed in this they cried out, '' There is no candour and no love of truth; everything is full of sarcasm and vile hypocrisy.'' Finally when they failed to carry their sentence of condemnation, aimed chiefly at Melanchthon, they presented their protest, which, however, was not entered on the minutes, but merely allowed as the expression of personal conviction.

In reply to the accusation of the Flacians, Melanchthon reaffirmed his adherence to the Confession, the Apology, the Schmalkald Articles, and the *Confessio Saxonica*. He said· '' I wrote the Confession and the Apology which they are quoting. Now they are debating how to get rid of their author.'' [2]

When in the colloquy the Catholics asked whether the Protestants were agreed, he replied,

---

[1] *C. R.*, 9 : 185.
[2] *C. R.*, 9 : 260.

" We are all agreed on the Confession." Then the Flacians again presented their articles; but failing to have them recognised, they left the conference at the beginning of October, declaring that they had been excluded. The conference was now adjourned to hear the pleasure of the King. In the earlier sessions the Catholics had insisted on " the perpetual consent of the Church," as " the rule for deciding all controversies." The Protestants would admit no rule except the Holy Scriptures and the three ancient Creeds.

As·the conference was adjourned, Melanchthon now had leisure to visit Heidelberg on invitation of the Palatine Elector. Here he was received with extraordinary demonstrations of respect by the Prince and by the university. His pleasure was enhanced by meeting his brother George and his dear friend Camerarius. But the latter had been sent on a sad mission. Melanchthon's wife had died on the eleventh of October, and Camerarius had come to break the news to him. Finding how happy he had made him by his visit, Camerarius postponed the announcement to the second day, when the two were walking together in the Prince's garden. Melanchthon heard the sorrowful intelligence with composure, and, looking up to heaven, exclaimed: " Fare thee well. I shall soon follow thee." He then spoke to his friend on the distressed condition of the Church, and on the terrible events that threatened, so that he seemed almost to bury his own sorrow in his thought of the common distress of the Fatherland.[1]

---

[1] Camerarius, p. 335.

In November, he returned to Worms, where he prepared " A Formula of Agreement touching Certain Disputed Articles." This formula gives the clearest proof of his adherence to the Confession and Apology, and to the whole Lutheran doctrinal system. It will stand forever in the estimation of fair and honest men as an all-sufficient refutation of the outrageous slanders of his baleful enemies, who were still boasting that they would drive him out of Germany.[1]

As the Protestants had been invited to recognise Ferdinand as Emperor, it was thought desirable to hold a convention for the consideration of religious questions. As usual, Melanchthon was commissioned to prepare an *Opinion*. This *Opinion* became the basis of the *Frankfort Recess* already referred to, which in time called forth the Weimar *Confutation Book*.

Melanchthon was now more than ever pained by the extravagance and violence of the Flacians. His distress was increased by the death, April 20, 1558, of his dear friend and colleague, Pastor Bugenhagen, and by the imprisonment of Victorin Strigel and Pastor Hugel of Jena, because they would not subscribe the *Confutation Book*.

Nothing could be farther from the spirit of Melanchthon than the application of such a method to secure uniformity in faith. Gladly would he have kept aloof from all further controversy with the Weimarians. But when the Elector of Saxony required of his theologians an *Opinion* of the *Confuta-*

[1] *C. R.*, 9 : 401.

tion Book, it fell to the lot of Melanchthon to write it. Among other things he declared that the Weimarians make such statements in regard to the Lord's Supper " as no one in the Church from the beginning has made, not even the Papists; viz., that the body of Christ is in all places, in stone and in wood." He refutes " the Stoic and Manichæan absurdities " of the Weimarians, as that " all the actions of men are necessitated." On the contrary, he says: " We begin with the Word of God, which condemns sin, and which offers forgiveness and grace for Christ's sake; and we say that thereby God works alarm and comfort, as is foreshown in David's conversion." He lays down the rule: " *Grace precedes; the Will follows; God draws, but he draws him that is willing.*" [1]

There were also outside enemies whom Melanchthon had to meet and refute during this last year of his life. The Jesuits had worked their way into Bavaria, and were expelling every person who would not accept the thirty-one articles of their *Inquisition*, which " had been prepared by a disreputable, raving monk." Melanchthon first saw these articles in September, 1558. In August of the following year he published his *Reply to the Impious Articles of the Bavarian Inquisition.*[2] The *Reply* ranks as one of its author's great apologetic writings, and has been called his swan's song, or dying confession, inasmuch as in his last Will and Testament, written the day before his death, he reaffirms it as his " Con-

---

[1] *C. R.*, 9 : 765-769.
[2] *Corpus Doctrinæ Christianæ.*

fession against the Papists, the Anabaptists, the Flacians, and the like."[1]

The *Reply* deals not only with the thirty-one articles of the *Inquisition*, but also with the various discussions which had risen among the Protestants themselves. It is direct and positive in tone, and leaves nothing to be desired from the standpoint of a true, evangelical Lutheranism. It affirms the real and substantial presence of Christ in the Eucharist and the communication of his body and blood. In regard to the Will he reaffirms the rule: "Grace precedes; the Will follows. The Word begins, the Will is called and drawn. God draws, but draws him who is willing."

A month later Melanchthon published the German edition of his *Corpus Doctrinæ Christianæ*, or, *A Complete Summary of the Correct, True, Christian Doctrine of the Holy Gospel*. It contains the *Augsburg Confession*, the *Apology*, the *Saxon Confession* of 1551, the *Loci*, the *Examen Ordinandorum*, *The Reply to the Bavarian Articles*, *A Refutation* of the Mohammedan Error of Servetus. The Preface bears date, September 29, 1559. The same book, with only slight deviations in contents, was prepared also in Latin, and published the following year. The Preface is dated, February 16, 1560.

Melanchthon, now grown weary of life, and still more weary of the quarrels of the theologians, was destined to have his soul vexed again over a most disreputable quarrel in regard to the Lord's Supper. He had recommended Tillman Heshuss, a former

[1] *C. R.*, 9: 1099.

pupil of his, to a professorship and to the superin-
tendency at Heidelberg.   Heshuss and one of his
deacons, Klebitz by name, actually fought over the
communion cup at the altar.   The Elector deposed
both of them, and sent his secretary to Wittenberg
to obtain the advice of Melanchthon.   Under the
circumstances it would have been useless to propose
new dogmatic formulas.   Hence Melanchthon treated
the subject of the Lord's Supper wholly on its practical side as " a communion of the body," as " a
consociation with the body of Christ," and appealed to the *Examen Ordinandorum* for " the form
of words concerning the Supper."   He rejects the
transubstantiation of the Catholics, as also the dic-
tum of the Bremen theologians that " the bread is
the substantial body of Christ," and that of Heshuss
that " the bread is the true body of Christ." [1]

The Elector Frederick, in his revulsion from the
disgraceful conduct of Heshuss and Klebitz, banished the Lutheran doctrine and introduced the
Reformed.   This so excited the aged John Brentz
that he assembled a synod at Stuttgart, and procured the adoption of articles which set forth a most
extreme doctrine of the Lord's Supper, including
oral manducation and a declaration of the abso
lute ubiquity of the human nature of Christ.   Mel
anchthon in a letter to George Cracovius complains
of " the decree of the Würtemberg abbots " as
written in barbarous Latin, and as presenting a doctrine " clearly in conflict with the ancient purer
Church "; and affirms that he still retains the form

---

[1] *C. R.*, 9: 962.

of words published many years ago in the *Examen Ordinandorum.*[1]

In this same letter he says that he " is cruelly tortured by many hostile armies." But this torture was not to last long. On the fifth of April, returning from Leipzig, whither he had gone to examine the Elector's Stipendiaries, he caught a cold. This affection was followed by a fever, which gradually grew worse, but did not at once prostrate the patient, nor wholly incapacitate him for work. He continued to lecture, to converse with his friends, to write letters, and to revise manuscripts for the press. A few days before the end came, he wrote on the left and right margins of a sheet of paper the reasons why he should not fear death·

" Thou shalt depart from sin. Thou shalt be set free from vexations, and from the rage of the theologians."

" Thou shalt come into the light. Thou shalt see God. Thou shalt behold the Son of God. Thou shalt learn those wonderful mysteries which in this life thou couldst not understand, as why we were created as we are, and what is the character of the union of the two natures in Christ." [2]

As his weakness increased and his end drew nigh, Dr. Peucer asked him if he wished anything else. He answered, " Nothing else but heaven. Do not ask me any more." The pastor then prayed, all present falling on their knees. At evening the pastor

---

[1] *C. R.*, 9: 1036.

[2] A detailed account of Melanchthon's last sickness and death is given in *C. R.*, 10: 235 *et seqq.*

pronounced the blessing on him, and Professor
Winsheim quoted for him from the Psalmist: " Into
thy hands I commend my spirit; thou hast redeemed me, thou faithful and true God." His lips
moved as if in prayer. At a quarter before seven
o'clock in the evening of April 19, 1560, Philip
Melanchthon fell on sleep, aged sixty-three years,
two months, and three days. The earthly house of
his tabernacle was dissolved. He had fought a good
fight, he had finished his course, he had kept the
faith.

The body was placed in a tin coffin, and this in a
wooden one with an inscription in Latin which re-
counts the chief events of his life, as that he had
served the University of Wittenberg forty-two
years, was the faithful assistant of Luther in the
purification of doctrine, was the author of the Augsburg Confession, and the firm defender of divine
truth, publicly and privately, in diets and by his
writings. The remains were first taken to the Parish
Church and placed before the altar where he had
been accustomed to kneel in prayer. Dr. Paul
Eber, the pastor, delivered a German sermon on the
hope of immortality. The remains were then removed to Castle Church, where Dr. Veit Winsheim,
professor of Greek, pronounced a Latin funeral oration. At five o'clock P.M., April 21st, all that was
mortal of Philip Melanchthon was sunk into the
grave by the side of the mortal remains of Martin
Luther—" lovely and pleasant in their lives, and
in their death they were not divided."

The funeral cortège, consisting of students, relat-

ives, professors, officials, citizens, and nobles, was
the largest ever seen in Wittenberg. Men and
women alike testified their grief by their tears and
lamentations. To all parts of Germany, except to
those parts estranged by the Flacians, the news of
" the dear father and preceptor's death brought
sorrow." At Strassburg and Tübingen meetings
were held and memorial addresses were delivered.
Strangers who had never seen him sent letters of
condolence, and many Greek and Latin elegies were
written on his death. Yet death, the great recon-
ciler, did not soften the wrath of his enemies. The
Flacians pursued his memory with calumnies more
virulent and malicious than ever. They charged
him with heresy and with the betrayal of the Lutheran doctrine. Even at the beginning of the
seventeenth century, Leonhard Hutter, a Wittenberg professor of theology, during a public discussion, tore Melanchthon's picture down from the
wall and trampled it under foot. But History has
vindicated him against " the wrath of the theologians." To-day the Lutheran Church places him
on a pedestal by the side of Luther, and honours
the two together as the fathers and founders of the
Lutheran Church. Germany proclaims him her Preceptor. Protestantism venerates him as the witness
of her spirit, as the prophet of her future.

APPENDIX

FUNERAL ORATION OVER LUTHER

" THOUGH amid the public sorrow my voice is obstructed by grief and tears, yet in this vast assembly something ought to be said, not, as among the heathen, only in praise of the deceased. Much rather is this assembly to be reminded of the wonderful government of the Church, and of her perils, that in our distress we may consider what we are, most of all, to desire, and by what examples we are to regulate our lives. There are ungodly men, who, in the confused condition of human affairs, think that everything is the result of accident. But we who are illumined by the many explicit declarations of God, distinguish the Church from the profane multitude; and we know that it is in reality governed and preserved by God. We fix our eye on this Church. We acknowledge lawful rulers, and consider their manner of life. We also select suitable leaders and teachers, whom we may piously follow and reverence.

" It is necessary to think on, and to speak of these things, so often as we name the name of the Reverend Doctor Martin Luther, our most dear Father and Preceptor, whom many wicked men have most bitterly hated; but whom we, who know that he was a minister of the Gospel raised up by God, love and applaud. We also have the evidence to show that his doctrine did not consist of seditious opinions scattered by blind impulse, as men of Epicurean tastes suppose; but that it is an exhibition of the will of God, and of true worship, an exposition of the Holy Scriptures, a preaching of the Word of God, that is, of the Gospel of Jesus Christ.

" In orations delivered on occasions like the present, it is the custom to say many things about the personal endowments of those who are panegyrised. But I will omit this, and will speak only on the main subject, viz., his relation to the Church; for good men will always judge that if he promoted sound and necessary doctrine in the Church, we should give thanks to God because he raised him up; and all good men should praise his labours, fidelity, constancy, and other virtues, and should most affectionately cherish his memory.

" So much for the exordium of my oration. The Son of God, as Paul observes, sits at the right hand of the Eternal Father, and gives gifts unto men, viz., the Gospel and the Holy Spirit. That he might bestow these he raises up Prophets, Apostles, Teachers, and Pastors, and selects from our midst those who study, hear, and delight in the writings of the Prophets and Apostles. Nor does he call into this service only those who occupy the ordinary stations; but he often makes war upon those very ones by teachers chosen from other stations. It is both pleasant and profitable to contemplate the Church of all ages, and to consider the goodness of God, in sending useful teachers, one after another, that as some fall in the ranks, others may at once press into their places.

" Behold the Patriarchs, Adam, Seth, Enoch, Methu-

❧ ORATIO ☙

Uber der Leich

des Ehrwirdigen herrn D. Mar-
tini Luthers / gethan durch Philip-
pum Melanthon / Am rrij.
tag Februarij.

Verdeudscht aus dem Latin
durch D. Caspar Creu-
tziger
⸪

Gedruckt zu Wittemberg
durch Georgen Rhaw
Anno XLVI.

TITLE-PAGE OF MELANCHTHON'S FUNERAL ORATION ON LUTHER, 1546.

selah, Noah, Shem. When in the time of the last named, who lived in the neighbourhood of the Sodomites, the nations forgot the teaching of Noah and Shem, and worshipped idols, Abraham was raised up to be Shem's companion and to assist him in his great work and in propagating sound doctrine. He was succeeded by Isaac, Jacob, and Joseph, which last lighted the torch of truth in all the land of Egypt, which at that time was the most flourishing kingdom in all the world. Then came Moses, Joshua, Samuel, David, Elijah, Elisha, Isaiah, Jeremiah, Daniel, Zechariah. Then Ezra, Onias, and the Maccabees. Then Simeon, Zacharias, the Baptist, Christ, and the Apostles. It is a delight to contemplate this unbroken succession, inasmuch as it is a manifest proof of the presence of God in the Church.

" After the Apostles comes a long line, inferior, indeed, but distinguished by the divine attestations: Polycarp, Irenæus, Gregory of Neocæsarea, Basil, Augustin, Prosper, Maximus, Hugo, Bernard, Tauler, and others. And though these later times have been less fruitful, yet God has always preserved a remnant; and that a more splendid light of the Gospel has been kindled by the voice of Luther, cannot be denied.

" To that splendid list of most illustrious men raised up by God to gather and establish the Church, and recognised as the chief glory of the human race, must be added the name of Martin Luther. Solon, Themistocles, Scipio, Augustus, and others, who established, or ruled over vast empires, were great men, indeed, but far inferior were they to our leaders, Isaiah, John the Baptist, Paul, Augustin, and Luther. It is proper that we of the Church should understand this manifest difference.

" What, then, are the great and splendid things disclosed by Luther which render his life illustrious ? Many are crying out that confusion has come upon the Church, and that inexplicable controversies have arisen. I reply that this belongs to the regulation of the Church. When the Holy Spirit reproves the world, disorders arise on account of the obstinacy of the wicked. The fault is with those who will not hear the Son of God, of whom the Heavenly Father says: 'Hear ye him.' Luther brought to light the true and necessary doctrine. That the densest darkness existed touching the doctrine of repentance, is evident. In his discussions he showed what true repentance is, and what is the refuge and the sure comfort of the soul which quails under the sense of the wrath of God. He expounded Paul's doctrine, which says that man is justified by faith. He showed the difference between the Law and the Gospel, between the righteousness of faith and civil righteousness. He also showed what the true worship of God is, and recalled the Church from heathenish superstition, which imagines that God is worshipped, even though the mind, agitated by some academic doubt, turns away from God. He bade us worship in faith and with a good conscience, and led us to the one Mediator, the Son of God, who sits at the right hand of the Eternal Father and makes intercession for us—not to images or to dead men, that by a shocking superstition impious men might worship images and dead men.

" He also pointed out other services acceptable to God, and so adorned and guarded civil life, as it had never been adorned and guarded by any other man's writings. Then from necessary services he separated the puerilities of human ceremonies, the rites and institutions which hinder the true worship of God. And that the heavenly truth might be handed down to posterity he translated the Prophetical and Apostolic Scriptures into the German language with so much accuracy that his version is more easily understood by the reader than most commentaries.

" He also published many expositions, which Erasmus was wont to say excelled all others. And as it is recorded respecting the rebuilding of Jerusalem that with one hand they builded and with the other they held the sword, so he fought with the enemies of the true doctrine, and at the same time composed annotations replete with heavenly truth, and by his pious counsel brought assistance to the consciences of many.

" Inasmuch as a large part of the doctrine cannot be understood by human reason, as the doctrine of the remission of sins and of faith, it must be acknowledged that he was taught of God; and many of us witnessed the struggles through which he passed, in establishing the principle that by faith are we received and heard of God.

" Hence throughout eternity pious souls will magnify the benefits which God has bestowed on the Church through Luther. First they will give thanks to God. Then they will own that they owe much to the labours of this man, even though atheists who mock the Church declare that these splendid achievements are empty and superstitious nothings.

" It is not true, as some falsely affirm, that intricate disputes have arisen, that the apple of discord has been thrown into the Church, that the riddles of the Sphynx have been proposed. It is an easy matter for discreet and pious persons, and for those who do not judge maliciously, to see, by a comparison of views, which accord with the heavenly doctrine, and which do not. Yea, without doubt these controversies have already been settled in the minds of all pious persons. For since God

wills to reveal himself and his purposes in the language
of Prophets and Apostles, it is not to be imagined that
that language is as ambiguous as the leaves of the Sibyl,
which, when disturbed, fly away, the sport of the winds.

" Some, by no means evil-minded persons, have complained that Luther displayed too much severity.   I will
not deny this.   But I answer in the language of Erasmus: ' Because of the magnitude of the disorders God
gave this age a violent physician.'   When God raised up
this instrument against the proud and impudent enemies
of the truth, he spoke as he did to Jeremiah: ' Behold I
place my words in thy mouth; destroy and build.'   Over
against these enemies God set this mighty destroyer.   In
vain do they find fault with God.   Moreover, God does
not govern the Church by human counsels; nor does he
choose instruments very like those of men.   It is natural
for mediocre and inferior minds to dislike those of more
ardent character, whether good or bad.   When Aristides
saw Themistocles by the mighty impulse of genius undertake and successfully accomplish great achievements,
though he congratulated the State, he sought to turn the
zealous mind of Themistocles from its course.

" I do not deny that the more ardent characters sometimes make mistakes, for amid the weakness of human
nature no one is without fault.   But we may say of such
a one what the ancients said of Hercules, Cimon, and
others: Ἄκομψος μὲν, ἄλλα τὰ μέγιστα αγαϑὸς—
' rough indeed, but worthy of all praise.'   And in the
Church, if, as Paul says, he wars a good warfare, holding
faith and a good conscience, he is to be held in the highest esteem by us.

" That Luther was such we do know, for he constantly
defended purity of doctrine and kept a good conscience.
There is no one who knew him, who does not know that

he was possessed of the greatest kindness, and of the greatest affability in the society of his friends, and that he was in no sense contentious or quarrelsome.   He also exhibited, as such a man ought, the greatest dignity of demeanour.   He possessed

$$\mathring{a}\psi\varepsilon\upsilon\delta\grave{\varepsilon}\varsigma\ \mathring{\eta}\vartheta o\varsigma,\ \varepsilon\mathring{\upsilon}\pi\rho o\sigma\acute{\eta}\gamma o\rho o\nu\ \sigma\tau\acute{o}\mu\alpha,$$

'An upright character, a gracious speech.'

" Rather may we apply to him the words of Paul: ' Whatsoever things are true, whatsoever things are honest, whatsoever things are just, whatsoever things are pure, whatsoever things are lovely, whatsoever things are of good report.'   If he was severe, it was the severity of zeal for the truth, not the love of strife, or of harshness.   Of these things we and many others are witnesses. To his sixty-third year he spent his life in the most ardent study of religion and of all the liberal arts.   No speech of mine can worthily set forth the praises of such a man. No lewd passions were ever detected in him, no seditious counsels.   He was emphatically the advocate of peace. He never mingled the arts of politics with the affairs of the Church for the purpose of augmenting his own authority, or that of his friends.   Such wisdom and virtue, I am persuaded, do not arise from mere human diligence.   Brave, lofty, ardent souls, such as Luther had, must be divinely guided.

" What shall I say of his other virtues ?   Often have I found him weeping and praying for the whole Church. He spent a part of almost every day reading the Psalms, with which he mingled his own supplications amid tears and groans.   Often did he express his indignation at those who through indifference or pretence of other occupations, are indifferent in the matter of prayer.   On this account, he said, Divine Wisdom has prescribed forms of prayer, that by reading them our minds may be quickened, and the voice ever may proclaim the God we worship.

" In the many grave deliberations incident to the public perils, we observed the transcendent vigour of his mind, his valour, his unshaken courage, where terror reigned.   God was his anchor, and faith never failed him.

" As regards the penetration of his mind, in the midst of uncertainties he alone saw what was to be done.   Nor was he indifferent, as many suppose, to the public weal. On the contrary he knew the wants of the state, and clearly understood the feelings and wishes of his fellow-citizens.   And though his genius was so extraordinary, yet he read with the greatest eagerness both ancient and modern ecclesiastical writings and all histories, that he might find in them examples applicable to present conditions.

" The immortal monuments of his eloquence remain, nor has the power of his oratory ever been surpassed.

" The removal of such a man from our midst, a man of the most transcendent genius, skilled in learning, trained by long experience, adorned with many superb and heroic virtues, chosen of God for the reformation of the Church, loving us all with a paternal affection—the removal of such a man from our midst calls for tears and lamentations.   We are like orphans bereft of a distinguished and faithful father.   But though we must bow to God, yet let us not permit the memory of his virtues and of his good offices to perish from among us.   And let us rejoice that he now holds that familiar and delightful intercourse with God and his Son, our Lord Jesus Christ, which by faith in the Son of God he always sought and expected, where, by the manifestations of God, and by the testimony of the whole Church in heaven, he not only hears the applause of his toils in the service of the Gospel, but is also delivered from the mortal body as from a prison, and has entered that vastly higher school, where he can contemplate the essence of God, the two natures joined in Christ, and the whole purpose set forth in founding and redeeming the Church,— which great things, contained and set forth in the sacred oracles, he contemplated by faith; but seeing them now face to face, he rejoices with unspeakable joy; and with his whole soul he ardently pours forth thanks to God for his great goodness.

" There he knows why the Son of God is called the Word and the Image of the Eternal Father, and in what way the Holy Spirit is the bond of mutual affection, not only between the Father and Son, but also between them and the Church. The first principles of these truths he had learned in this mortal life, and often did he most earnestly and wisely discourse on these lofty themes, on the distinction between true and false worship, on the true knowledge of God and of divine revelation, on the true God as distinguished from false deities.

" Many persons in this assembly have heard him discourse on these words: ' Ye shall see the heaven open, and the angels of God ascending and descending upon the Son of man.' He bade his hearers fix their minds on that large word of comfort which declares that heaven is open, that God is revealed to us; that the bolts of the divine wrath are turned away from those who flee to the Son; that God is now with us, and that those who call upon him, are received, guided, and kept by him.

" This purpose of God, pronounced by atheists to be a fable, admonishes us to banish doubt, and to cast out those fears which restrain our timid souls from calling on God and from resting in Him.

" He was wont to say that the angels, ascending and descending in the body of Christ, are ministers of the Gospel, who first under the direction of Christ ascend to God and receive from him the light of the Gospel and the Holy Spirit. Then they descend, that is, discharge the office of teaching among men. He was also accustomed to add that these heavenly spirits, these angels who behold the Son, study and rejoice over the mysterious union of the two natures; and that since they are the armed servants of the Lord in defending the Church, they are directed by his hand.

" Of these glorious things he is now a spectator, and as once under the direction of Christ he ascended and descended among the ministers of the Gospel, so now he beholds the angels sent by Christ, and enjoys with them the contemplation of the divine wisdom and the divine works.

" We remember the great delight with which he recounted the course, the counsels, the perils, and escapes of the Prophets, and the learning with which he discoursed on all the ages of the Church, thereby showing that he was inflamed by no ordinary passion for those wonderful men. Now he embraces them and rejoices to hear them speak, and to speak to them in turn. Now they hail him gladly as a companion, and thank God with him for having gathered and preserved the Church.

" Hence we do not doubt that Luther is eternally happy. We mourn over our bereavement, and though it is necessary to bow to the will of God who has called him hence, let us know that it is the will of God that we should cherish the memory of this man's virtues and services. That duty let us now discharge. Let us acknowledge that this man was a blessed instrument of God, and let us studiously learn his doctrine. Let us in

our humble station imitate his virtues, so necessary for
us: His fear of God, his faith, his devoutness in prayer,
his uprightness in the ministry, his chastity, his diligence
in avoiding seditious counsels, his eagerness for learning.
And as we ought frequently to reflect on those other
pious leaders of the Church, Jeremiah, John the Baptist,
and Paul, so let us consider the doctrine and course of
this man.   Let us also join in thanksgiving and prayer,
as is meet in this assembly.   Follow me then with devout hearts:—We give thanks to thee, Almighty God, the
Eternal Father of our Lord Jesus Christ, the Founder of
thy Church, together with thy Coëternal Son, and the
Holy Spirit, wise, good, merciful, just, true, powerful
Sovereign, because thou dost gather a heritage for thy
Son from among the human race, and dost maintain the
ministry of the Gospel, and hast now reformed thy
Church by means of Luther.   We present our ardent
supplications that thou wouldst henceforth preserve, fix,
and impress upon our hearts the doctrines of truth, as
Isaiah prayed for his disciples; and that by thy Holy
Spirit thou wouldst inflame our minds with a pure de-
votion, and direct our feet into the paths of holy
obedience.

" As the death of illustrious rulers often portends dire
punishment to the survivors, we beseech you, we, especially, to whom is committed the office of teaching, beseech you to reflect on the perils that now threaten the
whole world.   Yonder, the Turks are advancing ; here,
civil discord is threatened; there, other adversaries, re-
leased at last from the fear of Luther's censure, will
corrupt the truth more boldly than ever.

" That God may avert these calamities, let us be more
diligent in regulating our lives and in directing our
studies, always holding fast this sentiment, that so long

as we retain, hear, learn, and love the pure teaching of
the Gospel, we shall be the House and Church of God,
as the Son of God says: ' If a man love me, he will keep
my words; and my Father will love him, and we will
come unto him, and make our abode with him.' Encouraged by this ample promise, let us be quickened in
teaching the truth of Heaven, and let us not forget that
the human race and governments are preserved for the
sake of the Church; and let us fix our eyes on that
eternity to which God has called our attention, who has
not revealed himself by such splendid witnesses and sent
his Son in vain, but truly loves and cares for those who
magnify his benefits. Amen.'' [1]

[1] *C. R.*, 11   726 *et seqq.*

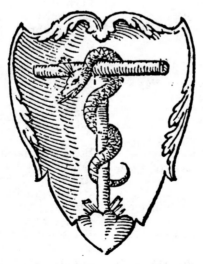

MELANCHTHON'S COAT OF ARMS.

INDEX

A

Adams, Melchior, 175
Adiaphoristic Controversy, 338 *sqq.*
Agricola, John, 50, 58, 79, 167–170, 175
Agricola, Rudolph, 13, 15
Agricola, Stephen, 185, 187, 189, 192, 258, 335, 350, 351
Alber, 254
Albert, Cardinal, 312
Alesius, Alexander, 265
Alliance against the Protestants, 314
Altenburg, 49
Amberg, 2
Amsdorf, Nicholas, 50, 72, 80, 87, 225, 257, 265, 281
Anabaptists, 170, 171
Andreæ, 369
Anshelm, Thomas, 22, 24
Antonius (Barnes), Dr., 229
Apology of the Augsburg Confession, 216, 217
Aquila, Caspar, 326
Articles of 1535, the Thirteen, 229
Articles of the Peasants, 145, 146
Augsburg Confession, 190–207, 218
Augsburg, Diet of, 191–201
Augsburg *Interim*, 329
Augsburg Religious Peace, 362
Aurogallus, 72

B

Bacchanti, 8
Baier, Dr., 81, 91, 200
Baptism, 170, 171
Barnes, Dr. Anthony, 228
Baumgartner, Hieronimus, 131, 182
Bebel, Heinrich, 20
Beckman, Otto, 37
Bellay, John, 224, 227
Bellay, William, 224, 227
Bern, 10
Bernhard, Bartholomew, 78, 79
Biel, Gabriel, 20
Bigamy, the Landgrave's, 274 *sqq.*
Billican, Theobald, 18
Billich, 297
Bindseil, 281
Blaurer, Ambrose, 225
Bodenstein (Carlstadt), Andrew, 37
Bora, Katharine von, 152, 153
Borner, Caspar, 37
Brassican, John, 19, 24
Bread-worship, 364
Brentz, John, 18, 185, 187, 189, 225, 235, 243
Bretschneider, 21, 26
Bretten, 1–4, 8, 31, 33, 36, 114–117, 121, 175, 256
Brismann, 152
Brück, Chancellor, 80, 192, 214, 216, 221, 290, 303, 305, 306
Bucer, Martin, 185, 188, 225, 227, 250–253

Bugenhagen, 127, 161, 162, 168, 169, 229, 254, 257
Bullinger, 363
Burkhard, Francis, 113, 117, 290, 337
Busch, Hermann, 115

C

Cajetan, Cardinal, 47, 49
Calvin, John, 264, 301, 363, 365, 366
Camerarius, Joachim, 35, 64, 114, 117, 119, 125–127, 131, 132, 136, 140, 152, 157, 160, 173, 176, 216, 225, 230, 232, 256, 280, 290, 295, 296, 329, 335, 353, 361, 370, 372
Campanius, 359, 361
Campeggius, Lorenzo, 115, 122, 190, 199, 209, 211, 212, 214, 215
Capito, 253
Carlowitz, Christopher von, 310, 330–332
Carlstadt, 47, 49, 50, 52, 53, 79, 80, 82, 83, 85, 91, 92, 107, 126, 144, 195
Cassel, Bucer and Melanchthon at, 251
Celibacy, 156, 157
Cellarius, Martin, 85, 91
Celle *Interim*, 334
Celtis, Conrad, 13
Chemnitz, Martin, 103, 283, 284, 369
Chilius, Dr. Ulrich, 224
Chrysostom, John, 88, 233
Chytræus, David, 283, 284
Coburg, 140, 194, 195, 216 ; *see* Luther
Cochlæus, John, 102, 211
Cologne Reformation, 296 *sqq.*
Comitianus, Andrew Francis, 35
Confession, *see* Augsburg
Confessio Saxonica, 354
Confessio Variata, 281 *sqq.*
Confutation, the Papal, 211
Constance, Council of, 76
Consultation, Hermann's, 296 *sqq.*

Cordatus, Conrad, 240, 257
Cracovius, 371, 376
Crotus, John, 13
Crotus, Richard, 24
Cruciger, 185, 229, 240, 252, 269, 272, 300, 319

D

Dalberg, John von, 13
Denck, John, 195
Diatribe, Erasmus's, 118
Dietrich, Dr. Leonhard, 18
Dietrich, Veit, 212, 259, 285
Diets, *see* Augsburg, Regensburg, Spires, Worms
Döllinger, Dr., 137
Doltsk, 80
Dringenberg, Ludwig, 9
Düben, 35
Dürer, Albrecht, 130, 140

E

Eber, Paul, 298, 324, 371, 378
Eberbach, Peter, 24
Eberhard, Duke, 19
Ebner, Hieronimus, 131
Eck, Dr. John, 32, 49–53, 55, 56, 67, 68, 74, 102, 195, 197, 202, 211, 283, 284, 286, 289–292 ; his 404 Articles, 195
Eckinger, John, 190
Education, oration on, 132, 133
Einsiedel, Haubold von, 87, 91
Emser, Jerome, 70, 71
Epistolæ Obscurorum Virorum, 25–27
Erasmus, 27, 32, 48, 67, 102, 103, 113, 117–121, 233, 312
Erfurt, 30
Examen Ordinandorum, 357

F

Fabri, John, 176, 177, 211
Family, Melanchthon's, 64
Fanaticism at Wittenberg, 80, 84
Faventinus, Didymus, 70

Faventraut, Alexius, 190
Ferdinand, 174, 177, 190
Flacius, 205, 284, 322, 339, 340, 342–344, 346–351, 359, 360, 366, 367, 369
Forster, John, 361
Frankenhausen, 148
Frankfort Convention, 263
Frankfort Recess, 368
Frederick, George, 354
Frederick, John, 220, 223, 270, 320–322, 325, 332, 356
Frederick the Wise, 30, 31, 48, 82, 142
Free Will, doctrine of, 233 *sqq.*
Friedlieb, Francis, 10
Fürstenschulen, 135
Funeral oration, 142, 143, 381

G

Gallus, Nicholas, 339, 364, 367
Gerbel, Nicholas, 10, 101
Gingelm, Nicholas, 36
Glass, Solomon, 272
Granvella, Chancellor, 290–292
Greek Letter, Melanchthon's, 152
Gresser, 335
Gropper, John, 291, 297
Grumbach, Chilian, 4
Grynæus, Simon, 10, 115
Gymnasia, 135, 137

H

Hagenau, Colloquy of, 272
Haller, Berthold, 10
Haugwitz, Erasmus von, 159
Hawerer, 4
Hedio, 185, 188
Heidelberg, University of, 13, 15
Heilbron, 4
Helvetius, Conrad, 9, 15
Henry VIII., King of England, 227 *sqq.*
Hermann, Archbishop, 296, 298
Hermann, Count, 24
Heshuss, Tillman, 375

Hess, Eoban, 24, 108, 132
Hess, John, 60, 94, 265
Hesse, Landgrave of, 121–124, 154, 171, 172, 174, 229, 250, 251
Heynlin, John, 20
Hiltebrant, John, 9, 24
Hochstratten, Jacob, 23
Höchel, Melchior, 115
House, Melanchthon's, 65
Hubmeier, Balthaser, 195
Hugel, 373
Hyperaspistes, Erasmus's, 120

I

Inaugural, Melanchthon's, 37, 38
Infant baptism, 241
Ingolstadt, 16, 28, 32, 34, 49, 66, 67
Inquisition, the Bavarian, 374
Instruction on Lord's Supper, Luther's, 251
Interim, *see* Augsburg, Celle, Leipzig

J

Jena, University of, 139
John, Elector of Saxony, 220
John, Margrave, 354
Jonas, Justus, 72, 80, 82, 127, 162, 169, 175, 185, 187, 189, 192, 193, 229, 240, 251; Jr., 296; 309, 358
Jüterbok, 334, 335

K

Kaden, Michael, 190
Kaisersburg, Geiler von, 16
Kecheln, Peter, 4
Kessler, John, 112
Klebitz, 376
Koch, John, 64
Königsberg, University of, 139
Kolbe, Christopher, 115
Kraft, Adam, 114, 130
Krapp, Hieronimus, 63
Krapp, Katharine, 63

L

Lambert, Francis, 155
Lange, Dr. John, 50, 58, 59, 63, 69
Latin schools, 134
League, Holy, 263
Leipzig Disputation, 50, 51
Leipzig *Interim*, 337
Lemp, Jacob, 20, 22, 27
Loci Communes, 94 *sqq.*, 231 *sqq.*
Locker, Jacob, 16
Lord's Supper, doctrine of, 178–180, 242, 361
Lowenstein, Count von, 16
Luther, Martin, called to Wittenberg, 30; his Theses, 31; compared with Melanchthon, 41–43; at the Leipzig Disputation, 50; burns the Pope's Bull, 68; writes two important works, 68, 69; returns from the Wartburg, 89; his eight sermons, 90; publishes the New Testament in German, 93; controversy with Erasmus on the Will, 120; relation to the Peasants' War, 147; his marriage, 154; at Marburg, 185–187; at Coburg, 194; approves Melanchthon's *Loci*, 247; instruction on the Lord's Supper, 251; his death, 309

M

Major, Dr., 306, 360
Maltz, Dietrich von, 311
Mandari, Fandius, 5
Mansfeld, 78, 79
Marburg, University of, 138; Colloquy of, 185–189; articles, 187
Martyr, Peter, 298, 363
Mass, 155–156
Matthesius, John, 350
Maurer, Bernhard, 27
Maximilian, Emperor, 5, 20, 24
Medler, Nicholas, 323

Melanchthon, Anna, 64
Melanchthon, George, 64
Melanchthon, Magdalena, 64
Melanchthon, Philip, birth and early years, 1–11; student at Heidelberg, 12–18; student, teacher, proof-reader, and editor at Tübingen, 19–28; call to Wittenberg, 32; Inaugural, 37; friendship with Luther, 40; attends the Leipzig Disputation, 50; controversy with Eck, 53; Theses, 58; marriage, family, salary, 63–66; controversy with Rhadinus and the Sorbonne, 71, 74; relation to the Wittenberg fanaticism, 85 *sqq.*; writes the *Loci Communes*, 94; wishes to relinquish theology, a compromise, 108–111; call to Nuremberg and services in the cause of education, 131, 133–140; relation to the Peasants' War, 149; writes the Saxon *Visitation Articles*, 161; controversy with Agricola, 167; tracts against the Anabaptists, 170, 171; attends the Diet of Spires and the Marburg Colloquy, 176, 186; writes the Augsburg Confession, 193 *sqq.*; negotiations with the Papists, 210–215; publishes the Confession and Apology, 218; called to England, to Tübingen, and to France, 224, 225, 229; new edition of the *Loci*, 231; his theology, 232; relation to the Wittenberg *Concord*, 251 *sqq.*; at Schmalkald, 261, 262; his Will, 268–271; his sickness and relation to the Landgrave's bigamy, 272, 274–280; revises the Augsburg Confession, 280–282; at Worms and Regensburg, 289, 290; aphorisms on the Lord's Supper, 292; assists in the Cologne Reformation,

Melanchthon, Philip—*Continued* 296 *sqq.*; writes the Wittenberg *Reformation*, 303 ; funeral oration over Luther, 310 ; letter to Carlowitz, 311 ; in exile, 319 ; relation to the Gymnasium and University of Jena, 322 ; relation to the Interims, 329 *sqq* ; defamed by Flacius, 339 ; letter of defence, 342–349 ; writes the Saxon Confession, 353 ; Mecklenburg Liturgy and the *Examen Ordinandorum*, 357 ; controversies on the Lord's Supper, 364 *sqq.*; the Flacian party, 369 ; reply to the Bavarian Articles, 374 ; last sickness and death, 377–379

Melanchthon, Philip, Jr., 64
Menius, Justus, 159, 185, 254
Miltitz, 49
Mosellanus, Peter, 32, 35, 114
Mühlberg, battle of, 318
Münzer, Thomas, 85, 144, 145
Musa of Jena, 192
Musculus, Andrew, 359
Myconius, Frederick, 159, 254, 280

N

Naucler, John, 22
Naumburg, Convention of, 361
Nausea, Frederick, 116
Neander, 136
Nesen, William, 113, 114, 125, 126
New Testament, 93
Nützel, Caspar, 131
Nuremberg, 130 *sqq.*; peace of, 220

O

Oberlanders (South Germans), 252 *sqq.*
Obscurantism, 26, 27
Œcolampadius, 15, 20, 23, 52, 180, 182, 183, 185, 186, 188, 243, 301

Order of service, 91, 92
Osiander, Andrew, 140, 185, 187, 189, 258, 357, 361, 369

P

Pacæus, 361
Pack, Dr. Otto von, 171, 173
Parma, 190
Paulsen, 138
Peace of Nuremberg, 220
Peasants' War, 142 *sqq.*
Pellican, Conrad, 31
Peucer, Caspar, 64, 281, 282, 371, 377
Pfefferkorn, John, 23, 24
Pfeffinger, 335
Pflug, Julius von, 291
Pforzheim, 6, 7, 9–11, 33, 67
Philip, Count Palatine, 2–5, 13
Philip, Landgrave, *see* Hesse
Piacenza, 190
Pirkheimer, Wilibald, 24, 28, 34, 117, 130, 140
Pistorius, John, 291, 297
Planitz, John von, 159
Pletner, 80
Pollich, Dr. Martin, 30
Pontanus, Chancellor, 270
Pope Leo X., 46, 48–50, 52
Pope Paul III., 260
Preceptor of Germany, 125 *sqq.*
Predestination, 236
Prettin, 87
Protest, Protestants, 177

R

Ranke, 151, 191, 332
Regensburg, Diet of, 291 ; Book, 291
Regius, Urban, 185
Reuchlin, Dionysius, 13
Reuchlin, John, 6, 8–11, 13, 14, 16, 19–21, 23, 24, 28, 31, 32, 51, 66, 67
Reuter, Barbara, 4
Reuter, Elizabeth, 8
Reuter, Hans, 3, 4
Rhadinus, Thomas, 70, 100

Rhagius, John, 37
Riccius, Dr. Paul, 31
Rochlitz, 64
Rorer, George, 284
Roting, Michael, 132, 141
Rubianus, Crotus, 25, 114

S

Sabinus, George, 64
Sachs, Hans, 130
Sacraments, number of, 240
Sadolet, Cardinal, 257
Salary, Melanchthon's, 66
Salmut, 361
Schemer, John, 19
Schenk, Jacob, 245, 257
Scheurl, Christopher, 35
Schleiz, 188
Schmalkald Articles, 260 ; Appendix to, 261 ; Convention, 260 ; League, 219, 304 ; War, 316 *sqq.*
Schmidt, Dr. Carl, 35, 184, 286
Schnepf, Erhard, 285
Scholasticism, 13
Schoner, John, 132
Schreiber, Jerome, 296
Schurf, Augustin, 323, 324
Schurf, Jerome, 37, 80, 83, 91, 159
Schwabach, 188, 189, 193, 194 ; Articles, 189
Schwartzerd, Anna, 4
Schwartzerd, Barbara, 4
Schwartzerd, Claus, 2
Schwartzerd, Elizabeth, 2
Schwartzerd, George, 2–5
Schwartzerd, George, Jr., 4, 115, 175, 372
Schwartzerd, John, 2
Schwartzerd, Margaretha, 4
Schwebel, John, 10, 57, 59, 60, 101, 185
Schwenckfeld, 359
Seidler, Jacob, 78, 79
Selneccer, Nicholas, 271, 281, 283, 284, 369
Servetus, 359
Sickingen, Conrad von, 34

Sickingen, Francis von, 24
Sigismund, 266
Silverborn, John, 113, 117
Simler, George, 9, 10, 14, 19, 20, 23, 27, 34
Sleidan, 314
Sorbil, 16
Sorbonne, 73–76, 226
Spalatin, 32, 33, 40, 41, 44, 45, 48, 55, 57, 62, 69, 77, 87, 101, 107–110, 113, 119, 162, 192, 202, 217
Spangel, Dr. Pallas, 114
Spengler, Lazarus, 131
Spires, Diet of, 174–178
Stadian, Francis, 20, 23, 27
Stadion, Bishop, 198
Stancar, Francis, 359, 369
Staupitz, Dr. John von, 30, 59
Stichs, Andrew, 4
Stigel, 322
Stöffler, Professor, 20, 23
Storch, Nicholas, 85
Strigel, Victorine, 103, 284, 322, 373
Stübner, Marcus Thomas, 85, 88, 91
Sturm, Jacob, 18, 176, 185, 226, 264
Sturm, John, 136
Sturm, Peter, 18

T

Theology, Melanchthon's, 231 *sqq.*
Torgau Articles, 193
Trent, Council of, 352
Trotzendorf, 136
Tübingen, Melanchthon's call to, 224, 225
Tübingen, University of, 19, 20

U

Ulrich, Duke, 144, 223
Unger, John, 6, 7

V

Valdesius, Alphonsus, 198
Vienna, Council of, 76

Vischer, Peter, 130
Visitation Articles, 161 *sqq.*
Voreus, Barnabas, 225

W

Weimar, *Confutation Book*, 373
Wessel, John, 13, 21
Westphal, Joachim, 363, 364
Wigand, 339
Wiland, Ulrich, 184
Will, controversy on, 118, 119
Will, Melanchthon's, 268–271
Wimpfeling, Jacob, 13, 16
Wimpina, 211, 265
Winsheim, Professor, 378
Winter, Balthaser, 284

Wittenberg, 29 *sqq.* ; *Concord*,
254, 255
Wolf, 136
Works, good, 360
Worms, Diet of, 289

Z

Zeigler, Bernhard, 265
Zoch, Dr., 306
Zweibrücken, 10
Zwickau Prophets, 85, 86, 92,
107
Zwilling, Gabriel, 80, 91
Zwingli, 178, 180–186, 188, 195,
211, 243, 300

Heroes of the Reformation.

EDITED BY

SAMUEL MACAULEY JACKSON,

Professor of Church History, New York University.

FULLY ILLUSTRATED

A SERIES of biographies of the leaders in the Protestant Reformation.

The literary skill and the standing as scholars of the writers who have agreed to prepare these biographies will, it is believed, ensure for them a wide acceptance on the part not only of special students of the period but of the general reader. Full use will be made in them of the correspondence of their several subjects and of any other autobiographical material that may be available. The general reader will be pleased to find all these citations translated into English and the scholar to find them referred specifically to their source. The value of these volumes will be furthered by comprehensive literary and historical references and adequate indexes.

It is, of course, the case that each one of the great teachers whose career is to be presented in this series looked at religious truth and at the problems of Christianity from a somewhat different point of view. On this ground an important feature in each volume of the series will be a precise and comprehensive statement, given as nearly as practicable in the language of the original writer, of the essential points in his theology.

It is planned that the narratives shall be not mere eulogies, but critical biographies; and the defects of judgment or sins of omission or commission on the parts of the subjects will not be passed by or extenuated. On the other hand they will do full justice to the nobility of character and to the distinctive contribution to human progress made by each one of these great Protestant leaders of the Reformation period. The series will avoid the partisanship of writers like Merle d'Aubigné, and, in the opposite direction, of the group of which Johannes Janssen may be taken as a type.

HEROES OF THE REFORMATION

I.—MARTIN LUTHER (1483-1546). The Hero of the Reformation.

By HENRY EYSTER JACOBS, D.D., LL.D. (Thiel College, 1877 and 1891, respectively); Professor of Systematic Theology, Evangelical Lutheran Seminary, Philadelphia, Pa.; author of "The Lutheran Movement in England during the Reigns of Henry VIII. and Edward VI., and its Literary Monuments." With 73 illustrations. 12°, $1.50.

II. PHILIP MELANCHTHON (1497-1560). The Protestant Preceptor of Germany.

By JAMES WILLIAM RICHARD, D.D. (Pennsylvania College, 1886); Professor of Homiletics, Lutheran Theological Seminary, Gettysburg, Pa. With 35 illustrations. 12°, $1.50.

III.—DESIDERIUS ERASMUS (1467-1536). The Humanist in the Service of the Reformation.

By EPHRAIM EMERTON, Ph.D. (Leipzig University, 1876); Professor of Ecclesiastical History, Harvard University, Cambridge, Mass.; author of "The Middle Ages (375–1300)." With 36 illustrations. 12°, $1.50.

IV.—THEODORE BEZA (1519-1605). The Counsellor of the French Reformation.

By HENRY MARTYN BAIRD, Ph.D. (College of New Jersey, 1867); D.D. (Rutgers College, 1877); LL.D. (College of New Jersey, 1882); L.H.D. (Princeton University, 1896); Professor of the Greek Language and Literature, New York University; author of "The Huguenots." With 24 illustrations. 12°, $1.50.

V. HULDREICH ZWINGLI (1484-1531). The Reformer of German Switzerland.

By SAMUEL MACAULEY JACKSON, LL.D. (Washington and Lee University, 1892); D.D. (New York University, 1893); Professor of Church History, New York University. Editor of the Series. With 30 illustrations, a special map, battle plan, and a facsimile letter. 12°, $2.00.

The following are in preparation :—

VI.—JOHN CALVIN (1509-1564). The Founder of Re-formed Protestantism.

By WILLISTON WALKER, Ph.D. (Leipzig University, 1888) ; D.D. (Adelbert College, 1894, Amherst College, 1895); Professor of Germanic and Western Church History, Theological Seminary, Hartford, Conn.; author of "The Creeds and Platforms of Congregationalism."

VII.—JOHN KNOX (1505-1572). The Hero of the Scotch Reformation.

By HENRY COWAN, D.D. (Aberdeen, 1888), Professor of Church History, the University of Aberdeen, Scotland; author of "Landmarks of Church History," "The Influence of the Scottish Church upon Christendom."

VIII.—THOMAS CRANMER (1489-1556). The English Reformer. *(Author will be announced later.)*

IX.—THE SATIRISTS AND SATIRES OF THE RE-FORMATION, BOTH PROTESTANT AND RO-MAN CATHOLIC.

By OLIPHANT SMEATON, M.A., Edinburgh, Scotland ; author of "English Satires."

X.—*a*. LÆLIUS (1525-1562) and FAUSTUS (1539-1604) SOCINUS. The Founders of the Unitarian Movement.

By Rev. ALEXANDER GORDON, M.A., Principal of the Unitarian Theological College, Manchester, England.

***b*. BALTHASAR HUBMAIER (1484-1528). The Theologian of the Early Baptists.**

By HENRY C. VEDDER, D.D. (University of Rochester, N. Y., 1897); Professor of Church History, Crozer Theological Seminary ; author of "Short History of the Baptists."

G. P. PUTNAM'S SONS

New York and London

Lightning Source UK Ltd.
Milton Keynes UK
UKOW02f0309070117

291594UK00011B/125/P